MW00612144

Python 3 Object Oriented Programming

Harness the power of Python 3 objects

Dusty Phillips

BIRMINGHAM - MUMBAI

Python 3 Object Oriented Programming

Copyright © 2010 Packt Publishing

All rights reserved. No part of this book may be reproduced, stored in a retrieval system, or transmitted in any form or by any means, without the prior written permission of the publisher, except in the case of brief quotations embedded in critical articles or reviews.

Every effort has been made in the preparation of this book to ensure the accuracy of the information presented. However, the information contained in this book is sold without warranty, either express or implied. Neither the author nor Packt Publishing, and its dealers and distributors will be held liable for any damages caused or alleged to be caused directly or indirectly by this book.

Packt Publishing has endeavored to provide trademark information about all of the companies and products mentioned in this book by the appropriate use of capitals. However, Packt Publishing cannot guarantee the accuracy of this information.

First published: July 2010

Production Reference: 1160710

Published by Packt Publishing Ltd.
32 Lincoln Road
Olton
Birmingham, B27 6PA, UK.

ISBN 978-1-849511-26-1

www.packtpub.com

Cover Image by Asher Wishkerman (a.wishkerman@mpic.de)

Credits

Author
Dusty Phillips

Reviewers
Jason Chu

Michael Driscoll

Dan McGee

Lawrence Oluyede

Acquisition Editor
Steven Wilding

Development Editor
Mayuri Kokate

Technical Editor
Vanjeet D'souza

Indexer
Hemangini Bari

Editorial Team Leader
Mithun Sehgal

Project Team Leader
Lata Basantani

Project Coordinator
Jovita Pinto

Proofreader
Chris Smith

Graphics
Geetanjali Sawant

Production Coordinator
Shantanu Zagade

Cover Work
Shantanu Zagade

About the Author

Dusty Phillips is a Canadian freelance software developer, teacher, martial artist, and open source aficionado. He is closely affiliated with the Arch Linux community and other open source projects. He maintains the Arch Linux storefronts, and compiled the popular Arch Linux Handbook. Dusty holds a Master's degree in Computer Science specializing in Human-Computer Interaction. He currently has six different Python interpreters installed on his computer.

I would like to thank my editors, Steven Wilding and Mayuri Kokate for well-timed encouragement and feedback. Many thanks to friend and mentor Jason Chu for getting me started in Python and for patiently answering numerous questions on Python, GIT, and life over the years. Thanks to my father, C. C. Phillips, for inspiring me to write while editing his terrific works of fiction. Finally, thanks to every person who has said they can't wait to buy my book; your enthusiasm has been a huge motivational force.

About the Reviewers

Jason Chu is the CTO and part founder of Oprius Software Inc. He's developed software professionally for over 8 years. Chu started using Python in 2003 with version 2.2. When not developing personal or professional software, he spends his time teaching karate, playing go, and having fun in his hometown: Victoria, BC, Canada. You'll often find him out drinking the Back Hand of God Stout at Christie's Carriage House.

Michael Driscoll has been programming Python for almost 4 years and has dabbled in other languages since the late nineties. He graduated from university with a Bachelor's degree in Science, majoring in Management Information Systems. Michael enjoys programming for fun and profit. His hobbies include biblical apologetics, blogging about Python at http://www.blog.pythonlibrary.org/, and learning photography. Michael currently works for the local government where he programs with Python as much as possible. This is his first book as a technical reviewer.

> I would like to thank my mom without whom I never would have grown to love learning as much as I do. I would also like to thank Scott Williams for forcing me to learn Python as, without him, I wouldn't have even known that the language existed. Most of all, I want to thank Jesus for saving me from myself.

Dan McGee is a software developer currently living in Chicago, Illinois. He has several years of experience working full-time in the Chicago area doing primarily Java web development; however, he has also been spotted working in a variety of other languages. Dan has also worked on a handful of freelance projects. In 2007, Dan became a developer for the Arch Linux distribution and has been doing various projects related to that since, including hacking on the package manager code, being a part-time system admin, and helping maintain and improve the website.

Lawrence Oluyede is a 26 years old software development expert in Python and web programming. He's glad that programming is going parallel and functional languages are becoming mainstream. He has been a co-author and reviewer for the first Ruby book in Italian (*Ruby per applicazioni web*) published by *Apogeo*. He has also contributed to other books in the past like the *Python Cookbook* (http://www.amazon.com/Python-Cookbook-Alex-Martelli/dp/0596007973/) and *The Definitive Guide to Django* (http://www.amazon.com/Definitive-Guide-Django-Development-Right/dp/1590597257).

Table of Contents

Preface

This book will introduce you to the terminology of the object-oriented paradigm, focusing on object-oriented design with step-by-step examples. It will take you from simple inheritance, one of the most useful tools in the object-oriented programmer's toolbox, all the way through to cooperative inheritance, one of the most complicated. You will be able to raise, handle, define, and manipulate exceptions.

You will be able to integrate the object-oriented and not-so-object-oriented aspects of Python. You will also be able to create maintainable applications by studying higher-level design patterns. You'll learn the complexities of string and file manipulation and how Python distinguishes between binary and textual data. Not one, but two very powerful automated testing systems will be introduced to you. You'll understand the joy of unit testing and just how easy unit tests are to create. You'll even study higher-level libraries such as database connectors and GUI toolkits and how they apply object-oriented principles.

What this book covers

Chapter 1, Object-oriented Design covers important object-oriented concepts. It deals mainly with abstraction, classes, encapsulation, and inheritance. We also briefly look into UML to model our classes and objects.

Chapter 2, Objects in Python discusses classes and objects and how they are used in Python. We will learn about attributes and behaviors in Python objects, and also the organization of classes into packages and modules. And lastly we shall see how to protect our data.

Chapter 3, When Objects are Alike gives us a more in-depth look into inheritance. It covers multiple inheritance and shows us how to inherit from built-ins. This chapter also covers polymorphism and duck typing.

Chapter 4, Expecting the Unexpected looks into exceptions and exception handling. We shall learn how to create our own exceptions. It also deals with the use of exceptions for program flow control.

Chapter 5, When to Use Object-oriented Programming deals with objects; when to create and use them. We will see how to wrap data using properties, and restricting data access. This chapter also discusses the DRY principle and how not to repeat code.

Chapter 6, Python Data Structures covers object-oriented features of data structures. This chapter mainly deals with tuples, dictionaries, lists, and sets. We will also see how to extend built-in objects.

Chapter 7, Python Object-oriented Shortcuts as the name suggests, deals with little time-savers in Python. We shall look at many useful built-in functions, then move on to using comprehensions in lists, sets, and dictionaries. We will learn about generators, method overloading, and default arguments. We shall also see how to use functions as objects.

Chapter 8, Python Design Patterns I first introduces us to Python design patterns. We shall then see the decorator pattern, observer pattern, strategy pattern, state pattern, singleton pattern, and template pattern. These patterns are discussed with suitable examples and programs implemented in Python.

Chapter 9, Python Design Patterns II picks up where the previous chapter left us. We shall see the adapter pattern, facade pattern, flyweight pattern, command pattern, abstract pattern, and composite pattern with suitable examples in Python.

Chapter 10, Files and Strings looks at strings and string formatting. Bytes and byte arrays are also discussed. We shall also look at files, and how to write and read data to and from files. We shall look at ways to store and pickle objects, and finally the chapter discusses serializing objects.

Chapter 11, Testing Object-oriented Programs opens with the use of testing and why testing is so important. It focuses on test-driven development. We shall see how to use the `unittest` module, and also the `py.test` automated testing suite. Lastly we shall cover code coverage using `coverage.py`.

Chapter 12, Common Python 3 Libraries concentrates on libraries and their utilization in application building. We shall build databases using SQLAlchemy, and user interfaces TkInter and PyQt. The chapter goes on to discuss how to construct XML documents and we shall see how to use ElementTree and lxml. Lastly we will use CherryPy and Jinja to create a web application.

What you need for this book

In order to compile and run the examples mentioned in this book you require the following software:

- Python version 3.0 or higher
- py.test
- coverage.py
- SQLAlchemy
- pygame
- PyQt
- CherryPy
- lxml

Who this book is for

If you're new to object-oriented programming techniques, or if you have basic Python skills, and wish to learn in depth how and when to correctly apply object-oriented programming in Python, this is the book for you.

If you are an object-oriented programmer for other languages you will also find this book a useful introduction to Python, as it uses terminology you are already familiar with.

Python 2 programmers seeking a leg up in the new world of Python 3 will also find the book beneficial but you need not necessarily know Python 2.

Conventions

In this book, you will find a number of styles of text that distinguish between different kinds of information. Here are some examples of these styles, and an explanation of their meaning.

Code words in text are shown as follows: "We can access other Python modules through the use of the import statement."

A block of code is set as follows:

```
class Friend(Contact):
    def __init__(self, name, email, phone):
        self.name = name
        self.email = email
        self.phone = phone
```

When we wish to draw your attention to a particular part of a code block, the relevant lines or items are set in bold:

```
class Friend(Contact):
    def __init__(self, name, email, phone):
        self.name = name
        self.email = email
        self.phone = phone
```

Any command-line input or output is written as follows:

```
>>> e = EmailableContact("John Smith", "jsmith@example.net")
>>> Contact.all_contacts
```

New terms and **important words** are shown in bold. Words that you see on the screen, in menus or dialog boxes for example, appear in the text like this: "We use this feature to update the label to a new random value every time we click the **Roll!** button".

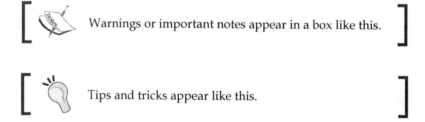

Warnings or important notes appear in a box like this.

Tips and tricks appear like this.

Reader feedback

Feedback from our readers is always welcome. Let us know what you think about this book—what you liked or may have disliked. Reader feedback is important for us to develop titles that you really get the most out of.

To send us general feedback, simply send an e-mail to feedback@packtpub.com, and mention the book title via the subject of your message.

If there is a book that you need and would like to see us publish, please send us a note in the **SUGGEST A TITLE** form on www.packtpub.com or e-mail suggest@packtpub.com.

If there is a topic that you have expertise in and you are interested in either writing or contributing to a book, see our author guide on www.packtpub.com/authors.

Customer support

Now that you are the proud owner of a Packt book, we have a number of things to help you get the most from your purchase.

Downloading the example code for this book

You can download the example code files for all Packt books you have purchased from your account at http://www.PacktPub.com. If you purchased this book elsewhere, you can visit http://www.PacktPub.com/support and register to have the files e-mailed directly to you.

Errata

Although we have taken every care to ensure the accuracy of our content, mistakes do happen. If you find a mistake in one of our books—maybe a mistake in the text or the code—we would be grateful if you would report this to us. By doing so, you can save other readers from frustration and help us improve subsequent versions of this book. If you find any errata, please report them by visiting http://www.packtpub.com/support, selecting your book, clicking on the **let us know** link, and entering the details of your errata. Once your errata are verified, your submission will be accepted and the errata will be uploaded on our website, or added to any list of existing errata, under the Errata section of that title. Any existing errata can be viewed by selecting your title from http://www.packtpub.com/support.

Piracy

Piracy of copyright material on the Internet is an ongoing problem across all media. At Packt, we take the protection of our copyright and licenses very seriously. If you come across any illegal copies of our works, in any form, on the Internet, please provide us with the location address or website name immediately so that we can pursue a remedy.

Please contact us at copyright@packtpub.com with a link to the suspected pirated material.

We appreciate your help in protecting our authors, and our ability to bring you valuable content.

Questions

You can contact us at questions@packtpub.com if you are having a problem with any aspect of the book, and we will do our best to address it.

Object-oriented Design

1

In software development, design is often considered the step done **before** programming. This isn't true; in reality, analysis, programming, and design tend to overlap, combine, and interweave. In this chapter, we will learn:

- What object-oriented means
- The difference between object-oriented design and object-oriented programming
- The basic principles of object-oriented design
- Basic Unified Modeling Language and when it isn't evil

Object-oriented?

Everyone knows what an object is: a tangible "something" that we can sense, feel, and manipulate. The earliest objects we interact with are typically baby toys. Wooden blocks, plastic shapes, and over-sized puzzle pieces are common first objects. Babies learn quickly that certain objects do certain things. Triangles fit in triangle-shaped holes. Bells ring, buttons press, and levers pull.

The definition of an object in software development is not so very different. Objects are not typically *tangible somethings* that you can pick up, sense, or feel, but they are models of *somethings* that can do certain things and have certain things done to them. Formally, an object is a collection of **data** and associated **behaviors**.

So knowing what an object is, what does it mean to be object-oriented? Oriented simply means directed toward. So object-oriented simply means, "functionally directed toward modeling objects". It is one of many techniques used for modeling complex systems by describing a collection of interacting objects via their data and behavior.

If you've read any hype, you've probably come across the terms object-oriented analysis, object-oriented design, object-oriented analysis and design, and object-oriented programming. These are all highly related concepts under the general object-oriented umbrella.

In fact, analysis, design, and programming are all stages of software development. Calling them object-oriented simply specifies what style of software development is being pursued.

Object-oriented Analysis (OOA) is the process of looking at a problem, system, or task that somebody wants to turn into an application and identifying the objects and interactions between those objects. The analysis stage is all about *what* needs to be done. The output of the analysis stage is a set of requirements. If we were to complete the analysis stage in one step, we would have turned a task, such as, "I need a website", into a set of requirements, such as:

Visitors to the website need to be able to (*italic* represents actions, **bold** represents objects):

- *review* our **history**
- *apply* for **jobs**
- *browse*, *compare*, and *order* our **products**

Object-oriented Design (OOD) is the process of converting such requirements into an implementation specification. The designer must name the objects, define the behaviors, and formally specify what objects can activate specific behaviors on other objects. The design stage is all about *how* things should be done. The output of the design stage is an implementation specification. If we were to complete the design stage in one step, we would have turned the requirements into a set of classes and interfaces that could be implemented in (ideally) any object-oriented programming language.

Object-oriented Programming (OOP) is the process of converting this perfectly defined design into a working program that does exactly what the CEO originally requested.

Yeah, right! It would be lovely if the world met this ideal and we could follow these stages one by one, in perfect order like all the old textbooks told us to. As usual, the real world is much murkier. No matter how hard we try to separate these stages, we'll always find things that need further analysis while we're designing. When we're programming, we find features that need clarification in the design. In the fast-paced modern world, most development happens in an **iterative development model**. In iterative development, a small part of the task is modeled, designed, and programmed, then the program is reviewed and expanded to improve each feature and include new features in a series of short cycles.

The rest of this book is about object-oriented programming, but in this chapter we will cover the basic object-oriented principles in the context of design. This allows us to understand these rather simple concepts without having to argue with software syntax or interpreters.

Objects and classes

So, an object is a collection of data with associated behaviors. How do we tell two types of objects apart? Apples and oranges are both objects, but it is a common adage that they cannot be compared. Apples and oranges aren't modeled very often in computer programming, but let's pretend we're doing an inventory application for a fruit farm! As an example, we can assume that apples go in barrels and oranges go in baskets.

Now, we have four kinds of objects: apples, oranges, baskets, and barrels. In object-oriented modeling, the term used for kinds of objects is **class**. So, in technical terms, we now have four **classes** of objects.

What's the difference between an object and a class? Classes describe objects. They are like blueprints for creating an object. You might have three oranges sitting on the table in front of you. Each orange is a distinct object, but all three have the attributes and behaviors associated with one class: the general class of oranges.

The relationship between the four classes of objects in our inventory system can be described using a **Unified Modeling Language** (invariably referred to as **UML**, because three letter acronyms are *cool*) **class diagram**. Here is our first class diagram:

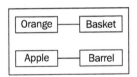

This diagram simply shows that an **Orange** is somehow associated with a **Basket** and that an **Apple** is also somehow associated with a **Barrel**. **Association** is the most basic way for two classes to be related.

UML is very popular among managers, and occasionally disparaged by programmers. The syntax of a UML diagram is generally pretty obvious; you don't have to read a tutorial to (mostly) understand what is going on when you see one. UML is also fairly easy to draw, and quite intuitive. After all, many people, when describing classes and their relationships, will naturally draw boxes with lines between them. Having a standard based on these intuitive diagrams makes it easy for programmers to communicate with designers, managers, and each other.

However, some programmers think UML is a waste of time. Citing iterative development, they will argue that formal specifications done up in fancy UML diagrams are going to be redundant before they're implemented, and that maintaining those formal diagrams will only waste time and not benefit anyone.

This is true of some organizations, and hogwash in other corporate cultures. However, every programming team consisting of more than one person will occasionally have to sit down and hash out the details of part of the system they are currently working on. UML is extremely useful, in these brainstorming sessions, for quick and easy communication. Even those organizations that scoff at formal class diagrams tend to use some informal version of UML in their design meetings, or team discussions.

Further, the most important person you ever have to communicate with is yourself. We all think we can remember the design decisions we've made, but there are always, "Why did I do that?" moments hiding in our future. If we keep the scraps of paper we did our initial diagramming on when we started a design, we'll eventually find that they are a useful reference.

This chapter, however, is not meant to be a tutorial in UML. There are many of those available on the Internet, as well as numerous books available on the topic. UML covers far more than class and object diagrams; it also has syntax for use cases, deployment, state changes, and activities. We'll be dealing with some common class diagram syntax in this discussion of object-oriented design. You'll find you can pick up the structure by example, and you'll subconsciously choose UML-inspired syntax in your own team or personal design sessions.

Our initial diagram, while correct, does not remind us that apples go in barrels or how many barrels a single apple can go in. It only tells us that apples are somehow associated with barrels. The association between classes is often obvious and needs no further explanation, but the option to add further clarification is always there. The beauty of UML is that most things are optional. We only need to specify as much information in a diagram as makes sense for the current situation. In a quick whiteboard session, we might just quickly draw lines between boxes. In a formal document that needs to make sense in six months, we might go into more detail. In the case of apples and barrels, we can be fairly confident that the association is, "many apples go in one barrel", but just to make sure nobody confuses it with, "one apple spoils one barrel", we can enhance the diagram as shown:

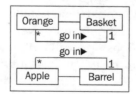

This diagram tells us that oranges **go in** baskets with a little arrow showing what goes in what. It also tells us the **multiplicity** (number of that object that can be used in the association) on both sides of the relationship. One **Basket** can hold many (represented by a *) **Orange** objects. Any one **Orange** can go in exactly one **Basket**.

It can be easy to confuse which side of a relationship the multiplicity goes on. The multiplicity is the number of objects of **that** class that can be associated with **any one** object at the other end of the association. For the apple goes in barrel association, reading from left to right, many instances of the **Apple** class (that is many **Apple** objects) can **go in** any one **Barrel**. Reading from right to left, **exactly** one **Barrel** can be associated with any one **Apple**.

Specifying attributes and behaviors

We now have a grasp on some basic object-oriented terminology. Objects are **instances** of classes that can be associated with each other. An object instance is a specific object with its own set of data and behaviors; a specific orange on the table in front of us is said to be an instance of the general class of oranges. That's simple enough, but what are these data and behaviors that are associated with each object?

Data describes objects

Let's start with data. Data typically represents the individual characteristics of a certain object. A class of objects can define specific characteristics that are shared by all instances of that class. Each instance can then have different data values for the given characteristics. For example, our three oranges on the table (if we haven't eaten any) could each have a different weight. The orange class could then have a weight **attribute**. All instances of the orange class have a weight attribute, but each orange might have a different value for this weight. Attributes don't have to be unique though; any two oranges may weigh the same amount. As a more realistic example, two objects representing different customers might have the same value for a first name attribute.

Attributes are frequently referred to as **properties**. Some authors suggest that the two terms have different meanings, usually that attributes are settable, while properties are read only. In Python, the concept of "read only" is not really used, so throughout this book we'll see the two terms used interchangeably. In addition, as we'll discuss in *Chapter 5*, the property keyword has a special meaning in Python for a particular kind of attribute.

In our fruit inventory application, the fruit farmer may want to know what orchard the orange came from, when it was picked, and how much it weighs. They might also want to keep track of where each basket is stored. Apples might have a color attribute and barrels might come in different sizes. Some of these properties may also belong to multiple classes (we may want to know when apples are picked, too), but for this first example, let's just add a few different attributes to our class diagram:

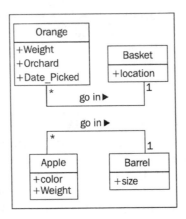

Depending on how detailed our design needs to be, we can also specify the type for each attribute. Attribute types are often primitives that are standard to most programming languages, such as integer, floating-point number, string, byte, or boolean. However, they can also represent data structures such as lists, trees, or graphs, or, most notably, other classes. This is one area where the design stage can overlap with the programming stage. The various primitives or objects available in one programming language may be somewhat different from what is available in other languages. Usually we don't need to concern ourselves with this at the design stage, as implementation-specific details are chosen during the programming stage. Use generic names and we'll be fine. If our design calls for a list container type, the Java programmers can choose to use a LinkedList or an ArrayList when implementing it, while the Python programmers (that's us!) can choose between the list built-in and a tuple.

In our fruit farming example, so far, our attributes are all basic primitives. But there are implicit attributes that we can make explicit: the associations. For a given orange, we might have an attribute containing the basket that holds that orange. Alternatively, one basket might contain a list of the oranges it holds. The next diagram adds these attributes as well as including type descriptions for our current properties:

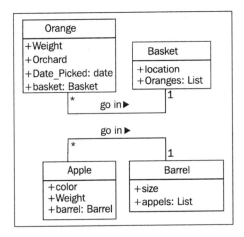

Behaviors are actions

Now we know what data is, but what are behaviors? Behaviors are actions that can occur on an object. The behaviors that can be performed on a specific class of objects are called **methods**. At the programming level, methods are like functions in structured programming, but they magically have access to all the data associated with that object. Like functions, methods can also accept **parameters**, and return **values**.

Parameters to a method are a list of objects that need to be **passed** into the method that is being called. These objects are used by the method to perform whatever behavior or task it is meant to do. Return values are the results of that task. Here's a concrete example; if our objects are numbers, the number class might have an add method that accepts a second number as a parameter. The first number object's add method will return the sum when the second number is passed to it. Given an object and it's method name, a calling object can call, or **invoke** the method on the target object. Invoking a method, at the programming level, is the process of telling the method to execute itself by passing it the required parameters as arguments.

We've stretched our, "comparing apples and oranges" example into a basic (if far-fetched) inventory application. Let's stretch it a little further and see if it breaks. One action that can be associated with oranges is the **pick** action. If you think about implementation, **pick** would place the orange in a basket by updating the **basket** attribute on the orange, and by adding the orange to the **oranges** list on the **Basket**. So **pick** needs to know what basket it is dealing with. We do this by giving the **pick** method a **basket** parameter. Since our fruit farmer also sells juice, we can add a **squeeze** method to **Orange**. When squeezed, **squeeze** might return the amount of juice retrieved, while also removing the **Orange** from the **basket** it was in.

Basket can have a sell action. When a basket is sold, our inventory system might update some data on as-yet unspecified objects for accounting and profit calculations. Alternatively, our basket of oranges might go bad before we can sell them, so we add a **discard** method. Let's add these methods to our diagram:

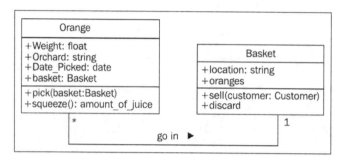

Adding models and methods to individual objects allows us to create a **system** of interacting objects. Each object in the system is a member of a certain class. These classes specify what types of data the object can hold and what methods can be invoked on it. The data in each object can be in a different state from other objects of the same class, and each object may react to method calls differently because of the differences in state.

Object-oriented analysis and design is all about figuring out what those objects are and how they should interact. The next section describes principles that can be used to make those interactions as simple and intuitive as possible.

Hiding details and creating the public interface

The key purpose of modeling an object in object-oriented design is to determine what the public **interface** of that object will be. The interface is the collection of attributes and methods that other objects can use to interact with that object. They do not need, and are often not allowed, to access the internal workings of the object. A common real-world example is the television. Our interface to the television is the remote control. Each button on the remote control represents a method that can be called on the television object. When we, as the calling object, access these methods, we do not know or care if the television is getting its signal from an antenna, a cable connection, or a satellite dish. We don't care what electronic signals are being sent to adjust the volume, or whether that volume is being output to speakers or a set of headphones. If we open the television to access the internal workings, for example to split the output signal to both external speakers and a set of headphones, we will void the warranty.

This process of hiding the implementation, or functional details, of an object is suitably called **information hiding**. It is also sometimes referred to as **encapsulation**, but encapsulation is actually a more all-encompassing term. Encapsulated data is not necessarily hidden. Encapsulation is, literally, creating a capsule, so think of creating a time capsule. If you put a bunch of information into a time capsule, lock and bury it, it is both encapsulated and the information is hidden. On the other hand, if the time capsule has not been buried and is unlocked or made of clear plastic, the items inside it are still encapsulated, but there is no information hiding.

The distinction between encapsulation and information hiding is largely irrelevant, especially at the design level. Many practical references use the terms interchangeably. As Python programmers, we don't actually have or need true information hiding, (we'll discuss the reasons for this in *Chapter 2*) so the more encompassing definition for encapsulation is suitable.

The public interface, however, is very important. It needs to be carefully designed as it is difficult to change it in the future. Changing the interface will break any client objects that are calling it. We can change the internals all we like, for example, to make it more efficient, or to access data over the network as well as locally, and the client objects will still be able to talk to it, unmodified, using the public interface. On the other hand, if we change the interface, by changing attribute names that are publicly accessed or by altering the order or types of arguments that a method can accept, all client objects will also have to be modified.

Remember, program objects represent real objects, but they are not real objects. They are models. One of the greatest gifts of modeling is the ability to ignore details that are irrelevant. A model car may look like a real 1956 Thunderbird on the outside, but it doesn't run and the driveshaft doesn't turn, as these details are overly complex and irrelevant to the youngster assembling the model. The model is an **abstraction** of a real concept.

Abstraction is another object-oriented buzzword that ties in with encapsulation and information hiding. Simply put, abstraction means dealing with the level of detail that is most appropriate to a given task. It is the process of extracting a public interface from the inner details. A driver of a car needs to interact with steering, gas pedal, and brakes. The workings of the motor, drive train, and brake subsystem don't matter to the driver. A mechanic, on the other hand works at a different level of abstraction, tuning the engine and bleeding the breaks. Here's an example of two abstraction levels for a car:

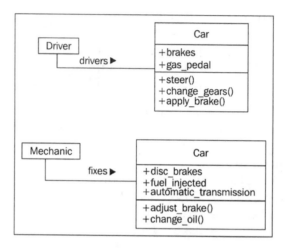

Now we have several new terms that refer to similar concepts. Condensing all this jargon into a single sentence, abstraction is the process of encapsulating information with separate public and private interfaces. The private interfaces can be subject to information hiding.

The important thing to bring from all these definitions is to make our models understandable to the other objects that have to interact with them. This means paying careful attention to small details. Ensure methods and properties have sensible names. When analyzing a system, objects typically represent nouns in the original problem, while methods are normally verbs. Attributes can often be picked up as adjectives, although if the attribute refers to another object that is part of the current object, it will still likely be a noun. Name classes, attributes, and methods accordingly. Don't try to model objects or actions that **might** be useful in the future. Model exactly those tasks that the system needs to perform and the design will naturally gravitate towards one that has an appropriate level of abstraction. This is not to say we should not think about possible future design modifications. Our designs should be open ended so that future requirements can be satisfied. However, when abstracting interfaces, try to model exactly what needs to be modeled and nothing more.

When designing the interface, try placing yourself in the object's shoes and imagine that the object has a strong preference for privacy. Don't let other objects have access to data about you unless you feel it is in your best interest for them to have it. Don't give them an interface to force you to perform a specific task unless you are certain you want them to be able to do that to you.

This is also a good practice for ensuring privacy on your social networking accounts!

Composition and inheritance

So far, we've learned to design systems as a group of interacting objects, where each interaction is viewing the objects involved at an appropriate level of abstraction. But we don't know yet how to create those levels of abstraction. There are a variety of ways to do this; we'll discuss some advanced design patterns in *Chapter 8* and *Chapter 9*. But even most design patterns rely on two basic principles known as **composition** and **inheritance**.

Composition is the act of collecting together several objects to compose a new one. Composition is usually a good choice when one object is part of another object. We've already seen a first hint of composition in the mechanic example. A car is composed of an engine, transmission, starter, headlights, and windshield, among numerous other parts. The engine, in turn, is composed of pistons, a crank shaft, and valves. In this example, composition is a good way to provide levels of abstraction. The car object can provide the interface required by a driver, while also providing access to its component parts, which offers a deeper level of abstraction suitable for a mechanic. Those component parts can, of course, be further broken down if the mechanic needs more information to diagnose a problem or tune the engine.

This is a common first example of composition, bit it's not a very good one when it comes to designing computer systems. Physical objects are easy to break into component objects. People have been doing it at least since the ancient Greeks originally postulated that atoms were the smallest unit of matter (they, of course, didn't have access to particle accelerators). Computer systems are generally less complicated than physical objects, yet identifying the component objects in such systems does not happen as naturally. The objects in an object-oriented system occasionally represent physical objects like people, books, or telephones. More often, however, they represent abstract ideas. People have names, books have titles, and telephones are used to make calls. Calls, titles, accounts, names, appointments, and payments are not usually considered objects in the physical world, but they are all frequently modeled components in computer systems.

Let's try modeling a more computer-oriented example to see composition in action. We'll be looking at the design of a computerized chess game. This was a very popular pastime among academics in the '80s and '90s. People were predicting that computers would one day be able to defeat a human chess master. When this happened in 1997 (IBM's Deep Blue defeated world chess champion, Gary Kasparov), interest in the problem waned, although there are still contests between computer and human chess players, and the program has not yet been written that can defeat a human chess master 100% of the time.

As a basic, high-level analysis: a game of chess is **played** between two *players*, using a *chess set* featuring a *board* containing sixty-four *positions* in an 8x8 grid. The board can have two sets of sixteen *pieces* that can be **moved**, in alternating *turns* by the two players in different ways. Each piece can **take** other pieces. The board will be required to **draw** itself on the computer *screen* after each turn.

I've identified some of the possible objects in the description using *italics*, and a few key methods using **bold**. This is a common first step in turning an object-oriented analysis into a design. At this point, to emphasize composition, we'll focus on the board, without worrying too much about the players or the different types of pieces.

Let's start at the highest level of abstraction possible. We have two players interacting with a chess set by taking turns making moves.

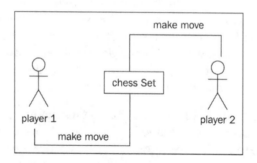

What is that? It doesn't quite look like our earlier class diagrams. That's because it isn't a class diagram! This is an **object diagram**, also called an instance diagram. It describes the system at a specific state in time, and is describing specific instances of objects, not the interaction between classes. Remember, both players are members of the same class, so the class diagram looks a little different:

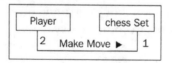

The diagram shows that exactly two players can interact with one chess set. It also indicates that any one player can be playing with only one chess set at a time.

But we're discussing composition, not UML, so let's think about what the **Chess Set** is composed of. We don't care what the player is composed of at this time. We can assume that the player has a heart and brain, among other organs, but these are irrelevant to our model. Indeed, there is nothing stopping said player from being Deep Blue itself, which has neither a heart nor brain.

The chess set, then, is composed of a board and thirty-two pieces. The board is further comprised of sixty-four positions. You could argue that pieces are not part of the chess set because you could replace the pieces in a chess set with a different set of pieces. While this is unlikely or impossible in a computerized version of chess, it introduces us to **aggregation**. Aggregation is almost exactly like composition. The difference is that aggregate objects can exist independently. It would be impossible for a position to be associated with a different chess board, so we say the board is composed of positions. But the pieces, which might exist independently of the chess set, are said to be in an aggregate relationship with that set.

Another way to differentiate between aggregation and composition is to think about the lifespan of the object. If the composite (outside) object controls when the related (inside) objects are created and destroyed, composition is most suitable. If the related object is created independently of the composite object, or can outlast that object, an aggregate relationship makes more sense. Also keep in mind that composition is aggregation; aggregation is simply a more general form of composition. Any composite relationship is also an aggregate relationship, but not vice versa.

Let's describe our current chess set composition and add some attributes to the objects to hold the composite relationships:

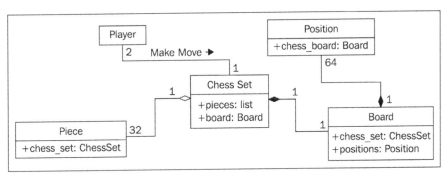

The composition relationship is represented in UML as a solid diamond. The hollow diamond represents the aggregate relationship. You'll notice that the board and pieces are stored as part of the chess set in exactly the same way a reference to them is stored as an attribute on the chess set. This shows that once again, in practice, the distinction between aggregation and composition is often irrelevant once you get past the design stage. When implemented, they behave in much the same way. However, it can help to differentiate between the two when your team is discussing how the different objects interact. Often you can treat them as the same thing, but when you need to distinguish between them, it's great to know the difference (this is abstraction at work).

Inheritance

We have discussed three types of relationships between objects: association, composition, and aggregation. But we have not fully specified our chess set, and these tools don't seem to give us all the power we need. We discussed the possibility that a player might be a human or it might be a piece of software featuring artificial intelligence. It doesn't seem right to say that a Player is *associated* with a human, or that the artificial intelligence implementation is *part of* the Player object. What we really need is the ability to say that "Deep Blue *is a* player" or that "Gary Kasparov *is a* player".

The *is a* relationship is formed by **inheritance**. Inheritance is the most famous, well-known, and over-used relationship in object-oriented programming. Inheritance is sort of like a family tree. My grandfather's last name was Phillips and my father inherited that name. I inherited it from him (along with blue eyes and a penchant for writing). In object-oriented programming, instead of inheriting features and behaviors from a person, one class can inherit attributes and methods from another class.

For example, there are thirty-two chess pieces in our chess set, but there are only six different types of pieces (pawns, rooks, bishops, knights, king, and queen), each of which behaves differently when it is moved. All of these classes of piece have properties, like color and the chess set they are part of, but they also have unique shapes when drawn on the chess board, and make different moves. See how the six types of pieces can inherit from a **Piece** class:

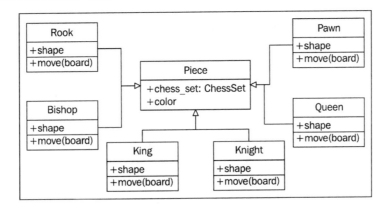

The hollow arrows, of course, indicate that the individual classes of pieces inherit from the **Piece** class. All the subtypes automatically have a **chess_set** and **color** attribute inherited from the base class. Each piece provides a different shape property (to be drawn on the screen when rendering the board), and a different **move** method to move the piece to a new position on the board at each turn.

We actually know that all subclasses of the **Piece** class need to have a **move** method, otherwise when the board tries to move the piece it will get confused. It is possible we want to create a new version of the game of chess that has one additional piece (the wizard). Our current design would allow us to design this piece without giving it a **move** method. The board would then choke when it asked the piece to move itself.

We can implement this by creating a dummy move method on the **Piece** class. The subclasses can then **override** this method with a more specific implementation. The default implementation might, for example, pop up an error message that says, **That piece cannot be moved**. Overriding methods in subtypes allows very powerful object-oriented systems to be developed. For example, if we wanted to implement a player class with artificial intelligence, we might provide a `calculate_move` method that takes a **Board** object and decides which piece to move where. A very basic class might randomly choose a piece and direction and move it. We could then override this method in a subclass with the Deep Blue implementation. The first class would be suitable for play against a raw beginner, the latter would challenge a grand master. The important thing is that other methods on the class, such as the ones that inform the board as to which move was chosen would not need to be changed; this implementation can be shared between the two classes.

In the case of chess pieces, it doesn't really make sense to provide a default implementation of the move method. All we need to do is specify that the move method is required in any subclasses. This can be done by making **Piece** an **abstract class** with the move method declared **abstract**. Abstract methods basically say "We need this method in a subclass, but we are declining to specify an implementation in this class."

Indeed, it is possible to make a class that does not implement any methods at all. Such a class would simply tell us what the class should do, but provides absolutely no advice on how to do it. In object-oriented parlance, such classes are called **interfaces**.

Inheritance provides abstraction

Now it's time for another long buzzword. **Polymorphism** is the ability to treat a class differently depending on which subclass is implemented. We've already seen it in action with the pieces system we've described. If we took the design a bit further, we'd probably see that the **Board** object can accept a move from the player and call the **move** function on the piece. The board need not ever know what type of piece it is dealing with. All it has to do is call the **move** method and the proper subclass will take care of moving it as a **Knight** or a **Pawn**.

Polymorphism is pretty cool, but it is a word that is rarely used in Python programming. Python goes an extra step past allowing a subclass of an object to be treated like a parent class. A board implemented in Python could take any object that has a move method, whether it is a Bishop piece, a car, or a duck. When **move** is called, the Bishop will move diagonally on the board, the car will drive someplace, and the duck will swim or fly, depending on its mood.

This sort of polymorphism in Python is typically referred to as **duck typing**: "If it walks like a duck or swims like a duck, it's a duck". We don't care if it really *is a* duck (inheritance), only that it swims or walks. Geese and swans might easily be able to provide the duck-like behavior we are looking for. This allows future designers to create new types of birds without actually specifying an inheritance hierarchy for aquatic birds. It also allows them to create completely different drop-in behaviors that the original designers never planned for. For example, future designers might be able to make a walking, swimming penguin that works with the same interface without ever suggesting that penguins are ducks.

Multiple inheritance

When we think of inheritance in our own family tree, we can see that we inherit features from more than just one parent. When strangers tell a proud mother that her son has, "his fathers eyes", she will typically respond along the lines of, "yes, but he got my nose".

Object-oriented design can also feature such **multiple inheritance**, which allows a subclass to inherit functionality from multiple parent classes. In practice, multiple inheritance can be tricky business, and some programming languages, (most notably, Java) strictly prohibit it. But multiple inheritance can have its uses. Most often, it can be used to create objects that have two distinct sets of behaviors. For example, an object designed to connect to a scanner and send a fax of the scanned document might be created by inheriting from two separate `scanner` and `faxer` objects.

As long as two classes have distinct interfaces, it is not normally harmful for a subclass to inherit from both of them. But it gets messy if we inherit from two classes that provide overlapping interfaces. For example, if we have a motorcycle class that has a `move` method, and a boat class also featuring a `move` method, and we want to merge them into the ultimate amphibious vehicle, how does the resulting class know what to do when we call `move`? At the design level, this needs to be explained, and at the implementation level, each programming language has different ways of deciding which parent class's method is called, or in what order.

Often, the best way to deal with it is to avoid it. If you have a design showing up like this, you're *probably* doing it wrong. Take a step back, analyze the system again, and see if you can remove the multiple inheritance relationship in favor of some other association or composite design.

Inheritance is a very powerful tool for extending behavior. It is also one of the most exciting advancements of object-oriented design over earlier paradigms. Therefore, it is often the first tool that object-oriented programmers reach for. However, it is important to recognize that owning a hammer does not turn screws into nails. Inheritance is the perfect solution for obvious *is a* relationships but it can be abused. Programmers often use inheritance to share code between two kinds of objects that are only distantly related, with no *is a* relationship in sight. While this is not necessarily a bad design, it is a terrific opportunity to ask just why they decided to design it that way, and if a different relationship or design pattern would have been more suitable.

Case study

Let's tie all our new object-oriented knowledge together by going through a few iterations of object-oriented design on a somewhat real-world example. The system we'll be modeling is a library catalog. Libraries have been tracking their inventory for centuries, originally using card catalogs, and, more recently, electronic inventories. Modern libraries have web-based catalogs that we can query from our home.

Let's start with an analysis. The local librarian has asked us to write a new card catalog program because their ancient DOS based program is ugly and out of date. That doesn't give us much detail, but before we start asking for more information, let's consider what we already know about library catalogs:

Catalogs contain lists of books. People search them to find books on certain subjects, with specific titles, or by a particular author. Books can be uniquely identified by an **International Standard Book Number (ISBN)**. Each book has a **Dewey Decimal System (DDS)** number assigned to help find it on a particular shelf.

This simple analysis tells us some of the obvious objects in the system. We quickly identify *Book* as the most important object, with several attributes already mentioned, such as author, title, subject, ISBN, and DDS number, and catalog as a sort of manager for books.

We also notice a few other objects that may or may not need to be modeled in the system. For cataloging purposes, all we need to search a book by author is an author_name attribute on the book. But authors are also objects, and we might want to store some other data about the author. As we ponder this, we might remember that some books have multiple authors. Suddenly, the idea of having a single author_name attribute on objects seems a bit silly. A list of authors associated with each book is clearly a better idea. The relationship between author and book is clearly association, since you would never say "book is an author" (it's not inheritance), and saying "book has an author", though grammatically correct, does not imply that authors are part of books (it's not aggregation). Indeed, any one author may be associated with multiple books.

We should also pay attention to the noun (nouns are always good candidates for objects) *shelf*. Is a shelf an object that needs to be modeled in a cataloging system? How do we identify an individual shelf. What happens if a book is stored at the end of one shelf, and later moved to the beginning of the next shelf because another book was inserted in the previous shelf?

DDS was designed to help locate physical books in a library. As such, storing a DDS attribute with the book should be enough to locate it, regardless of which shelf it is stored on. So we can, at least for the moment, remove shelf from our list of contending objects.

Another questionable object in the system is the user. Do we need to know anything about a specific user? Their name, address, or list of overdue books? So far the librarian has told us only that they want a catalog; they said nothing about tracking subscriptions or overdue notices. In the back of our minds, we also note that authors and users are both specific kinds of people; there might be a useful inheritance relationship here in the future.

For cataloging purposes, we decide we don't need to identify the user, for now. We can assume that a user will be searching the catalog, but we don't have to actively model them in the system, beyond providing an interface that allows them to search.

We have identified a few attributes on the book, but what properties does a catalog have? Does any one library have more than one catalog? Do we need to uniquely identify them? Obviously, the catalog has to have a list of the books it contains, somehow, but this list is probably not part of the public interface.

What about behaviors? The catalog clearly needs a search method, possibly separate ones for authors, titles, and subjects. Are there any behaviors on books? Would it need a preview method? Or could preview be identified by a first pages attribute, instead of a method?

The questions in the preceding discussion are all part of the object-oriented analysis phase. But intermixed with the questions, we have already identified a few key objects that are part of the design. Indeed, what you have just seen is several micro-iterations between analysis and design. Likely, these iterations would all occur in an initial meeting with the librarian. Before this meeting, however, we can already sketch out a most basic design for the objects we have concretely identified:

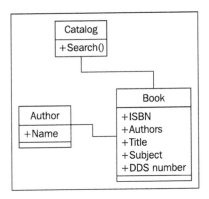

Armed with this basic diagram and a pencil to interactively improve it, we meet up with the librarian. They tell us that this is a good start, but libraries don't serve only books, they also have DVDs, magazines, and CDs, none of which have an ISBN or DDS number. All of these types of items can be uniquely identified by a UPC number, though. We remind the librarian that they have to find the items on the shelf, and these items probably aren't organized by UPC. The librarian explains that each type is organized in a different way. The CDs are mostly audio books and they only have a couple dozen in stock, so they are organized by the author's last name. DVDs are divided into genre and further organized by title. Magazines are organized by title and then refined by volume and issue number. Books are, as we had guessed, organized by DDS number.

With no previous object-oriented design experience, we might consider adding separate lists of DVDs, CDs, magazines, and books to our catalog, and search each one in turn. The trouble is, except for certain extended attributes, and identifying the physical location of the item, these items all behave in much the same. This is a job for inheritance! We quickly update our UML diagram:

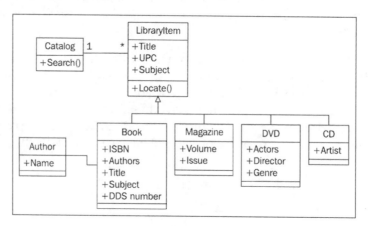

The librarian understands the gist of our sketched diagram, but is a bit confused by the **locate** functionality. We explain using a specific use case where the user is searching for the word "bunnies". The user first sends a search request to the catalog. The catalog queries its internal list of items and finds a book and a DVD with "bunnies" in the title. At this point, the catalog doesn't care if it is holding a DVD, book, CD or magazine; all items are the same, as far as the catalog is concerned. But the user wants to know how to find the physical items, so the catalog would be remiss if it simply returned a list of titles. So it calls the **locate** method on the two items it has uncovered. The book's **locate** method returns a DDS number that can be used to find the shelf holding the book. The DVD is located by returning the genre and title of the DVD. The user can then visit the DVD section, find the section containing that genre, and find the specific DVD as sorted by title.

As we explain, we sketch a UML **sequence diagram** explaining how the various objects are communicating:

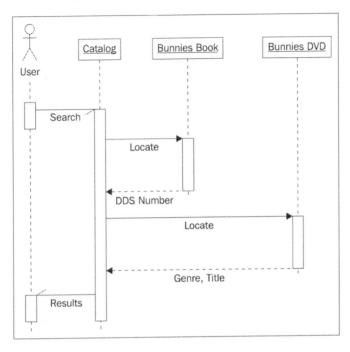

Where class diagrams describe the relationships between classes, sequence diagrams describe specific sequences of messages passed between objects. The dashed line hanging from each object is a **lifeline** describing the lifetime of the object. The wider boxes on each lifeline represent active processing in that object (where there's no box, the object is basically sitting idle, waiting for something to happen). The horizontal arrows between the lifelines indicate specific messages. The solid arrows represent methods being called, while the dashed arrows with solid heads represent the method return values. The half arrowheads indicate asynchronous messages sent to or from an object. An asynchronous message typically means the first object calls a method on the second object which returns immediately. After some processing, the second object calls a method on the first object to give it a value. This is in contrast to normal method calls, which do the processing in the method, and return a value immediately.

Sequence diagrams, like all UML diagrams, are best used when they are needed. There is no point in drawing a UML diagram for the sake of drawing a diagram. But when you need to communicate a series of interactions between two objects, the sequence diagram is a very useful tool.

Unfortunately, our class diagram so far is still a messy design. We notice that actors on DVDs and artists on CDs are all types of people, but are being treated differently from the book authors. The librarian also reminds us that most of their CDs are audio books, which have authors instead of artists.

How can we deal with different kinds of people that contribute to a title? An obvious implementation is to create a `Person` class with the person's name and other relevant details and then create subclasses of this for the artists, authors, and actors. But is inheritance really necessary here? For searching and cataloging purposes, we don't really care that acting and writing are two very different activities. If we were doing an economic simulation, it would make sense to give separate actor and author classes different `calculate_income` and `perform_job` methods, but for cataloging purposes, it is probably enough to know how the person contributed to the item. We recognize that all items have one or more **Contributor** objects, so we move the author relationship from the book to its parent class:

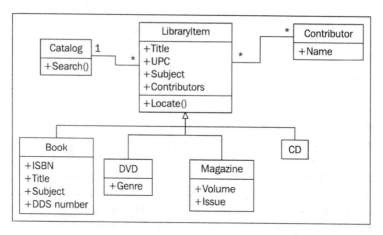

The multiplicity of the **Contributor/LibraryItem** relationship is **many-to-many**, as indicated by the * at each end of the relationship. Any one library item might have more than one contributor (for example, several actors and a director on DVD). And many authors write many books, so they would be attached to multiple library items.

This little change, while it looks a bit cleaner and simpler has lost some vital information. We can still tell who contributed to a specific library item, but we don't know how they contributed. Were they the director or an actor? Did they write the audio book, or were they the voice that narrated the book?

It would be nice if we could just add a `contributor_type` attribute on the
Contributor class, but this will fall apart when dealing with multi-talented people
who have both authored books and directed movies.

One option is to add attributes to each of our **LibraryItem** subclasses that hold the
information we need, such as **Author** on **Book**, or **Artist** on **CD**, and then make the
relationship to those properties all point to the **Contributor** class. The problem with
this is that we lose a lot of polymorphic elegance. If we want to list the contributors
to an item, we have to look for specific attributes on that item, such as **Authors**
or **Actors**. We can alleviate this by adding a **GetContributors** method on the
LibraryItem class that subclasses can override. Then the catalog never has to know
what attributes the objects are querying; we've abstracted the public interface:

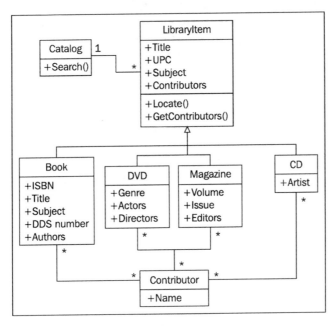

Just looking at this class diagram, it feels like we are doing something wrong. It is
bulky and fragile. It may do everything we need, but it feels like it will be hard to
maintain or extend. There are too many relationships, and too many classes would
be affected by modifications to any one class. It looks like spaghetti and meatballs.

Now that we've explored inheritance as an option, and found it wanting, we might look back at our previous composition-based diagram, where **Contributor** was attached directly to **LibraryItem**. With some thought, we can see that we actually only need to add one more relationship to a brand-new class to identify the type of contributor. This is an important step in object-oriented design. We are now adding a class to the design that is intended to *support* the other objects, rather than modeling any part of the initial requirements. We are **refactoring** the design to facilitate the objects in the system, rather than objects in real life. Refactoring is an essential process in the maintenance of a program or design. The goal of refactoring is to improve the design by moving code around, removing duplicate code or complex relationships in favor of simpler, more elegant designs.

This new class is composed of a **Contributor** and an extra attribute identifying the type of contribution the person has made to the given **LibraryItem**. There can be many such contributions to a particular **LibraryItem**, and one contributor can contribute in the same way to different items. The diagram communicates this design very well:

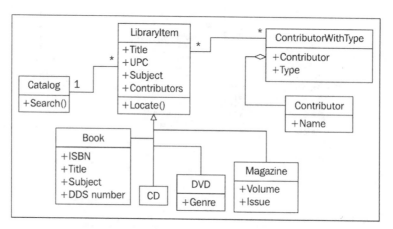

At first, this composition relationship looks less natural than the inheritance-based relationships. But it has the advantage of allowing us to add new types of contributions without adding a new class to the design. Inheritance is most useful when the subclasses have some kind of specialization. Specialization is creating or changing attributes or behaviors on the subclass to make it somehow different from the parent class. It seems silly to create a bunch of empty classes solely for identifying different types of objects (this attitude is less prevalent among Java and other "everything is an object" programmers, but it is common among more practical Python designers). If we look at the inheritance version of the diagram, we can see a bunch of subclasses that don't actually do anything:

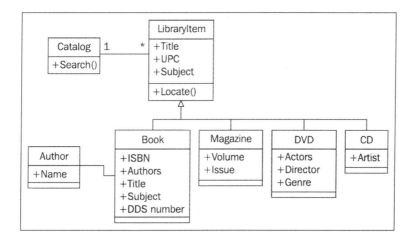

Sometimes it is important to recognize when not to use object-oriented principles. This example of when not to use inheritance is a good reminder that objects are just tools, and not rules.

Exercises

This is a practical book, not a textbook. As such, I'm not about to assign you a bunch of fake object-oriented analysis problems to create designs for. Instead, I want to give you some things to think about that you can apply to your own projects. If you have previous object-oriented experience, you won't need to put much effort into these. But they are useful mental exercises if you've been using Python for a while but never really cared about all that class stuff.

First, think about a recent programming project you've completed. Identify the most prominent object in the design. Try to think of as many attributes for this object as possible. Did it have: Color? Weight? Size? Profit? Cost? Name? ID number? Price? Style? Think about the attribute types. Were they primitives or classes? Were some of those attributes actually behaviors in disguise? Sometimes what looks like data is actually calculated from other data on the object, and you can use a method to do those calculations. What other methods or behaviors did the object have? What objects called those methods. What kinds of relationships did they have to this object?

Now think about an upcoming project. It doesn't matter what the project is; it might be a fun free-time project or a multi-million dollar contract. It doesn't have to be a complete application; it could just be one subsystem. Perform a basic object-oriented analysis. Identify the requirements and the interacting objects. Sketch out a class diagram featuring the very highest level of abstraction on that system. Identify the major interacting objects. Identify minor supporting objects. Go into detail for the attributes and methods of some of the most interesting ones. Take different objects to different levels of abstraction. Look for places you can use inheritance or composition. Look for places you should avoid inheritance.

The goal is not to design a system (although you're certainly welcome to do so if inclination meets both ambition and available time). The goal is to think about object-oriented designs. Focusing on projects that you have worked on or are expecting to work on in the future simply makes it real.

Now visit your favorite search engine and look up some tutorials on UML. There are dozens, so find the one that suits your preferred method of study. Sketch some class diagrams or a sequence diagram for the objects you identified earlier. Don't get too hung up on memorizing the syntax (after all, if it is important, you can always look it up again), just get a feel for the language. Something will stay lodged in your brain, and it can make communicating a bit easier if you can quickly sketch a diagram for your next OOP discussion.

Summary

In this chapter, we took a whirlwind tour through the terminology of the object-oriented paradigm, focusing on object-oriented design. We learned how to separate different objects into a taxonomy of different classes and to describe the attributes and behaviors of those objects via the class interface. In particular, we covered:

- Classes and objects
- Abstraction, encapsulation, and information hiding
- Designing a public interface
- Object relations: association, composition, and inheritance
- Basic UML syntax for fun and communication

In the next chapter, we'll explore how to implement classes and methods in Python.

2
Objects in Python

So, we now have a design in hand and are ready to turn that design into a working program! Of course, it doesn't usually happen that way, but this book is about programming in Python. We'll be seeing examples and hints for good software design throughout the book, but our focus is object-oriented programming. So let's have a look at the Python syntax that allows us to create object-oriented software.

After completing this chapter we will understand:

- How to create classes and instantiate objects in Python
- How to add attributes and behaviors to Python objects
- How to organize classes into packages and modules
- How to suggest people don't clobber our data

Creating Python classes

We don't have to write much Python code to realize that Python is a very "clean" language. When we want to do something, we just do it, without having to go through a lot of setup. The ubiquitous, "hello world" in Python, as you've likely seen, is only one line.

Similarly, the simplest class in Python 3 looks like this:

```python
class MyFirstClass:
    pass
```

There's our first object-oriented program! The class definition starts with the `class` keyword. This is followed by a name (of our choice) identifying the class, and is terminated with a colon.

The class name must follow standard Python variable naming rules (must start with a letter or underscore, can only be comprised of letters, underscores, or numbers). In addition, the Python style guide (search the web for "PEP 8"), recommends that classes should be named using **CamelCase** notation (start with a capital letter, any subsequent words should also start with a capital).

The class definition line is followed by the class contents, indented. As with other Python constructs, indentation is used to delimit the classes, rather than braces or brackets as many other languages use. Use four spaces for indentation unless you have a compelling reason not to (such as fitting in with somebody else's code that uses tabs for indents). Any decent programming editor can be configured to insert four spaces whenever the *Tab* key is pressed.

Since our first class doesn't actually do anything, we simply use the pass keyword on the second line to indicate that no further action needs to be taken.

We might think there isn't much we can do with this most basic class, but it does allow us to instantiate objects of that class. We can load the class into the Python 3 interpreter so we can play with it interactively. To do this, save the class definition mentioned earlier into a file named first_class.py and then run the command python -i first_class.py. The -i argument tells Python to "run the code and then drop to the interactive interpreter". The following interpreter session demonstrates basic interaction with this class:

```
>>> a = MyFirstClass()
>>> b = MyFirstClass()
>>> print(a)
<__main__.MyFirstClass object at 0xb7b7faec>
>>> print(b)
<__main__.MyFirstClass object at 0xb7b7fbac>
>>>
```

This code instantiates two objects from the new class, named a and b. Creating an instance of a class is a simple matter of typing the class name followed by a pair of parentheses. It looks much like a normal function call, but Python knows we're "calling" a class and not a function, so it understands that its job is to create a new object. When printed, the two objects tell us what class they are and what memory address they live at. Memory addresses aren't used much in Python code, but here, it demonstrates that there are two distinctly different objects involved.

Adding attributes

Now, we have a basic class, but it's fairly useless. It doesn't contain any data, and it doesn't **do** anything. What do we have to do to assign an attribute to a given object?

It turns out that we don't have to do anything special in the class definition. We can set arbitrary attributes on an instantiated object using the dot notation:

```
class Point:
    pass

p1 = Point()
p2 = Point()

p1.x = 5
p1.y = 4

p2.x = 3
p2.y = 6

print(p1.x, p1.y)
print(p2.x, p2.y)
```

If we run this code, the two print statements at the end tell us the new attribute values on the two objects:

```
5 4

3 6
```

This code creates an empty `Point` class with no data or behaviors. Then it creates two instances of that class and assigns each of those instances x and y coordinates to identify a point in two dimensions. All we need to do to assign a value to an attribute on an object is use the syntax *<object>.<attribute>* = *<value>*. This is sometimes referred to as **dot notation**. The value can be anything: a Python primitive, a built-in data type, another object. It can even be a function or another class!

Making it do something

Now, having objects with attributes is great, but object-oriented programming is really about the interaction between objects. We're interested in invoking actions that cause things to happen to those attributes. It is time to add behaviors to our classes.

Let's model a couple of actions on our `Point` class. We can start with a **method** called `reset` that moves the point to the origin (the origin is the point where `x` and `y` are both zero). This is a good introductory action because it doesn't require any parameters:

```
class Point:
    def reset(self):
        self.x = 0
        self.y = 0

p = Point()
p.reset()
print(p.x, p.y)
```

That print statement shows us the two zeros on the attributes:

```
0 0
```

A method in Python is identical to defining a function. It starts with the keyword `def` followed by a space and the name of the method. This is followed by a set of parentheses containing the parameter list (we'll discuss the `self` parameter in just a moment), and terminated with a colon. The next line is indented to contain the statements inside the method. These statements can be arbitrary Python code operating on the object itself and any parameters passed in as the method sees fit.

The one difference between methods and normal functions is that all methods have one required argument. This argument is conventionally named `self`; I've never seen a programmer use any other name for this variable (convention is a very powerful thing). There's nothing stopping you, however, from calling it `this` or even `Martha`.

The `self` argument to a method is simply a reference to the object that the method is being invoked on. We can access attributes and methods of that object as if it were any other object. This is exactly what we do inside the `reset` method when we set the `x` and `y` attributes of the `self` object.

Notice that when we call the `p.reset()` method, we do not have to pass the `self` argument into it. Python automatically takes care of this for us. It knows we're calling a method on the `p` object, so it automatically passes that object to the method.

However, the method really is just a function that happens to be on a class. Instead of calling the method on the object, we could invoke the function on the class, explicitly passing our object as the `self` argument:

```
p = Point()
Point.reset(p)
print(p.x, p.y)
```

The output is the same as the previous example because, internally, the exact same process has occurred.

What happens if we forget to include the self argument in our class definition? Python will bail with an error message:

```
>>> class Point:
...     def reset():
...         pass
...
>>> p = Point()
>>> p.reset()
Traceback (most recent call last):
  File "<stdin>", line 1, in <module>
TypeError: reset() takes no arguments (1 given)
```

The error message is not as clear as it could be ("You silly fool, you forgot the self argument" would be more informative). Just remember that when you see an error message that indicates missing arguments, the first thing to check is whether you forgot self in the method definition.

So how do we pass multiple arguments to a method? Let's add a new method that allows us to move a point to an arbitrary position, not just the origin. We can also include one that accepts another Point object as input and returns the distance between them:

```
import math

class Point:
    def move(self, x, y):
        self.x = x
        self.y = y

    def reset(self):
        self.move(0, 0)

    def calculate_distance(self, other_point):
        return math.sqrt(
                (self.x - other_point.x)**2 +
                (self.y - other_point.y)**2)

# how to use it:
point1 = Point()
```

```
point2 = Point()

point1.reset()
point2.move(5,0)
print(point2.calculate_distance(point1))
assert (point2.calculate_distance(point1) ==
        point1.calculate_distance(point2))
point1.move(3,4)
print(point1.calculate_distance(point2))
print(point1.calculate_distance(point1))
```

The print statements at the end give us the following output:

```
5.0
```

```
4.472135955
```

```
0.0
```

A lot has happened here. The class now has three methods. The move method accepts two arguments, x and y, and sets the values on the self object, much like the old reset method from the previous example. The old reset method now calls move, since a reset is just a move to a specific known location.

The calculate_distance method uses the not-too-complex Pythagorean Theorem to calculate the distance between two points. I hope you understand the math (** means squared, and math.sqrt calculates a square root), but it's not a requirement for our current focus: learning how to write methods.

The example code at the end shows how to call a method with arguments; simply include the arguments inside the parentheses, and use the same dot notation to access the method. I just picked some random positions to test the methods. The test code calls each method and prints the results on the console. The assert function is a simple test tool; the program will bail if the statement after assert is False (or zero, empty, or None). In this case, we use it to ensure that the distance is the same regardless of which point called the other point's calculate_distance method.

Initializing the object

If we don't explicitly set the x and y positions on our Point object, either using move or by accessing them directly, we have a broken point with no real position. What will happen when we try to access it?

Well, let's just try it and see. "Try it and see" is an extremely useful tool for Python study. Open up your interactive interpreter and type away. The following interactive session shows what happens if we try to access a missing attribute. If you saved the previous example as a file or are using the examples distributed with the book, you can load it into the Python interpreter with the command `python -i filename.py`.

```
>>> point = Point()
>>> point.x = 5
>>> print(point.x)
5
>>> print(point.y)
Traceback (most recent call last):
  File "<stdin>", line 1, in <module>
AttributeError: 'Point' object has no attribute 'y'
```

Well, at least it threw a useful exception. We'll cover exceptions in detail in *Chapter 4*. You've probably seen them before (especially the ubiquitous **SyntaxError**, which means you typed something incorrectly!). At this point, simply be aware that it means something went wrong.

The output is useful for debugging. In the interactive interpreter it tells us the error occurred at **line 1**, which is only partially true (in an interactive session, only one line is executed at a time). If we were running a script in a file, it would tell us the exact line number, making it easy to find the offending code. In addition, it tells us the error is an **AttributeError**, and gives a helpful message telling us what that error means.

We can catch and recover from this error, but in this case, it feels like we should have specified some sort of default value. Perhaps every new object should be `reset()` by default or maybe it would be nice if we could force the user to tell us what those positions should be when they create the object.

Most object-oriented programming languages have the concept of a **constructor**, a special method that creates and initializes the object when it is created. Python is a little different; it has a constructor *and* an initializer. Normally, the constructor function is rarely ever used unless you're doing something exotic. So we'll start our discussion with the initialization method.

The Python initialization method is the same as any other method, except it has a special name: `__init__`. The leading and trailing double underscores mean, "this is a special method that the Python interpreter will treat as a special case". Never name a function of your own with leading and trailing double underscores. It may mean nothing to Python, but there's always the possibility that the designers of Python will add a function that has a special purpose with that name in the future, and when they do, your code will break.

Let's start with an initialization function on our `Point` class that requires the user to supply `x` and `y` coordinates when the `Point` object is instantiated:

```
class Point:
    def __init__(self, x, y):
        self.move(x, y)

    def move(self, x, y):
        self.x = x
        self.y = y

    def reset(self):
        self.move(0, 0)

# Constructing a Point
point = Point(3, 5)
print(point.x, point.y)
```

Now, our point can never go without a `y` coordinate! If we try to construct a point without including the proper initialization parameters, it will fail with a **not enough arguments** error similar to the one we received earlier when we forgot the `self` argument.

What if we don't want to make those two arguments required? Well then we can use the same syntax Python functions use to provide default arguments. The keyword argument syntax appends an equals sign after each variable name. If the calling object does not provide that argument, then the default argument is used instead; the variables will still be available to the function, but they will have the values specified in the argument list. Here's an example:

```
class Point:
    def __init__(self, x=0, y=0):
        self.move(x, y)
```

Most of the time, we put our initialization statements in an __init__ function. But as mentioned earlier, Python has a constructor in addition to its initialization function. You may never need to use the other Python constructor, but it helps to know it exists, so we'll cover it briefly.

The constructor function is called __new__ as opposed to __init__, and accepts exactly one argument, the class that is being constructed (it is called **before** the object is constructed, so there is no `self` argument). It also has to return the newly created object. This has interesting possibilities when it comes to the complicated art of meta-programming, but is not very useful in day-to-day programming. In practice, you will rarely, if ever, need to use __new__, and __init__ will be sufficient.

Explaining yourself

Python is an extremely easy-to-read programming language; some might say it is self-documenting. However, when doing object-oriented programming, it is important to write API documentation that clearly summarizes what each object and method does. Keeping documentation up-to-date is difficult; the best way to do it is to write it right into our code.

Python supports this through the use of **docstrings**. Each class, function, or method header can have a standard Python string as the first line following the definition (the line that ends in a colon). This line should be indented the same as the following code.

Docstrings are simply Python strings enclosed with apostrophe (') or quote (") characters. Often, docstrings are quite long and span multiple lines (the style guide suggests that line-length should not exceed 80 characters), which can be formatted as multi-line strings, enclosed in matching triple apostrophe (''') or triple quote (""") characters.

A docstring should clearly and concisely summarize the purpose of the class or method it is describing. It should explain any parameters whose usage is not immediately obvious, and is also a good place to include short examples of how to use the API. Any caveats or problems an unsuspecting user of the API should be aware of should also be noted.

To illustrate the use of docstrings, we will end this section with our completely documented `Point` class:

```python
import math

class Point:
    'Represents a point in two-dimensional geometric coordinates'

    def __init__(self, x=0, y=0):
        '''Initialize the position of a new point. The x and y
           coordinates can be specified. If they are not, the point
           defaults to the origin.'''
        self.move(x, y)

    def move(self, x, y):
        "Move the point to a new location in two-dimensional space."
        self.x = x
        self.y = y
```

```
    def reset(self):
        'Reset the point back to the geometric origin: 0, 0'
        self.move(0, 0)

    def calculate_distance(self, other_point):
        """Calculate the distance from this point to a second point
            passed as a parameter.

        This function uses the Pythagorean Theorem to calculate
        the distance between the two points. The distance is returned
        as a float."""

        return math.sqrt(
                (self.x - other_point.x)**2 +
                (self.y - other_point.y)**2)
```

Try typing or loading (remember, it's `python -i filename.py`) this file into the interactive interpreter. Then enter `help(Point)<enter>` at the Python prompt. You should see nicely formatted documentation for the class, as shown in the following screenshot:

Modules and packages

Now that we know how to create classes and instantiate objects, it is time to think about organizing them. For small programs, we can just put all our classes into one file and put some code at the end of the file to start them interacting. However, as our projects grow, it can become difficult to find one class that needs to be edited among the many classes we've defined. This is where **modules** come in. Modules are simply Python files, nothing more. The single file in our small program is a module. Two Python files are two modules. If we have two files in the same folder, we can load a class from one module for use in the other module.

For example, if we are building an e-commerce system, we will likely be storing a lot of data in a database. We can put all the classes and functions related to database access into a separate file (we'll call it something sensible: `database.py`). Then our other modules (for example: customer models, product information, and inventory) can import classes from that module in order to access the database.

The `import` statement is used for importing modules or specific classes or functions from modules. We've already seen an example of this in our `Point` class in the previous section. We used the `import` statement to get Python's built-in `math` module so we could use its `sqrt` function in our `distance` calculation.

Here's a concrete example. Assume we have a module called `database.py` that contains a class called `Database`, and a second module called `products.py` that is responsible for product-related queries. At this point, we don't need to think too much about the contents of these files. What we know is that `products.py` needs to instantiate the `Database` class from `database.py` so it can execute queries on the product table in the database.

There are several variations on the import statement syntax that can be used to access the class.

```
import database
db = database.Database()
# Do queries on db
```

This version imports the `database` module into the `products` namespace (the list of names currently accessible in a module or function), so any class or function in the `database` module can be accessed using `database.<something>` notation. Alternatively, we can import just the one class we need using the `from...` `import` syntax:

```
from database import Database
db = Database()
# Do queries on db
```

If, for some reason, `products` already has a class called `Database`, and we don't want the two names to be confused, we can rename the class when used inside the `products` module:

```
from database import Database as DB
db = DB()
# Do queries on db
```

We can also import multiple items in one statement. If our `database` module also contains a `Query` class, we can import both classes using:

```
from database import Database, Query
```

Some sources say that we can even import all classes and functions from the `database` module using this syntax:

```
from database import *
```

Don't do this. Every experienced Python programmer will tell you that you should never use this syntax. They'll use obscure justifications like, "it clutters up the namespace", which doesn't make much sense to beginners. One way to learn why to avoid this syntax is to use it and try to understand your code two years later. But we can save some time and two years of poorly written code with a quick explanation now!

When we explicitly import the database class at the top of our file using `from database import Database`, we can easily see where the `Database` class comes from. We might use `db = Database()` 400 lines later in the file, and we can quickly look at the imports to see where that `Database` class came from. Then if we need clarification as to how to use the `Database` class, we can visit the original file (or import the module in the interactive interpreter and use the `help(database.Database)` command). However, if we use `from database import *` syntax, it takes a lot longer to find where that class is located. Code maintenance becomes a nightmare.

In addition, many editors are able to provide extra functionality, such as reliable code completion or the ability to jump to the definition of a class if normal imports are used. The `import *` syntax usually completely destroys their ability to do this reliably.

Finally, using the `import *` syntax can bring unexpected objects into our local namespace. Sure, it will import all the classes and functions defined in the module being imported from, but it will also import any classes or modules that were themselves imported into that file!

In spite of all these warnings, you may think, "if I only use `from X import *` syntax for one module, I can assume any unknown imports come from that module". This is technically true, but it breaks down in practice. I promise that if you use this syntax, you (or someone else trying to understand your code) will have extremely frustrating moments of, "Where on earth can this class be coming from?" Every name used in a module should come from a well-specified place, whether it is defined in that module, or explicitly imported from another module. There should be no magic variables that seem to come out of thin air. We should **always** be able to immediately identify where the names in our current namespace originated.

Organizing the modules

As a project grows into a collection of more and more modules, we may find that we want to add another level of abstraction, some kind of nested hierarchy on our modules' levels. But we can't put modules inside modules; one file can only hold one file, after all, and modules are nothing more than Python files.

Files, however, can go in folders and so can modules. A **package** is a collection of modules in a folder. The name of the package is the name of the folder. All we need to do to tell Python that a folder is a package and place a (normally empty) file in the folder named `__init__.py`. If we forget this file, we won't be able to import modules from that folder.

Let's put our modules inside an `ecommerce` package in our working folder, which will also contain a `main.py` to start the program. Let's additionally add another package in the `ecommerce` package for various payment options. The folder hierarchy will look like this:

```
parent_directory/
    main.py
    ecommerce/
            __init__.py
        database.py
        products.py
        payments/
                __init__.py
            paypal.py
            authorizenet.py
```

When importing modules or classes between packages, we have to be cautious about the syntax. In Python 3, there are two ways of importing modules: absolute imports and relative imports.

Absolute imports

Absolute imports specify the complete path to the module, function, or path we want to import. If we need access to the `Product` class inside the `products` module, we could use any of these syntaxes to do an absolute import:

```
import ecommerce.products
product = ecommerce.products.Product()
```

or

```
from ecommerce.products import Product
product = Product()
```

or

```
from ecommerce import products
product = products.Product()
```

The `import` statements separate packages or modules using the period as a separator.

These statements will work from any module. We could instantiate a `Product` using this syntax in `main.py`, in the `database` module, or in either of the two payment modules. Indeed, so long as the packages are available to Python, it will be able to import them. For example, the packages can also be installed to the Python site packages folder, or the **PYTHONPATH** environment variable could be customized to dynamically tell Python what folders to search for packages and modules it is going to import.

So with these choices, which syntax do we choose? It depends on your personal taste and the application at hand. If there are dozens of classes and functions inside the `products` module that I want to use, I generally import the module name using the `from ecommerce import products` syntax and then access the individual classes using `products.Product`. If I only need one or two classes from the `products` module, I import them directly using the `from ecommerce.proucts import Product` syntax. I don't personally use the first syntax very often unless I have some kind of name conflict (for example, I need to access two completely different modules called `products` and I need to separate them). Do whatever you think makes your code look more elegant.

Relative imports

When working with related modules in a package, it seems kind of silly to specify the full path; we know what our parent module is named. This is where **relative imports** come in. Relative imports are basically a way of saying "find a class, function, or module as it is positioned relative to the current module". For example, if we are working in the `products` module and we want to import the `Database` class from the `database` module "next" to it, we could use a relative import:

```
from .database import Database
```

The period in front of `database` says, "Use the database module inside the current package". In this case, the current package is the package containing the `products.py` file we are currently editing, that is, the `ecommerce` package.

If we were editing the `paypal` module inside the `ecommerce.payments` package, we would want to say, "Use the database package inside the parent package", instead. That is easily done with two periods:

```
from ..database import Database
```

We can use more periods to go further up the hierarchy. Of course, we can also go down one side and back up the other. We don't have a deep enough example hierarchy to illustrate this properly, but the following would be a valid import if we had a `ecommerce.contact` package containing an `email` module and wanted to import the `send_mail` function into our `paypal` module:

```
from ..contact.email import send_mail
```

This import uses two periods to say, "the parent of the payments package", then uses normal `package.module` syntax to go back "up" into the contact package.

Inside any one module, we can specify variables, classes, or functions. They can be a handy way of storing global state without namespace conflicts. For example, we have been importing the `Database` class into various modules and then instantiating it, but it might make more sense to have only one `database` object globally available from the `database` module. The database module might look like this:

```
class Database:
    # the database implementation
    pass

database = Database()
```

Then we can use any of the import methods we've discussed to access the database object, for example:

```
from ecommerce.database import database
```

A problem with the above class is that the database object is created immediately when the module is first imported, which is usually when the program starts up. This isn't always ideal, since connecting to a database can take a while, slowing down startup, or the database connection information may not yet be available. We could delay creating the database until it is actually needed by calling an `initialize_database` function to create the module-level variable:

```
class Database:
    # the database implementation
    pass


database = None


def initialize_database():
    global database
    database = Database()
```

The `global` keyword tells Python that the database variable inside `initialize_database` is the module-level one we just defined. If we had not specified the variable as global, Python would have created a new local variable that would be discarded when the method exits, leaving the module-level value unchanged.

As these two examples illustrate, all code in a module is executed immediately at the time it is imported. However, if it is inside a method or function, the function will be created, but its internal code will not be executed until the function is called. This can be a tricky thing for scripts (like the main script in our e-commerce example) that perform execution. Often, we will write a program that does something useful, and then later find that we want to import a function or class from that module in a different program. But as soon as we import it, any code at the module level is immediately executed. If we are not careful, we can end up running the first program when we really only meant to access a couple functions inside that module.

To solve this, we should always put our startup code in a function (conventionally called main) and only execute that function when we know we are executing as a script, but not when our code is being imported from a different script. But how do we know that?:

```
class UsefulClass:
    '''This class might be useful to other modules.'''
    pass
```

```
def main():
    '''creates a useful class and does something with it for our
module.'''
    useful = UsefulClass()
    print(useful)


if __name__ == "__main__":
    main()
```

Every module has a __name__ special variable (remember, Python uses double underscores for special variables, like a class's __init__ method) that specifies the name of the module when it was imported. But when the module is executed directly with python module.py, it is never imported, so the __name__ is set to the string "__main__". Make it a policy to wrap all your scripts in an if __name__ == "__main__": test, just in case you write a function you will find useful to be imported by other code someday.

So methods go in classes, which go in modules, which go in packages. Is that all there is to it?

Actually, no. That is the typical order of things in a Python program, but it's not the only possible layout. Classes can be defined anywhere. They are typically defined at the module level, but they can also be defined inside a function or method, like so:

```
def format_string(string, formatter=None):
    '''Format a string using the formatter object, which
    is expected to have a format() method that accepts
    a string.'''
    class DefaultFormatter:
        '''Format a string in title case.'''
        def format(self, string):
            return str(string).title()

    if not formatter:
        formatter = DefaultFormatter()

    return formatter.format(string)

hello_string = "hello world, how are you today?"
print(" input: " + hello_string)
print("output: " + format_string(hello_string))
```

Output:

```
input: hello world, how are you today?
output: Hello World, How Are You Today?
```

The `format_string` function accepts a string and optional formatter object, and then applies the formatter to that string. If no formatter is supplied, it creates a formatter of its own as a local class and instantiates it. Since it is created inside the scope of the function, this class cannot be accessed from anywhere outside of that function. Similarly, functions can be defined inside other functions as well; in general, any Python statement can be executed at any time. These "inner" classes and functions are useful for "one-off" items that don't require or deserve their own scope at the module level, or only make sense inside a single method.

Who can access my data?

Most object-oriented programming languages have a concept of "access control". This is related to abstraction. Some attributes and methods on an object are marked "private", meaning only that object can access them. Others are marked "protected", meaning only that class and any subclasses have access. The rest are "public", meaning any other object is allowed to access them.

Python doesn't do that. Python doesn't really believe in enforcing laws that might someday get in your way. Instead, it provides unenforced guidelines and best practices. Technically, all methods and attributes on a class are publicly available. If we want to suggest that a method should not be used publicly, we can put a note in docstrings indicating if a method is meant for internal use only, (preferably with an explanation of how the public-facing API works!).

By convention, we can also prefix an attribute or method with an underscore character: _. Most Python programmers will interpret this as, "This is an internal variable, think three times before accessing it directly". But there is nothing stopping them from accessing it if they think it is in their best interest to do so. Yet, if they think so, why should we stop them? We may not have any idea what future uses our classes may be put to.

There's another thing you can do to strongly suggest that outside objects don't access a property or method. Prefix it with a double underscore: __. This will perform **name mangling** on the attribute in question. This basically means that the method can still be called by outside objects if they **really** want to do it, but it requires extra work and is a strong indicator that you think your attribute should remain private. For example:

```
class SecretString:
    '''A not-at-all secure way to store a secret string.'''

    def __init__(self, plain_string, pass_phrase):
        self.__plain_string = plain_string
        self.__pass_phrase = pass_phrase

    def decrypt(self, pass_phrase):
        '''Only show the string if the pass_phrase is correct.'''
        if pass_phrase == self.__pass_phrase:
            return self.__plain_string
        else:
            return ''
```

If we load this class and test it in the interactive interpreter, we can see that it hides the plaintext string from the outside world:

```
>>> secret_string = SecretString("ACME: Top Secret", "antwerp")
>>> print(secret_string.decrypt("antwerp"))
ACME: Top Secret
>>> print(secret_string.__plain_text)
Traceback (most recent call last):
  File "<stdin>", line 1, in <module>
AttributeError: 'SecretString' object has no attribute
'__plain_text'
>>>
```

It looks like it works. Nobody can access our `plain_text` attribute without the passphrase, so it must be safe. Before we get too excited, though, let's see how easy it can be to hack our security:

```
>>> print(secret_string._SecretString__plain_string)
ACME: Top Secret
```

Oh No! Somebody has hacked our secret string. Good thing we checked! This is Python name mangling at work. When we use a double underscore, the property is prefixed with _<classname>. When methods in the class internally access the variable, they are automatically unmangled. When external classes wish to access it, they have to do the name mangling themselves. So name mangling does not guarantee privacy, it only strongly recommends it. Most Python programmers will not touch a double-underscore variable on another object unless they have an extremely compelling reason to do so.

However, most Python programmers will not touch a single-underscore variable without a compelling reason either. For the most part, there is no good reason to use a name-mangled variable in Python, and doing so can cause grief. For example, a name-mangled variable may be useful to a subclass, and it would have to do the mangling itself. Let other objects access your hidden information if they want to, just let them know, using a single-underscore prefix or some clear docstrings that you think this is not a good idea.

Finally, we can import code directly from packages, as opposed to just modules inside packages. In our earlier example, we had an ecommerce package containing two modules named database.py and products.py. The database module contains a db variable that is accessed from a lot of places. Wouldn't it be convenient if this could be imported as import ecommerce.db instead of import ecommerce.database.db?

Remember the __init__.py file that defines a directory as a package? That file can contain any variables or class declarations we like, and they will be available as part of the package. In our example, if the ecommerce/__init__.py file contained this line:

```
from .database import db
```

We could then access the db attribute from main.py or any other file using this import:

```
from ecommerce import db
```

It might help to think of the __init__.py file as if it was an ecommerce.py file if that file were a module instead of a package. This can also be useful if you put all your code in a single module and later decide to break it up into a package of modules. The __init__.py file for the new package can still be the main point of contact for other modules talking to it, but the code can be internally organized into several different modules or subpackages.

Case study

To tie it all together, let's build a simple command-line notebook application. This is a fairly simple task, so we won't be experimenting with multiple packages. We will, however, see common usage of classes, functions, methods, and docstrings.

Let's start with a quick analysis: Notes are short memos stored in a notebook. Each note should record the day it was written and can have tags added for easy querying. It should be possible to modify notes. We also need to be able to search for notes. All of this should be done from the command-line.

The obvious object is the `Note`. Less obvious is a `Notebook` container object. Tags and dates also seem to be objects, but we can use dates from Python's standard library and a comma-separated string for tags. To avoid complexity at this point, let's not define separate classes for these objects.

`Note` objects have attributes for the `memo` itself, `tags`, and a `creation_date`. Each note will also need a unique integer `id`, so that users can select them in a menu interface. Notes could have a method to modify note content and another for tags, or we could just let the notebook access those attributes directly. To make searching easier, we should put a `match` method on the `Note`. This method will accept a string and can tell us if a note matches the string without accessing the attributes directly. That way, if we want to modify the search parameters (to search tags instead of note contents, for example, or to make the search case-insensitive), we only have to do it in one place.

The `Notebook` obviously has the list of `notes` as an attribute. It will also need a `search` method that returns a list of filtered notes.

But how do we interact with these objects? We've specified a command-line app, which can either mean we run the program with different options to add or edit commands, or we could have some kind of a menu that allows us to pick different things to do to the notebook. It would be nice if we could design it so that either interface was allowed, or we could add other interfaces such as a GUI toolkit or a web-based interface in the future.

As a design decision, we'll implement the menu interface now, but will keep the command-line options version in mind to ensure we design our `Notebook` class with extensibility in mind.

So if we have two command-line interfaces each interacting with the `Notebook`, then `Notebook` is going to need some methods for them to interact with. We'll need to be able to `add` a new note, and `modify` an existing note by `id`, in addition to the `search` method we've already discussed. The interfaces will also need to be able to list all notes, but they can do that by accessing the `notes` list attribute directly.

We may be missing a few details, but that gives us a really good overview of the code we need to write. We can summarize all this in a simple class diagram:

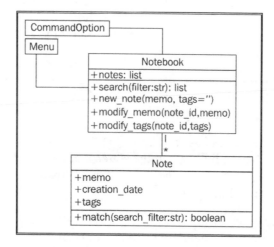

Before writing any code, let's define the folder structure for this project. The menu interface should clearly be in its own module, since it will be an executable script, and we may have other executable scripts accessing the notebook in the future. The `Notebook` and `Note` objects can live together in one module. These modules can both exist in the same top-level directory without having to put them in a package. An empty `command_option.py` module can help remind us in the future that we were planning to add new user interfaces.

```
parent_directory/
    notebook.py
    menu.py
    command_option.py
```

Now, on to the code. Let's start by defining the `Note` class, as it seems simplest. The following example presents `Note` in its entirety. Docstrings within the example explain how it all fits together.

```
import datetime

# Store the next available id for all new notes
last_id = 0

class Note:
    '''Represent a note in the notebook. Match against a
    string in searches and store tags for each note.'''

    def __init__(self, memo, tags=''):
```

```
        '''initialize a note with memo and optional
        space-separated tags. Automatically set the note's
        creation date and a unique id.'''
        self.memo = memo
        self.tags = tags
        self.creation_date = datetime.date.today()
        global last_id
        last_id += 1
        self.id = last_id

    def match(self, filter):
        '''Determine if this note matches the filter
        text. Return True if it matches, False otherwise.

        Search is case sensitive and matches both text and
        tags.'''
        return filter in self.memo or filter in self.tags
```

Before continuing, we should quickly fire up the interactive interpreter and test our code so far. Test frequently and often, because things never work the way you expect them to. Indeed, when I tested my first version of this example I found out I had forgotten the `self` argument in the `match` function! We'll discuss automated testing in *Chapter 10*; for now, it suffices to check a few things using the interpreter:

```
>>> from notebook import Note
>>> n1 = Note("hello first")
>>> n2 = Note("hello again")
>>> n1.id
1
>>> n2.id
2
>>> n1.match('hello')
True
>>> n2.match('second')
False
>>>
```

It looks like everything is behaving as expected. Let's create our notebook next:

```python
class Notebook:
    '''Represent a collection of notes that can be tagged,
    modified, and searched.'''

    def __init__(self):
        '''Initialize a notebook with an empty list.'''
        self.notes = []

    def new_note(self, memo, tags=''):
        '''Create a new note and add it to the list.'''
        self.notes.append(Note(memo, tags))

    def modify_memo(self, note_id, memo):
        '''Find the note with the given id and change its
        memo to the given value.'''
        for note in self.notes:
            if note.id == note_id:
                note.memo = memo
                break

    def modify_tags(self, note_id, tags):
        '''Find the note with the given id and change its
        tags to the given value.'''
        for note in self.notes:
            if note.id == note_id:
                note.tags = tags
                break

    def search(self, filter):
        '''Find all notes that match the given filter
        string.'''
        return [note for note in self.notes if
                note.match(filter)]
```

We'll clean that up in a minute. First let's test it to make sure it works:

```python
>>> from notebook import Note, Notebook
>>> n = Notebook()
>>> n.new_note("hello world")
>>> n.new_note("hello again")
>>> n.notes
```

```
[<notebook.Note object at 0xb730a78c>, <notebook.Note object at
  0xb73103ac>]
>>> n.notes[0].id
1
>>> n.notes[1].id
2
>>> n.notes[0].memo
'hello world'
>>> n.search("hello")
[<notebook.Note object at 0xb730a78c>, <notebook.Note object at
  0xb73103ac>]
>>> n.search("world")
[<notebook.Note object at 0xb730a78c>]
>>> n.modify_memo(1, "hi world")
>>> n.notes[0].memo
'hi world'
>>>
```

It does work. The code is a little messy though; our `modify_tags` and `modify_memo` methods are almost identical. That's not good coding practice. Let's see if we can fix it.

Both methods are trying to identify the note with a given ID before doing something to that note. So let's add a method to locate the note with a specific ID. We'll prefix the method name with an underscore to suggest that the method is for internal use only, but of course, our menu interface can access the method if it wants to.

```
    def _find_note(self, note_id):
        '''Locate the note with the given id.'''
        for note in self.notes:
            if note.id == note_id:
                return note
        return None

    def modify_memo(self, note_id, memo):
        '''Find the note with the given id and change its
        memo to the given value.'''
        self._find_note(note_id).memo = memo
```

That should work for now; let's have a look at the menu interface. The interface simply needs to present a menu and allow the user to input choices. Here's a first try:

```python
import sys
from notebook import Notebook, Note

class Menu:
    '''Display a menu and respond to choices when run.'''
    def __init__(self):
        self.notebook = Notebook()
        self.choices = {
                "1": self.show_notes,
                "2": self.search_notes,
                "3": self.add_note,
                "4": self.modify_note,
                "5": self.quit
                }

    def display_menu(self):
        print("""
Notebook Menu

1. Show all Notes
2. Search Notes
3. Add Note
4. Modify Note
5. Quit
""")

    def run(self):
        '''Display the menu and respond to choices.'''
        while True:
            self.display_menu()
            choice = input("Enter an option: ")
            action = self.choices.get(choice)
            if action:
                action()
            else:
                print("{0} is not a valid choice".format(choice))

    def show_notes(self, notes=None):
        if not notes:
            notes = self.notebook.notes
```

```
        for note in notes:
            print("{0}: {1}\n{2}".format(
                note.id, note.tags, note.memo))

    def search_notes(self):
        filter = input("Search for: ")
        notes = self.notebook.search(filter)
        self.show_notes(notes)

    def add_note(self):
        memo = input("Enter a memo: ")
        self.notebook.new_note(memo)
        print("Your note has been added.")

    def modify_note(self):
        id = input("Enter a note id: ")
        memo = input("Enter a memo: ")
        tags = input("Enter tags: ")
        if memo:
            self.notebook.modify_memo(id, memo)
        if tags:
            self.notebook.modify_tags(id, tags)

    def quit(self):
        print("Thank you for using your notebook today.")
        sys.exit(0)

if __name__ == "__main__":
    Menu().run()
```

This code first imports the notebook objects using an absolute import. Relative imports wouldn't work because we haven't placed our code inside a package. The Menu class's run method repeatedly displays a menu and responds to choices by calling functions on the notebook. This is done using an idiom that is rather peculiar to Python. The choices entered by the user are strings. In the menu's __init__ we create a dictionary that maps strings to functions on the menu object itself. Then when the user makes a choice, we retrieve the object from the dictionary. The action variable actually refers to a specific method and is called by appending empty brackets (since none of the methods require parameters) to the variable. Of course, the user might have entered an inappropriate choice, so we check if the action really exists before calling it.

The various methods each request user input and call appropriate methods on the Notebook object associated with it. For the search implementation, we notice that after we've filtered the notes, we need to show them. So we make the show_notes function serve double duty; it accepts an optional notes parameter. If it's supplied, it displays only the filtered notes, but if it's not, it displays all notes. Since the notes parameter is optional, show_notes can still be called with no parameters as an empty menu item.

If we test this code, we'll find that modifying notes doesn't work. There are two bugs, namely:

- The notebook crashes when we enter a note ID that does not exist. We should never trust our users to enter correct data!

- Even if we enter a correct ID, it will crash because the note IDs are integers, but our menu is passing a string.

The latter bug can be solved by modifying the Notebook class's _find_note method to compare the values using strings instead of the integers stored in the note, as follows:

```python
def _find_note(self, note_id):
    '''Locate the note with the given id.'''
    for note in self.notes:
        if str(note.id) == str(note_id):
            return note
    return None
```

We simply convert both the input (note_id) and the note's ID to strings before comparing them. We could also convert the input to an integer, but then we'd have trouble if the user had entered the letter "a" instead of the number "1".

The problem with users entering note IDs that don't exist can be fixed by changing the two modify methods on the notebook to check if _find_note returned a note or not, like this:

```python
def modify_memo(self, note_id, memo):
    '''Find the note with the given id and change its
    memo to the given value.'''
    note = self._find_note(note_id)
    if note:
        note.memo = memo
        return True
    return False
```

This method has been updated to return `True` or `False`, depending on whether a note has been found. The menu could use this return value to display an error if the user entered an invalid note. This code is a bit unwieldy though; it would look a bit better if it raised an exception instead. We'll cover those in *Chapter 4*.

Exercises

Write some object-oriented code. The goal is to use the principles and syntax you learned in this chapter to ensure you can use it, instead of just reading about it. If you've been working on a Python project, go back over it and see if there are some objects you can create and add properties or methods to. If it's large, try dividing it into a few modules or even packages and play with the syntax.

If you don't have such a project, try starting a new one. It doesn't have to be something you intend to finish, just stub out some basic design parts. You don't need to fully implement everything, often just a `print("this method will do something")` is all you need to get the overall design in place. This is called **top-down design**, when you work out the different interactions and describe how they should work before actually implementing what they do. The converse, **bottom-up design**, implements details first and then ties them all together. Both patterns are useful at different times, but for understanding object-oriented principles, a top-down workflow is more suitable.

If you're having trouble coming up with ideas, try writing a TO DO application. (Hint: It would be similar to the design of the notebook application, but with extra date management methods.) It can keep track of things you want to do each day, and allow you to mark them as completed.

Now, try designing a bigger project; it doesn't have to actually do anything, but make sure you experiment with the package and module importing syntax. Add some functions in various modules and try importing them from other modules and packages. Use relative and absolute imports. See the difference, and try to imagine scenarios where you would want to use each one.

Summary

In this chapter, we learned how simple it is to create classes and assign properties and methods in Python. We also covered access control and different levels of scope (packages, modules, classes, and functions). In particular, we covered:

- Class syntax
- Attributes and methods
- Initializers and constructors
- Modules and packages
- Relative and absolute imports
- Access control and its limitations

In the next chapter, we'll learn how to share implementation using inheritance.

3

When Objects are Alike

In the programming world, duplicate code is considered evil. We should not have multiple copies of the same, or similar code in different places.

There are many ways to merge similar pieces of code or objects with similar functionality. In this chapter, we'll be covering the most famous object-oriented principle: **inheritance**. As discussed in *Chapter 1*, inheritance allows us to create "is a" relationships between two or more classes, abstracting common details into superclasses and storing specific ones in the subclass. In particular, we'll be covering the Python syntax and principles for:

- Basic inheritance
- Inheriting from built-ins
- Multiple inheritance
- Polymorphism and duck typing

Basic inheritance

Technically, every class we create uses inheritance. All Python classes are subclasses of the special class named `object`. This class provides very little in terms of data and behaviors (those behaviors it does provide are all double-underscore methods intended for internal use only), but it does allow Python to treat all objects in the same way.

If we don't explicitly inherit from a different class, our classes will automatically inherit from `object`. However, we can openly state that our class derives from `object` using the following syntax:

```
class MySubClass(object):
    pass
```

This is inheritance! This example is, technically, no different from our very first example in *Chapter 2*, since Python 3 automatically inherits from `object` if we don't explicitly provide a different superclass. A **superclass**, or parent class, is a class that is being inherited from. A **subclass** is a class that is inheriting from a superclass. In this case, the superclass is `object`, and `MySubClass` is the subclass. A subclass is also said to be **derived** from its parent class or that the subclass **extends** the parent.

As you've probably figured out from the example, inheritance requires a minimal amount of extra syntax over a basic class definition. Simply include the name of the parent class inside a pair of parentheses after the class name, but before the colon terminating the class definition. This is all we have to do to tell Python that the new class should be derived from the given superclass.

How do we apply inheritance in practice? The simplest and most obvious use of inheritance is to add functionality to an existing class. Let's start with a simple contact manager that tracks the name and e-mail address of several people. The contact class is responsible for maintaining a list of all contacts in a class variable, and for initializing the name and address, in this simple class:

```python
class Contact:
    all_contacts = []

    def __init__(self, name, email):
        self.name = name
        self.email = email
        Contact.all_contacts.append(self)
```

This example introduces us to class variables. The `all_contacts` list, because it is part of the class definition, is actually shared by all instances of this class. This means that there is only **one** `Contact.all_contacts` list, and if we call `self.all_contacts` on any one object, it will refer to that single list. The code in the initializer ensures that whenever we create a new contact, the list will automatically have the new object added. Be careful with this syntax, for if you ever set the variable using `self.all_contacts`, you will actually be creating a **new** instance variable on the object; the class variable will still be unchanged and accessible as `Contact.all_contacts`.

This is a very simple class that allows us to track a couple pieces of data about our contacts. But what if some of our contacts are also suppliers that we need to order supplies from? We could add an order method to the Contact class, but that would allow people to accidentally order things from contacts who are customers or family friends. Instead, let's create a new Supplier class that acts like a Contact, but has an additional order method:

```
class Supplier(Contact):
    def order(self, order):
        print("If this were a real system we would send "
              "{} order to {}".format(order, self.name))
```

Now, if we test this class in our trusty interpreter, we see that all contacts, including suppliers, accept a name and e-mail address in their __init__, but only suppliers have a functional order method:

```
>>> c = Contact("Some Body", "somebody@example.net")
>>> s = Supplier("Sup Plier", "supplier@example.net")
>>> print(c.name, c.email, s.name, s.email)
Some Body somebody@example.net Sup Plier supplier@example.net
>>> c.all_contacts
[<__main__.Contact object at 0xb7375ecc>,
 <__main__.Supplier object at 0xb7375f8c>]
>>> c.order("Ineed pliers")
Traceback (most recent call last):
  File "<stdin>", line 1, in <module>
AttributeError: 'Contact' object has no attribute 'order'
>>> s.order("I need pliers")
If this were a real system we would send I need pliers order to
Supplier
>>>
```

So now our Supplier class can do everything a Contact can do (including adding itself to the list of all_contacts) and all the special things it needs to handle as a supplier. This is the beauty of inheritance.

Extending built-ins

One of the most interesting uses of this kind of inheritance is adding functionality to built-in classes. In the `Contact` class seen earlier, we are adding contacts to a list of all contacts. What if we also wanted to search that list by name? Well, we could add a method on the `Contact` class to search it, but it feels like this method actually belongs on the list itself. We can do this using inheritance:

```python
class ContactList(list):
    def search(self, name):
        '''Return all contacts that contain the search value
        in their name.'''
        matching_contacts = []
        for contact in self:
            if name in contact.name:
                matching_contacts.append(contact)
        return matching_contacts

class Contact:
    all_contacts = ContactList()

    def __init__(self, name, email):
        self.name = name
        self.email = email
        self.all_contacts.append(self)
```

Instead of instantiating a normal list as our class variable, we create a new `ContactList` class that extends the built-in `list`. Then we instantiate this subclass as our `all_contacts` list. We can test the new search functionality as follows:

```python
>>> c1 = Contact("John A", "johna@example.net")
>>> c2 = Contact("John B", "johnb@example.net")
>>> c3 = Contact("Jenna C", "jennac@example.net")
>>> [c.name for c in Contact.all_contacts.search('John')]
['John A', 'John B']
>>>
```

Are you wondering how we changed the built-in syntax `[]` into something we can inherit from? Creating an empty list with `[]` is actually a shorthand for creating an empty list using `list()`; the two syntaxes are identical:

```python
>>> [] == list()
True
```

So, the `list` data type is like a class that we can extend, not unlike `object`.

As a second example, we can extend the `dict` class, which is the long way of creating a dictionary (the `{ : }` syntax).

```
class LongNameDict(dict):
    def longest_key(self):
        longest = None
        for key in self:
            if not longest or len(key) > len(longest):
                longest = key
        return longest
```

This is easy to test in the interactive interpreter:

```
>>> longkeys = LongNameDict()
>>> longkeys['hello'] = 1
>>> longkeys['longest yet'] = 5
>>> longkeys['hello2'] = 'world'
>>> longkeys.longest_key()
'longest yet'
```

Most built-in types can be similarly extended. Commonly extended built-ins are `object`, `list`, `set`, `dict`, `file`, and `str`. Numerical types such as `int` and `float` are also occasionally inherited from.

Overriding and super

So inheritance is great for adding new behavior to existing classes, but what about changing behavior? Our `contact` class allows only a name and an e-mail address. This may be sufficient for most contacts, but what if we want to add a phone number for our close friends?

As we saw in *Chapter 2*, we can do this easily by just setting a phone attribute on the contact after it is constructed. But if we want to make this third variable available on initialization, we have to **override** `__init__`. Overriding is altering or replacing a method of the superclass with a new method (with the same name) in the subclass. No special syntax is needed to do this; the subclass's newly created method is automatically called instead of the superclass's method. For example:

```
class Friend(Contact):
    def __init__(self, name, email, phone):
        self.name = name
        self.email = email
        self.phone = phone
```

Any method can be overridden, not just __init__. Before we go on, however, we need to correct some problems in this example. Our Contact and Friend classes have duplicate code to set up the name and email properties; this can make maintenance complicated, as we have to update the code in two or more places. More alarmingly, our Friend class is neglecting to add itself to the all_contacts list we have created on the Contact class.

What we really need is a way to call code on the parent class. This is what the super function does; it returns the object as an instance of the parent class, allowing us to call the parent method directly:

```
class Friend(Contact):
    def __init__(self, name, email, phone):
        super().__init__(name, email)
        self.phone = phone
```

This example first gets the instance of the parent object using super, and calls __init__ on that object, passing in the expected arguments. It then does its own initialization, namely setting the phone attribute.

A super() call can be made inside any method, not just __init__. This means all methods can be modified via overriding and calls to super. The call to super can also be made at any point in the method; we don't have to make the call as the first line in the method. For example, we may need to manipulate the incoming parameters before forwarding them to the superclass.

Multiple inheritance

Multiple inheritance is a touchy subject. In principle, it's very simple: a subclass that inherits from more than one parent class is able to access functionality from both of them. In practice, this is much less useful than it sounds and many expert programmers recommend against using it. So we'll start with a warning:

> As a rule of thumb, if you think you need multiple inheritance, you're probably wrong, but if you know you need it, you're probably right.

The simplest and most useful form of multiple inheritance is called a **mixin**. A mixin is generally a superclass that is not meant to exist on its own, but is meant to be inherited by some other class to provide extra functionality. For example, let's say we wanted to add functionality to our Contact class that allows sending an e-mail to self.email. Sending e-mail is a common task that we might want to use on many other classes. So we can write a simple mixin class to do the e-mailing for us:

```
class MailSender:
    def send_mail(self, message):
        print("Sending mail to " + self.email)
        # Add e-mail logic here
```

For brevity, we won't include the actual e-mail logic here; if you're interested in studying how it's done, see the `smtplib` module in the Python standard library.

This class doesn't do anything special (in fact, it can barely function as a stand-alone class), but it does allow us to define a new class that is both a `Contact` and a `MailSender`, using multiple inheritance:

```
class EmailableContact(Contact, MailSender):
    pass
```

The syntax for multiple inheritance looks like a parameter list in the class definition. Instead of including one base class inside the parenthesis, we include two (or more), separated by a comma. We can test this new hybrid to see the mixin at work:

```
>>> e = EmailableContact("John Smith", "jsmith@example.net")
>>> Contact.all_contacts
[<__main__.EmailableContact object at 0xb7205fac>]
>>> e.send_mail("Hello, test e-mail here")
Sending mail to jsmith@example.net
```

The `Contact` initializer is still adding the new contact to the `all_contacts` list, and the mixin is able to send mail to `self.email` so we know everything is working.

That wasn't so hard, and you're probably wondering what the dire warnings about multiple inheritance are. We'll get into the complexities in a minute, but let's consider what options we had, other than using a mixin here:

- We could have used single inheritance and added the `send_mail` function to the subclass. The disadvantage here is that the e-mail functionality then has to be duplicated for any other classes that need e-mail.

- We can create a stand-alone Python function for sending mail, and just call that, with the correct e-mail address supplied as a parameter, when e-mail needs to be sent.

- We could **monkey-patch** (we'll briefly cover monkey-patching in *Chapter 7*) the `Contact` class to have a `send_mail` method after the class has been created. This is done by defining a function that accepts the `self` argument, and setting it as an attribute on an existing class.

Multiple inheritance works all right when mixing methods from different classes, but it gets very messy when we have to work with calling methods on the superclass. Why? Because there are multiple superclasses. How do we know which one to call? How do we know what order to call them in?

Let's explore these questions by adding a home address to our Friend class. What are some ways we could do this? An address is a collection of strings representing the street, city, country, and other related details of the contact. We could pass each of these strings as parameters into the Friend class's __init__ method. We could also store these strings in a tuple or dictionary and pass them into __init__ as a single argument. This is probably the best course of action if there is no additional functionality that needs to be added to the address.

Another option would be to create a new Address class to hold those strings together, and then pass an instance of this class into the __init__ in our Friend class. The advantage of this solution is that we can add behavior (say, a method to give directions to that address or to print a map) to the data instead of just storing it statically. This would be utilizing composition, the "has a" relationship we discussed in *Chapter 1*. Composition is a perfectly viable solution to this problem and allows us to reuse Address classes in other entities such as buildings, businesses, or organizations.

However, inheritance is also a viable solution, and that's what we want to explore, so let's add a new class that holds an address. We'll call this new class AddressHolder instead of Address, because inheritance defines an "is a" relationship. It is not correct to say a Friend is an Address, but since a friend can have an Address, we can argue that a Friend is an AddressHolder. Later, we could create other entities (companies, buildings) that also hold addresses. Here's our AddressHolder class:

```
class AddressHolder:
    def __init__(self, street, city, state, code):
        self.street = street
        self.city = city
        self.state = state
        self.code = code
```

Very simple; we just take all the data and toss it into instance variables upon initialization.

The diamond problem

But how can we use this in our existing `Friend` class, which is already inheriting from `Contact`? Multiple inheritance, of course. The tricky part is that we now have two parent `__init__` methods that both need to be initialized. And they need to be initialized with different arguments. How do we do that? Well, we could start with the naïve approach:

```
class Friend(Contact, AddressHolder):
    def __init__(self, name, email, phone,
            street, city, state, code):
        Contact.__init__(self, name, email)
        AddressHolder.__init__(
            self, street, city, state, code)
        self.phone = phone
```

In this example, we directly call the `__init__` function on each of the superclasses and explicitly pass the `self` argument. This example technically works; we can access the different variables directly on the class. But there are a few problems.

First, it is possible for a superclass to go uninitialized if we neglect to explicitly call the initializer. This is not bad in this example, but it could cause bad program crashes in common scenarios. Imagine, for example, trying to insert data into a database that has not been connected to.

Second, and more sinister, is the possibility of a superclass being called multiple times, because of the organization of the class hierarchy. Look at this inheritance diagram:

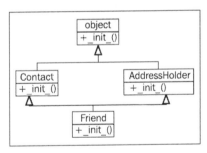

The `__init__` method from the `Friend` class first calls `__init__` on `Contact` which implicitly initializes the `object` superclass (remember, all classes derive from `object`). `Friend` then calls `__init__` on `AddressHolder`, which implicitly initializes the `object` superclass... *again*. The parent class has been set up twice. In this case, that's relatively harmless, but in some situations, it could spell disaster. Imagine trying to connect to a database twice for every request! The base class should only be called once. Once, yes, but when? Do we call `Friend` then `Contact` then `Object` then `AddressHolder`? Or `Friend` then `Contact` then `AddressHolder` then `Object`?

Technically, the order in which methods can be called can be adapted on the fly by modifying the __mro__ (**Method Resolution Order**) attribute on the class. This is beyond the scope of this book. If you think you need to understand it, I recommend *Expert Python Programming, Tarek Ziadé, Packt Publishing*, or read the original documentation on the topic at: http://www.python.org/download/releases/2.3/mro/

Let's look at a second contrived example that illustrates this problem more clearly. Here we have a base class that has a method named call_me. Two subclasses override that method, and then another subclass extends both of these using multiple inheritance. This is called diamond inheritance because of the diamond shape of the class diagram:

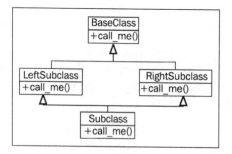

Diamonds are what makes multiple inheritance tricky. Technically, all multiple inheritance in Python 3 is diamond inheritance, because all classes inherit from object. The previous diagram, using object.__init__ is also such a diamond.

Converting this diagram to code, this example shows when the methods are called:

```
class BaseClass:
    num_base_calls = 0
    def call_me(self):
        print("Calling method on Base Class")
        self.num_base_calls += 1


class LeftSubclass(BaseClass):
    num_left_calls = 0
    def call_me(self):
        BaseClass.call_me(self)
        print("Calling method on Left Subclass")
        self.num_left_calls += 1
```

```
class RightSubclass(BaseClass):
    num_right_calls = 0
    def call_me(self):
        BaseClass.call_me(self)
        print("Calling method on Right Subclass")
        self.num_right_calls += 1


class Subclass(LeftSubclass, RightSubclass):
    num_sub_calls = 0
    def call_me(self):
        LeftSubclass.call_me(self)
        RightSubclass.call_me(self)
        print("Calling method on Subclass")
        self.num_sub_calls += 1
```

This example simply ensures each overridden call_me method directly calls the parent method with the same name. Each time it is called, it lets us know by printing the information to the screen, and updates a static variable on the class to show how many times it has been called. If we instantiate one Subclass object and call the method on it once, we get this output:

```
>>> s = Subclass()
>>> s.call_me()
Calling method on Base Class
Calling method on Left Subclass
Calling method on Base Class
Calling method on Right Subclass
Calling method on Subclass
>>> print(s.num_sub_calls, s.num_left_calls, s.num_right_calls,
s.num_base_calls)
1 1 1 2
>>>
```

The base class's call_me method has been called twice. This isn't expected behavior and can lead to some very difficult bugs if that method is doing actual work—like depositing into a bank account twice.

The thing to keep in mind with multiple inheritance is that we only want to call the "next" method in the class hierarchy, not the "parent" method. In fact, that next method may not be on a parent or ancestor of the current class. The super keyword comes to our rescue once again. Indeed, super was originally developed to make complicated forms of multiple inheritance possible. Here is the same code written using super:

```
class BaseClass:
    num_base_calls = 0
    def call_me(self):
        print("Calling method on Base Class")
        self.num_base_calls += 1

class LeftSubclass(BaseClass):
    num_left_calls = 0
    def call_me(self):
        super().call_me()
        print("Calling method on Left Subclass")
        self.num_left_calls += 1

class RightSubclass(BaseClass):
    num_right_calls = 0
    def call_me(self):
        super().call_me()
        print("Calling method on Right Subclass")
        self.num_right_calls += 1

class Subclass(LeftSubclass, RightSubclass):
    num_sub_calls = 0
    def call_me(self):
        super().call_me()
        print("Calling method on Subclass")
        self.num_sub_calls += 1
```

The change is pretty minor; we simply replaced the naïve direct calls with calls to super(). This is simple enough, but look at the difference when we execute it:

```
>>> s = Subclass()
>>> s.call_me()
Calling method on Base Class
Calling method on Right Subclass
Calling method on Left Subclass
Calling method on Subclass
```

```
>>> print(s.num_sub_calls, s.num_left_calls, s.num_right_calls,
s.num_base_calls)
1 1 1 1
```

Looks good, our base method is only being called once. But what is `super()` actually doing here? Since the `print` statements are executed after the `super` calls, the printed output is in the order each method is actually executed. Let's look at the output from back to front to see who is calling what.

First `call_me` of `Subclass` calls `super().call_me()`, which happens to refer to `LeftSubclass.call_me()`. `LeftSubclass.call_me()` then calls `super().call_me()`, but in this case, `super()` is referring to `RightSubclass.call_me()`. Pay particular attention to this; the `super` call is **not** calling the method on the superclass of `LeftSubclass` (which is `BaseClass`), it is calling `RightSubclass`, even though it is not a parent of `LeftSubclass`! This is the **next** method, not the parent method. `RightSubclass` then calls `BaseClass` and the `super` calls have ensured each method in the class hierarchy is executed once.

Different sets of arguments

Can you see how this is going to make things complicated when we return to our `Friend` multiple inheritance example? In the `__init__` method for `Friend`, we were originally calling `__init__` for both parent classes, *with different sets of arguments*:

```
Contact.__init__(self, name, email)
AddressHolder.__init__(self, street, city, state, code)
```

How can we convert this to using `super`? We don't necessarily know which class `super` is going to try to initialize first. Even if we did, we need a way to pass the "extra" arguments so that subsequent calls to `super`, on other subclasses, have the right arguments.

Specifically, if the first call to `super` passes the `name` and `email` arguments to `Contact.__init__`, and `Contact.__init__` then calls `super`, it needs to be able to pass the address related arguments to the "next" method, which is `AddressHolder.__init__`.

This is a problem whenever we want to call superclass methods with the same name, but different sets of arguments. Most often, the only time you would want to call a superclass with a completely different set of arguments is in `__init__`, as we're doing here. Even with regular methods, though, we may want to add optional parameters that only make sense to one subclass or a set of subclasses.

Sadly, the only way to solve this problem is to plan for it from the beginning. We have to design our base class parameter lists so that they accept keyword arguments for any argument that is not required by every subclass implementation. We also have to ensure the method accepts arguments it doesn't expect and pass those on in its super call, in case they are necessary to later methods in the inheritance order.

Python's function parameter syntax provides all the tools we need to do this, but it makes the overall code cumbersome. Have a look at the proper version of the Friend multiple inheritance code:

```python
class Contact:
    all_contacts = []

    def __init__(self, name='', email='', **kwargs):
        super().__init__(**kwargs)
        self.name = name
        self.email = email
        self.all_contacts.append(self)

class AddressHolder:
    def __init__(self, street='', city='', state='', code='',
            **kwargs):
        super().__init__(**kwargs)
        self.street = street
        self.city = city
        self.state = state
        self.code = code

class Friend(Contact, AddressHolder):
    def __init__(self, phone='', **kwargs):
        super().__init__(**kwargs)
        self.phone = phone
```

We've changed all arguments to keyword arguments by giving them an empty string as a default value. We've also ensured that a **kwargs parameter is included to capture any additional parameters that our particular method doesn't know what to do with. It passes these parameters up to the next class with the super call.

> If you aren't familiar with the **kwargs syntax, it basically collects any keyword arguments passed into the method that were not explicitly listed in the parameter list. These arguments are stored in a dictionary named kwargs (we can call the variable whatever we like, but convention suggests kw, or kwargs). When we call a different method (for example: super().__init__) with a **kwargs syntax, it unpacks the dictionary and passes the results to the method as normal keyword arguments. We'll cover this in detail in *Chapter 7*.

The previous example does what it is supposed to do. But it's starting to look messy, and it has become difficult to answer the question, "What arguments do we need to pass into `Friend.__init__`?" This is the foremost question for anyone planning to use the class, so a `docstring` should be added to the method to explain what is happening.

Further, even this implementation is insufficient if we want to "reuse" variables in parent classes. When we pass the `**kwargs` variable to `super`, the dictionary does not include any of the variables that were included as explicit keyword arguments. For example, in `Friend.__init__`, the call to `super` does not have `phone` in the `kwargs` dictionary. If **any** of the other classes need the `phone` parameter, we need to ensure it is in the dictionary that is passed. Worse, if we forget to do that, it will be tough to debug, because the superclass will not complain, but will simply assign the default value (in this case, an empty string) to the variable.

There are a few ways to ensure that the variable is passed upwards. Assume the `Contact` class does, for some reason, need to be initialized with a phone parameter, and the `Friend` class will also need access to it. We can do any of the following:

- Don't include `phone` as an explicit keyword argument. Instead, leave it in the `kwargs` dictionary. `Friend` can look it up using the syntax `kwargs['phone']`. When it passes `**kwargs` to the `super` call, `phone` will still be in the dictionary.

- Make `phone` an explicit keyword argument but update the `kwargs` dictionary before passing it to `super`, using the standard dictionary syntax `kwargs['phone'] = phone`.

- Make `phone` an explicit keyword argument, but update the `kwargs` dictionary using the `kwargs.update` method. This is useful if you have several arguments to update. You can create the dictionary passed into `update` using either the `dict(phone=phone)` constructor, or the dictionary syntax `{'phone': phone}`.

- Make `phone` an explicit keyword argument, but pass it to the super call explicitly with the syntax `super().__init__(phone=phone, **kwargs)`.

We have covered many of the caveats involved with multiple inheritance in Python. When we need to account for all the possible situations, we have to plan for them and our code will get messy. Basic multiple inheritance can be handy, but in many cases, we may want to choose a more transparent way of combining two disparate classes, usually using composition or one of the design patterns we'll be covering in *Chapter 8* and *Chapter 9*.

Polymorphism

We introduced polymorphism in *Chapter 1*. It is a fancy name describing a simple concept; different behaviors happen depending on which subclass is being used, without having to explicitly know what the subclass actually is. As an example, imagine a program that plays audio files. A media player might need to load an AudioFile object and then play it. We'd put a play() method on the object, which is responsible for decompressing or extracting the audio and routing it to the sound card and speakers. The act of playing an AudioFile could feasibly be as simple as:

```
audio_file.play()
```

However the process of decompressing and extracting an audio file is very different for different types of files. The .wav files are stored uncompressed, while .mp3, .wma, and .ogg files all have very different compression algorithms.

We can use inheritance with polymorphism to simplify the design. Each type of file can be represented by a different subclass of AudioFile, for example, WavFile, MP3File. Each of these would have a play() method, but that method would be implemented differently for each file to ensure the correct extraction procedure is followed. The media player object would never need to know which subclass of AudioFile it is referring to; it just calls play() and polymorphically lets the object take care of the actual details of playing. Let's look at a quick skeleton showing how this might look:

```
class AudioFile:
    def __init__(self, filename):
        if not filename.endswith(self.ext):
            raise Exception("Invalid file format")

        self.filename = filename

class MP3File(AudioFile):
    ext = "mp3"
    def play(self):
        print("playing {} as mp3".format(self.filename))

class WavFile(AudioFile):
    ext = "wav"
    def play(self):
        print("playing {} as wav".format(self.filename))

class OggFile(AudioFile):
    ext = "ogg"
    def play(self):
        print("playing {} as ogg".format(self.filename))
```

All audio files check to ensure that a valid extension was given upon initialization. But notice how the __init__ method in the parent class is able to access the ext class variable from different subclasses? That's polymorphism at work. If the filename doesn't end with the correct name, it raises an exception (exceptions will be covered in detail in the next chapter). The fact that AudioFile doesn't actually store a reference to the ext variable doesn't stop it from being able to access it on the subclass.

In addition, each subclass of AudioFile implements play() in a different way (this example doesn't actually play the music; audio compression algorithms really deserve a separate book!). This is also polymorphism in action. The media player can use the exact same code to play a file, no matter what type it is; it doesn't care what subclass of AudioFile it is looking at. The details of decompressing the audio file are *encapsulated*. If we test this example, it works as we would hope:

```
>>> ogg = OggFile("myfile.ogg")
>>> ogg.play()
playing myfile.ogg as ogg
>>> mp3 = MP3File("myfile.mp3")
>>> mp3.play()
playing myfile.mp3 as mp3
>>> not_an_mp3 = MP3File("myfile.ogg")
Traceback (most recent call last):
  File "<stdin>", line 1, in <module>
  File "polymorphic_audio.py", line 4, in __init__
    raise Exception("Invalid file format")
Exception: Invalid file format
```

See how AudioFile.__init__ is able to check the file type without actually knowing what subclass it is referring to?

Polymorphism is actually one of the coolest things about object-oriented programming, and it makes some programming designs obvious that weren't possible in earlier paradigms. However, Python makes polymorphism less cool because of duck typing. Duck typing in Python allows us to use **any** object that provides the required behavior without forcing it to be a subclass. The dynamic nature of Python makes this trivial. The following example does not extend AudioFile, but it can be interacted with in Python using the exact same interface:

```
class FlacFile:
    def __init__(self, filename):
        if not filename.endswith(".flac"):
```

```
        raise Exception("Invalid file format")

    self.filename = filename

def play(self):
    print("playing {} as flac".format(self.filename))
```

Our media player can play this object just as easily as one that extends `AudioFile`.

Polymorphism is one of the most important reasons to use inheritance in many object-oriented contexts. Because any objects that supply the correct interface can be used interchangeably in Python, it reduces the need for polymorphic common superclasses. Inheritance can still be useful for sharing code, but if all that is being shared is the public interface, duck typing is all that is required. This reduced need for inheritance also reduces the need for multiple inheritance; often, when multiple inheritance appears to be a valid solution, we just can use duck typing to mimic one of the multiple superclasses.

Of course, just because an object satisfies a particular interface (by providing required methods or attributes) does not mean it will simply work in all situations. It has to fulfill that interface in a way that makes sense in the overall system. Just because an object provides a `play()` method does not mean it will automatically work with a media player. For example, our chess AI object from *Chapter 1* may have a `play()` method that moves a chess piece. Even though it satisfies the interface, this class would likely break in spectacular ways if we tried to plug it into a media player!

Another useful feature of duck typing is that the duck-typed object only needs to provide those method and attributes that are actually being accessed. For example, if we needed to create a fake file object to read data from, we can create a new object that has a `read()` method; we don't have to override the `write` method if the code that is going to interact with the object will only be reading from the file. More succinctly, duck typing doesn't need to provide the entire interface of an object that is available, it only needs to fulfill the interface that is actually used.

Case study

Let's try to tie everything we've learned together with a larger example. We'll be designing a simple real estate application that allows an agent to manage properties available for purchase or rent. There will be two types of properties: apartments and houses. The agent needs to be able to enter a few relevant details about new properties, list all currently available properties, and mark a property as sold or rented. For brevity, we won't worry about editing property details or reactivating a property after it is sold.

The project will allow the agent to interact with the objects using the Python interpreter prompt. In this world of graphical user interfaces and web applications, you might be wondering why we're creating such old-fashioned looking programs. Simply put, both windowed programs and web applications require a lot of overhead knowledge and boilerplate code to make them do what is required. If we were developing software using either of these paradigms, we'd get so lost in "GUI programming" or "web programming" that we'd lose sight of the object-oriented principles we're trying to master.

Luckily, most GUI and web frameworks utilize an object-oriented approach, and the principles we're studying now will help in understanding those systems in the future. We'll discuss them both briefly, in *Chapter 12*, but complete details are far beyond the scope of a single book.

Looking at our requirements it seems like there are quite a few nouns that might represent classes of objects in our system. Clearly we'll need to represent a Property. Houses and apartments may need separate classes. Rentals and purchases also seem to require separate representation. Since we're focusing on inheritance right now, we'll be looking at ways to share behavior using inheritance or multiple inheritance.

Clearly, `House` and `Apartment` are both types of properties, so `Property` can be a superclass of those two classes. `Rental` and `Purchase` will need some extra thought; if we use inheritance, we'll need to have separate classes, for example, for `HouseRental` and `HousePurchase`, and use multiple inheritance to combine them. This feels a little clunky compared to a composition/association-based design, but let's run with it and see what we come up with.

Now then, what attributes might be associated with a `Property`? Regardless of whether it is an apartment or a house, most people will want to know the square footage, number of bedrooms, and number of bathrooms. (There are numerous other attributes that might be modeled, but we'll keep it simple for our prototype.)

If the property is a house, it will want to advertise the number of stories, whether it has a garage (attached, detached, or none), and whether the yard is fenced. An apartment will want to indicate if it has a balcony, and if laundry is en-suite, coin, or off-site.

Both property types will require a method to display the characteristics of that property. At the moment, no other behaviors are apparent.

Rental properties will need to store the rent per month, whether the property is furnished, and whether utilities are included, and if not, what they are estimated to be. Properties for purchase will need to store the purchase price and estimated annual property taxes. For our application, we'll only need to display this data, so we can get away with just adding a `display()` method similar to that used in the other classes.

Finally, we'll need an `Agent` object that holds a list of all properties, displays those properties, and allows us to create new ones. Creating properties will entail prompting the user for the relevant details for each property type. This could be done in the `Agent` object, but then `Agent` would need to know a lot of information about the types of properties. This is not taking advantage of polymorphism. Another alternative would be to put the prompts in the initializer or even a constructor for each class, but this would not allow the classes to be applied later in a GUI or web application in the future. A better idea is to create a static method that does the prompting and returns a dictionary of the prompted parameters. Then all the `Agent` has to do is prompt the user for the type of property and payment method, and ask the correct class to instantiate itself.

That's a lot of designing for a seemingly simple app! The following class diagram may communicate our design decisions a little more clearly:

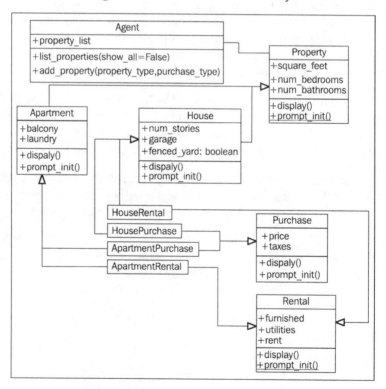

Wow, That's a lot of inheritance arrows! I don't think it would be possible to add another level of inheritance without crossing arrows. Multiple inheritance is messy business, even at the design stage.

Clearly, the trickiest aspects of these classes is going to be ensuring superclass methods get called in the inheritance hierarchy. Let's start with the `Property` implementation:

```python
class Property:
    def __init__(self, square_feet='', beds='',
            baths='', **kwargs):
        super().__init__(**kwargs)
        self.square_feet = square_feet
        self.num_bedrooms = beds
        self.num_baths = baths

    def display(self):
        print("PROPERTY DETAILS")
        print("================")
        print("square footage: {}".format(self.square_feet))
        print("bedrooms: {}".format(self.num_bedrooms))
        print("bathrooms: {}".format(self.num_baths))
        print()

    def prompt_init():
        return dict(square_feet=input("Enter the square feet: "),
                beds=input("Enter number of bedrooms: "),
                baths=input("Enter number of baths: "))
    prompt_init = staticmethod(prompt_init)
```

This class is pretty straightforward. We've already added the extra `**kwargs` parameter to `__init__` because we know it's going to be used in a multiple inheritance situation. We've also included a call to `super().__init__` in case we are not the last call in the multiple inheritance chain. In this case, we're "consuming" the keyword arguments because we know they won't be needed at other levels of the inheritance hierarchy.

We see something new in the `prompt_init` method. This method is made into a static method immediately after it is initially created. Static methods are associated only with a class (much like class variables), rather than a specific object instance. Hence, they have no `self` argument. Because of this, the `super` keyword won't work (there is no parent object, only a parent class), so we simply call the static method on the parent class directly. This method uses the Python `dict` constructor to create a dictionary of values that can be passed into `__init__`. The value for each key is prompted with a call to `input`.

The `Apartment` class extends `Property`, and is similar in structure:

```
class Apartment(Property):
    valid_laundries = ("coin", "ensuite", "none")
    valid_balconies = ("yes", "no", "solarium")

    def __init__(self, balcony='', laundry='', **kwargs):
        super().__init__(**kwargs)
        self.balcony = balcony
        self.laundry = laundry

    def display(self):
        super().display()
        print("APARTMENT DETAILS")
        print("laundry: %s" % self.laundry)
        print("has balcony: %s" % self.balcony)


        parent_init = Property.prompt_init()
        laundry = ''
        while laundry.lower() not in \
                Apartment.valid_laundries:
            laundry = input("What laundry facilities does "
                    "the property have? ({})".format(
                    ", ".join(Apartment.valid_laundries))
        balcony = ''
        while balcony.lower() not in \
                Apartment.valid_balconies:
            balcony = input(
                "Does the property have a balcony? "
                "({})".format(
                ", ".join(Apartment.valid_balconies))
        parent_init.update({
            "laundry": laundry,
            "balcony": balcony
        })
        return parent_init
    prompt_init = staticmethod(prompt_init)
```

The `display()` and `__init__()` methods call their respective parent class methods using `super()` to ensure the `Property` class is properly initialized.

The `prompt_init` static method is now getting dictionary values from the parent class, and then adding some additional values of its own. It calls the `dict.update` method to merge the new dictionary values into the first one. However, that `prompt_init` method is looking pretty ugly; it twice loops until the user enters a valid input using structurally similar code but different variables. It would be nice to extract this validation logic so we can maintain it in only one location; it will likely also be useful to later classes.

With all the talk on inheritance, we might think this is a good place to use a `mixin`. Instead, we have a chance to study a situation where inheritance is not the best solution. The method we want to create will be used in a static method. If we were to inherit from a class that provided validation functionality, the functionality would also have to be provided as a static method that did not access any instance variables on the class. If it doesn't access any instance variables, what's the point of making it a class at all? Why don't we just make this validation functionality a module-level function that accepts an input string and list of valid answers, and leave it at that?

Let's explore what this validation function would look like:

```
def get_valid_input(input_string, valid_options):
    input_string += " ({}) ".format(", ".join(valid_options))
    response = input(input_string)
    while response.lower() not in valid_options:
        response = input(input_string)
    return response
```

We can test this function in the interpreter, independently of all the other classes we've been working on. This is a good sign, it means different pieces of our design are not tightly coupled to each other and can later be improved independently, without affecting other pieces of code.

```
>>> get_valid_input("what laundry?", ("coin", "ensuite", "none"))
what laundry? (coin, ensuite, none) hi
what laundry? (coin, ensuite, none) COIN
'COIN'
```

Now, let's quickly update our `Apartment.prompt_init` method to use this new function for validation:

```
def prompt_init():
    parent_init = Property.prompt_init()
    laundry = get_valid_input(
            "What laundry facilities does "
            "the property have? ",
            Apartment.valid_laundries)
```

```
        balcony = get_valid_input(
            "Does the property have a balcony? ",
            Apartment.valid_balconies)
        parent_init.update({
            "laundry": laundry,
            "balcony": balcony
        })
        return parent_init
    prompt_init = staticmethod(prompt_init)
```

That's much easier to read (and maintain!) than our original version. Now we're ready to build the `House` class. This class has a parallel structure to `Apartment`, but refers to different prompts and variables:

```
class House(Property):
    valid_garage = ("attached", "detached", "none")
    valid_fenced = ("yes", "no")

    def __init__(self, num_stories='',
            garage='', fenced='', **kwargs):
        super().__init__(**kwargs)
        self.garage = garage
        self.fenced = fenced
        self.num_stories = num_stories

    def display(self):
        super().display()
        print("HOUSE DETAILS")
        print("# of stories: {}".format(self.num_stories))
        print("garage: {}".format(self.garage))
        print("fenced yard: {}".format(self.fenced))


    def prompt_init():
        parent_init = Property.prompt_init()
        fenced = get_valid_input("Is the yard fenced? ",
                House.valid_fenced)
        garage = get_valid_input("Is there a garage? ",
            House.valid_garage)
        num_stories = input("How many stories? ")

        parent_init.update({
            "fenced": fenced,
            "garage": garage,
```

```
                "num_stories": num_stories
        })
        return parent_init
    prompt_init = staticmethod(prompt_init)
```

There's nothing new to explore here, so let's move on to the `Purchase` and `Rental` classes. In spite of having apparently different purposes, they are also similar in design to the ones we just discussed:

```
class Purchase:
    def __init__(self, price='', taxes='', **kwargs):
        super().__init__(**kwargs)
        self.price = price
        self.taxes = taxes

    def display(self):
        super().display()
        print("PURCHASE DETAILS")
        print("selling price: {}".format(self.price))
        print("estimated taxes: {}".format(self.taxes))


    def prompt_init():
        return dict(
            price=input("What is the selling price? "),
            taxes=input("What are the estimated taxes? "))
    prompt_init = staticmethod(prompt_init)

class Rental:
    def __init__(self, furnished='', utilities='',
            rent='', **kwargs):
        super().__init__(**kwargs)
        self.furnished = furnished
        self.rent = rent
        self.utilities = utilities

    def display(self):
        super().display()
        print("RENTAL DETAILS")
        print("rent: {}".format(self.rent))
        print("estimated utilities: {}".format(
            self.utilities))
        print("furnished: {}".format(self.furnished))
```

```
def prompt_init():
    return dict(
        rent=input("What is the monthly rent? "),
        utilities=input(
            "What are the estimated utilities? "),
        furnished = get_valid_input(
            "Is the property furnished? ",
                ("yes", "no")))
prompt_init = staticmethod(prompt_init)
```

These two classes don't have a superclass (other than `object`), but we still call
`super().__init__` because they are going to be combined with the other classes,
and we don't know what order the `super` calls will be made in. The interface
is similar to that used for `House` and `Apartment`, which is very useful when we
combine the functionality of these four classes in separate subclasses. For example:

```
class HouseRental(Rental, House):
    def prompt_init():
        init = House.prompt_init()
        init.update(Rental.prompt_init())
        return init
    prompt_init = staticmethod(prompt_init)
```

This is slightly surprising, as it has neither an __init__ nor display method!
Because both parent classes appropriately call `super` in these methods, we only have
to extend those classes and the classes will behave in the correct order. This is not
the case with prompt_init, of course, since it is a static method that does not call
`super`, so we implement this one explicitly. We should test this class to make sure it
is behaving properly before we write the other three combinations:

```
>>> init = HouseRental.prompt_init()
Enter the square feet: 1
Enter number of bedrooms: 2
Enter number of baths: 3
Is the yard fenced?  (yes, no) no
Is there a garage?  (attached, detached, none) none
How many stories? 4
What is the monthly rent? 5
What are the estimated utilities? 6
Is the property furnished?  (yes, no) no
>>> house = HouseRental(**init)
>>> house.display()
```

```
PROPERTY DETAILS
================
square footage: 1
bedrooms: 2
bathrooms: 3


HOUSE DETAILS
# of stories: 4
garage: none
fenced yard: no


RENTAL DETAILS
rent: 5
estimated utilities: 6
furnished: no
```

It looks like it is working fine. The `prompt_init` method is prompting for initializers to all the super classes, and `display()` is also cooperatively calling all three superclasses.

Note: The order of the inherited classes in the preceding example is important. If we had written `class HouseRental(House, Rental)` instead of `class HouseRental(Rental, House)`, `display()` would not have called `Rental.display()`! When `display` is called on our version of `HouseRental`, it refers to the `Rental` version of the method, which calls `super.display()` to get the `House` version, which again calls `super.display()` to get the property version. If we reverse it, display would refer to the `House` class's `display()`. When super is called, it calls the method on the `Property` parent class. But `Property` does not have a call to super in its `display` method. This means `Rental` class's `display` method would not be called! By placing the inheritance list in the order we did, we ensure that `Rental` calls super, which then takes care of the `House` side of the hierarchy. You might think we could have added a `super` call to `Property.display()`, but that will fail because the next superclass of `Property` is `object`, and `object` does not have a `display` method. Another way to fix this is to allow `Rental` and `Purchase` to extend the `Property` class instead of deriving directly from `object`. (Or we could modify the method resolution order dynamically, but that is beyond the scope of this book.)

Now that we have tested it, we are prepared to create the rest of our combined subclasses:

```
class ApartmentRental(Rental, Apartment):
    def prompt_init():
        init = Apartment.prompt_init()
        init.update(Rental.prompt_init())
        return init
    prompt_init = staticmethod(prompt_init)

class ApartmentPurchase(Purchase, Apartment):
    def prompt_init():
        init = Apartment.prompt_init()
        init.update(Purchase.prompt_init())
        return init
    prompt_init = staticmethod(prompt_init)

class HousePurchase(Purchase, House):
    def prompt_init():
        init = House.prompt_init()
        init.update(Purchase.prompt_init())
        return init
    prompt_init = staticmethod(prompt_init)
```

That should be the most intense designing out of our way! Now all we have to do is create the Agent, which is responsible for creating new listings and displaying existing ones. Let's start with the simpler storing and listing of properties:

```
class Agent:
    def __init__(self):
        self.property_list = []

    def display_properties(self):
        for property in self.property_list:
            property.display()
```

Adding a property will require first querying the type of property and whether property is for purchase or rental. We can do this by displaying a simple menu. Once this has been determined, we can extract the correct subclass and prompt for all the details using the prompt_init hierarchy we've already developed. Sound simple? It is. Let's start by adding a dictionary class variable to the Agent class:

```
type_map = {
    ("house", "rental"): HouseRental,
    ("house", "purchase"): HousePurchase,
    ("apartment", "rental"): ApartmentRental,
    ("apartment", "purchase"): ApartmentPurchase
    }
```

That's some pretty funny looking code. This is a dictionary, where the keys are tuples of two distinct strings, and the values are class objects. Class objects? Yes, classes can be passed around, renamed, and stored in containers just like "normal" objects or primitive data types. With this simple dictionary, we can simply hijack our earlier `get_valid_input` method to ensure we get correct dictionary keys and look up the appropriate class, like so:

```
def add_property(self):
    property_type = get_valid_input(
            "What type of property? ",
            ("house", "apartment")).lower()
    payment_type = get_valid_input(
            "What payment type? ",
            ("purchase", "rental")).lower()

    PropertyClass = self.type_map[
        (property_type, payment_type)]
    init_args = PropertyClass.prompt_init()
    self.property_list.append(PropertyClass(**init_args))
```

This may look a bit funny, too! We look up the class in the dictionary and store it in a variable named `PropertyClass`. We don't know exactly which class we have available, but the class knows itself, so we can polymorphically call `prompt_init` to get a dictionary of values appropriate to pass into the constructor. Then we use the keyword argument syntax to convert the dictionary into arguments and construct the new object to load the correct data.

Now our user can use this `Agent` class to add and view lists of properties. It wouldn't take much work to add features to mark a property as available or unavailable or to edit and remove properties. Our prototype is now in a good enough state to take to a real estate `agent` and demonstrate its functionality. Here's how a demo session might work:

```
>>> agent = Agent()
>>> agent.add_property()
What type of property?  (house, apartment) house
What payment type?  (purchase, rental) rental
Enter the square feet: 900
Enter number of bedrooms: 2
Enter number of baths: one and a half
Is the yard fenced?  (yes, no) yes
Is there a garage?  (attached, detached, none) detached
How many stories? 1
```

```
What is the monthly rent? 1200
What are the estimated utilities? included
Is the property furnished?  (yes, no) no
>>> agent.add_property()
What type of property?  (house, apartment) apartment
What payment type?  (purchase, rental) purchase
Enter the square feet: 800
Enter number of bedrooms: 3
Enter number of baths: 2
What laundry facilities does the property have?  (coin, ensuite,
one) ensuite
Does the property have a balcony? (yes, no, solarium) yes
What is the selling price? $200,000
What are the estimated taxes? 1500
>>> agent.display_properties()
PROPERTY DETAILS
================
square footage: 900
bedrooms: 2
bathrooms: one and a half


HOUSE DETAILS
# of stories: 1
garage: detached
fenced yard: yes
RENTAL DETAILS
rent: 1200
estimated utilities: included
furnished: no
PROPERTY DETAILS
================
square footage: 800
bedrooms: 3
bathrooms: 2


APARTMENT DETAILS
```

```
laundry: ensuite
has balcony: yes
PURCHASE DETAILS
selling price: $200,000
estimated taxes: 1500
>>>
```

Exercises

Look around you at some of the physical objects in your workspace and see if you can describe them in an inheritance hierarchy. Humans have been dividing the world into taxonomies like this for centuries, so it shouldn't be difficult. Are there any non-obvious inheritance relationships between classes of objects? If you were to model these objects in a computer application, what properties and methods would they share? Which ones would have to be polymorphically overridden? What properties would be completely different between them?

Now, write some code. No, not for the physical hierarchy; that's boring. Physical items have more properties than methods. Just think about a pet programming project you've wanted to tackle in the past year, but never got around to. For whatever problem you want to solve, try to think of some basic inheritance relationships. Then implement them. Make sure you pay attention to the sorts of relationships that you actually don't need to use inheritance for, too! Are there any places where you might want to use multiple inheritance? Are you sure? Can you see any place you would want to use a mixin? Try to knock together a quick prototype. It doesn't have to be useful or even partially working. You've seen how you can test code using python3 -i already; just write some code and test it in the interactive interpreter. If it works, write some more. If it doesn't, fix it!

Now take a look at the real estate example. This turned out to be a quite effective use of multiple inheritance. I have to admit though, I had my doubts when I started the design. Have a look at the original problem and see if you can come up with another design to solve it that uses only single inheritance. What about a design that doesn't use inheritance at all? Of the three, which do you think is the most elegant solution? Elegance is a primary goal in Python development, but each programmer has a different opinion as to what is the most elegant solution. Some people tend to think and understand problems most clearly using composition, while others find multiple inheritance to be the most useful tool.

Finally, try adding some new features to the three designs. Whatever features strike your fancy are fine. I'd like to see a way to differentiate between available and unavailable properties, for starters. It's not much use to me if it's already rented!

Which design is easiest to extend? Which is hardest? If somebody asked you why you thought that, would you be able to explain yourself?

Summary

We've gone from simple inheritance, one of the most useful tools in the object-oriented programmer's toolbox, all the way through to multiple inheritance, one of the most complicated. We learned how to:

- Add functionality to existing classes and built-ins using inheritance
- Share similar code between classes by abstracting it into a parent class
- Combine multiple threads of functionality using multiple inheritance
- Call parent methods using `super`
- Format argument lists in multiple inheritance so super doesn't choke

In the next chapter, we'll cover the subtle art of handling exceptional circumstances.

4

Expecting the Unexpected

Programs are very fragile. It would be nice if code always returned a valid result, but sometimes a valid result can't be calculated. It's not possible to divide by zero, or to access the eighth item in a five-item list, for example.

In the old days, the only way around this was to rigorously check the inputs for every function to make sure they made sense. Typically functions had special return values to indicate an error condition; for example, they could return a negative number to indicate that a positive value couldn't be calculated. Different numbers might mean different errors occurred. Any code that called this function would have to explicitly check for an error condition and act accordingly. A lot of code didn't bother to do this, and programs simply crashed.

Not so in the object-oriented world! In this chapter we will study **exceptions**, special error objects that only need to be handled when it makes sense to handle them. In particular, we will cover:

- How to cause an exception to occur
- How to recover when an exception has occurred
- How to handle different exceptions with different code
- Cleaning up when an exception has occurred
- Creating new exceptions
- Using the exception syntax for flow control

Raising exceptions

So what is an exception, really? Technically, an exception is just an object. There are many different exception classes available and we can easily define more of our own. The one thing they all have in common is that they derive from a built-in class called `BaseException`.

These exception objects become special when they are handled inside the program's flow of control. When an exception occurs, everything that was supposed to happen doesn't happen, **unless** it was supposed to happen when an exception occurred. Make sense? Don't worry, it will!

So then, how do we cause an exception to occur? The easiest way is to do something stupid! Chances are you've done this already and seen the exception output. For example, any time Python encounters a line in your program that it can't understand, it bails with a SyntaxError, which is a type of exception. Here's a common one:

```
>>> print "hello world"
  File "<stdin>", line 1
    print "hello world"
                      ^
SyntaxError: invalid syntax
```

That print statement was a valid command in Python 2 and previous versions, but in Python 3, because print is a function, we have to enclose the arguments in parenthesis. So if we type the above into a Python 3 interpreter, we get the SyntaxError exception.

A SyntaxError, while common, is actually a special exception, because we can't handle it. It tells us that we typed something wrong and we better figure out what it is. Some other common exceptions, which we **can** handle, are shown in the following example:

```
>>> x = 5 / 0
Traceback (most recent call last):
  File "<stdin>", line 1, in <module>
ZeroDivisionError: int division or modulo by zero

>>> lst = [1,2,3]
>>> print(lst[3])
Traceback (most recent call last):
  File "<stdin>", line 1, in <module>
IndexError: list index out of range

>>> lst + 2
Traceback (most recent call last):
  File "<stdin>", line 1, in <module>
```

```
TypeError: can only concatenate list (not "int") to list


>>> lst.add
Traceback (most recent call last):
  File "<stdin>", line 1, in <module>
AttributeError: 'list' object has no attribute 'add'


>>> d = {'a': 'hello'}
>>> d['b']
Traceback (most recent call last):
  File "<stdin>", line 1, in <module>
KeyError: 'b'


>>> print(this_is_not_a_var)
Traceback (most recent call last):
  File "<stdin>", line 1, in <module>
NameError: name 'this_is_not_a_var' is not defined
>>>
```

Sometimes these exceptions are indicators of something wrong in our program (in which case we would go to the indicated line number and fix it), but they also occur in legitimate situations. A ZeroDivisionError doesn't always mean we received invalid input, just different input. The user may have entered a zero by mistake, or on purpose, or it may represent a legitimate value such as an empty bank account or the age of a newborn child.

You may have noticed all the above built-in exceptions end in the name Error. In Python, the words "error" and "exception" are used almost interchangeably. Errors are sometimes considered more dire than exceptions, but they are dealt with in exactly the same way. Indeed, all the error classes above have Exception (which extends BaseException) as their superclass.

Raising an exception

Now, then, what do we do if we're writing a program that needs to inform the user or a calling function that the inputs are somehow invalid? It would be nice if we could use the same mechanism that Python uses… and we can! Want to see how? Here's a simple class that adds items to a list **only** if they are even numbered integers:

```
class EvenOnly(list):
    def append(self, integer):
        if not isinstance(integer, int):
            raise TypeError("Only integers can be added")
        if integer % 2:
            raise ValueError("Only even numbers can be added")
        super().append(integer)
```

This class extends the `list` built-in, as we discussed in *Chapter 2*, and overrides the `append` method to check two conditions that ensure the item is an even integer. We first check if the input is an instance of the `int` type, and then use the modulus operator to ensure it is divisible by two. If either of the two conditions is not met, the `raise` keyword is used to cause an exception to occur. The `raise` keyword is simply followed by the object being raised as an exception. In the example above, two objects are newly constructed from the built-in classes `TypeError` and `ValueError`. The raised object could just as easily be an instance of a new exception class we create ourselves (we'll see how shortly), an exception that was defined elsewhere, or even an exception object that has been previously raised and handled.

If we test this class in the Python interpreter, we can see that it is outputting useful error information when exceptions occur, just as before:

```
>>> e = EvenOnly()
>>> e.append("a string")
Traceback (most recent call last):
  File "<stdin>", line 1, in <module>
  File "even_integers.py", line 7, in add
    raise TypeError("Only integers can be added")
TypeError: Only integers can be added

>>> e.append(3)
Traceback (most recent call last):
  File "<stdin>", line 1, in <module>
  File "even_integers.py", line 9, in add
```

```
     raise ValueError("Only even numbers can be added")
ValueError: Only even numbers can be added
>>> e.append(2)
```

 Note: While this class is effective for demonstrating exceptions in action, it isn't very good at its job. It is still possible to get other values into the list using index notation or slice notation. This can all be avoided by overriding other appropriate methods, some of which are double-underscore methods.

What happens when an exception occurs?

When an exception is raised, it appears to stop program execution immediately. Any lines that were supposed to happen after the exception are not executed, and, unless the exception is dealt with, the program will exit with an error message. Take a look at this simple function:

```
def no_return():
    print("I am about to raise an exception")
    raise Exception("This is always raised")
    print("This line will never execute")
    return "I won't be returned"
```

If we execute this function, we see that the first `print` call is executed and then the exception is raised. The second `print` statement is never executed, and the `return` statement never executes either:

```
>>> no_return()
I am about to raise an exception
Traceback (most recent call last):
  File "<stdin>", line 1, in <module>
  File "exception_quits.py", line 3, in no_return
    raise Exception("This is always raised")
Exception: This is always raised
```

Further, if we have a function that calls a second function that raises an exception, nothing will be executed in the first function after the point where the second function was called. Raising an exception stops all execution right up the function call stack until it is either handled, or forces the interpreter to exit. To demonstrate, let's add a second function that calls our first one:

```
def call_exceptor():
    print("call_exceptor starts here...")
    no_return()
    print("an exception was raised...")
    print("...so these lines don't run")
```

When we call this function, we see that the first print statement executes as well as the first line in the no_return function. But once the exception is raised, nothing else executes:

```
>>> call_exceptor()
call_exceptor starts here...
I am about to raise an exception
Traceback (most recent call last):
  File "<stdin>", line 1, in <module>
  File "method_calls_excepting.py", line 9, in call_exceptor
    no_return()
  File "method_calls_excepting.py", line 3, in no_return
    raise Exception("This is always raised")
Exception: This is always raised
```

We'll soon see that the interpreter is not actually taking a shortcut and exiting immediately; the exception can be handled inside either method. Indeed, exceptions can be handled at any level after they are initially raised. If we look at the exception's output (called a traceback) from bottom to top, we see both methods listed. Inside no_return, the exception is initially raised. Then just above that, we see that inside call_exceptor, that pesky no_return function was called and the exception "bubbled up" to the calling method. From there it went up one more level to the main interpreter, which finally printed the traceback.

Handling exceptions

Now let's look at the tail side of the exception coin. Namely, if we encounter an exception situation, how should our code react to, or recover from it? We handle exceptions by wrapping any code that might throw one (whether it is exception code itself, or a call to any function or method that may have an exception raised inside it) inside a try...except clause. The most basic syntax looks like this:

```
try:
    no_return()
except:
    print("I caught an exception")
print("executed after the exception")
```

If we run this simple script using our existing no_return function, which we know, very well, always throws an exception, we get this output:

```
I am about to raise an exception
I caught an exception
executed after the exception
```

The no_return function happily informs us that it is about to raise an exception. But we fooled it and caught the exception. Once caught, we were able to clean up after ourselves (in this case, by outputting that we were handling the situation), and continue on our way, with no interference from the offending function. The remainder of the code in the no_return function still went unexecuted, but the code that called the function was able to recover and continue.

Note the indentation around try and except. The try clause wraps any code that might throw an exception. The except clause is then back on the same indentation level as the try line. Any code to handle the exception is indented after the except clause. Then normal code resumes at the original indentation level.

The problem with the above code is that it will catch any type of exception. What if we were writing some code that could raise both a TypeError and a ZeroDivisionError? We might want to catch the ZeroDivisionError, but let the TypeError propagate to the console. Can you guess the syntax? Here's a rather silly function that does just that:

```
def funny_division(anumber):
    try:
        return 100 / anumber
    except ZeroDivisionError:
        return "Silly wabbit, you can't divide by zero!"
```

```
print(funny_division(0))
print(funny_division(50.0))
print(funny_division("hello"))
```

The function is tested with `print` statements that show it behaving as expected:

```
Silly wabbit, you can't divide by zero!
2.0
Traceback (most recent call last):
  File "catch_specific_exception.py", line 9, in <module>
    print(funny_division("hello"))
  File "catch_specific_exception.py", line 3, in funny_division
    return 100 / anumber
TypeError: unsupported operand type(s) for /: 'int' and 'str'
```

The first line of output shows that if we enter 0, we get properly mocked. If we call with a valid number (note that it's not an integer, but it's still a valid divisor), it operates correctly. Yet if we enter a string (you were wondering how to get a `TypeError`, weren't you?), it fails with an exception. If we had used an empty `except` clause, that didn't specify a `ZeroDivisionError`, it would have accused us of dividing by zero when we sent it a string, which is not proper behavior at all.

We can even catch two or more different exceptions and handle them with the same code. Here's an example that raises three different types of exceptions. It handles `TypeError` and `ZeroDivisionError` with the same exception handler, but it may also raise a `ValueError` if you supply the number 13:

```
def funny_division2(anumber):
    try:
        if anumber == 13:
            raise ValueError("13 is an unlucky number")
        return 100 / anumber
    except (ZeroDivisionError, TypeError):
        return "Enter a number other than zero"

for val in (0, "hello", 50.0, 13):
    print("Testing {}:".format(val), end=" ")
    print(funny_division2(val))
```

The `for` loop at the bottom simply loops over several test inputs and prints the results. If you're wondering about that `end` argument in the print statement, it simply turns the default trailing newline into a space so it's joined with the output from the next line. Here's a run of the script:

```
Testing 0: Enter a number other than zero
Testing hello: Enter a number other than zero
Testing 50.0: 2.0
Testing 13: Traceback (most recent call last):
  File "catch_multiple_exceptions.py", line 11, in <module>
    print(funny_division2(val))
  File "catch_multiple_exceptions.py", line 4, in funny_division2
    raise ValueError("13 is an unlucky number")
ValueError: 13 is an unlucky number
```

The number 0 and the string are both caught by the `except` clause and a suitable error message is printed. The exception from the number 13 is not caught, because it is a `ValueError`, which was not included in the types of exceptions being handled.

This is all well and good, but what if we want to catch different exceptions and do different things with them? Or maybe we want to do something with an exception and then allow it to continue to bubble up to the parent function, as if it had never been caught? We don't need any new syntax to deal with these cases. It's possible to stack `except` clauses, and only one will be executed. For the second question, the `raise` keyword, with no arguments, will re-raise the last exception if we're already inside an exception handler, observe:

```python
def funny_division3(anumber):
    try:
        if anumber == 13:
            raise ValueError("13 is an unlucky number")
        return 100 / anumber
    except ZeroDivisionError:
        return "Enter a number other than zero"
    except TypeError:
        return "Enter a numerical value"
    except ValueError:
        print("No, No, not 13!")
        raise raise
```

The last line re-raises the `ValueError`, so after outputting No, No, not 13!, it will raise the exception again; we'll still get the stack trace on the console.

If we stack exception clauses like we did above, only the first matching clause will be run, even if more than one of them fit. How can more than one clause match? Remember that exceptions are objects, and inheritance can take place. As we'll see in the next section, most exceptions extend the `Exception` class (which is, itself, derived from `BaseException`). If we catch `Exception` before we catch `TypeError`, then only the `Exception` handler will be executed, because `TypeError` is an `Exception`, by inheritance.

This can come in handy in cases where we want to handle some exceptions specifically, and then handle all remaining exceptions in a more general case. We can simply catch `Exception` after catching any specific exceptions and handle the general case there.

Sometimes when we catch an exception, we need a reference to the `Exception` object itself. This most often happens if we define our own exceptions with custom arguments, but can also be relevant with standard exceptions. Most exception classes accept a set of arguments in their constructor, and we might want to access those attributes in the exception handler. If we define our own exception class, we can even call custom methods on it when we catch it. The syntax for capturing an exception as a variable uses the `as` keyword:

```
try:
    raise ValueError("This is an argument")
except ValueError as e:
    print("The exception arguments were", e.args)
```

If we run this simple snippet, it prints out the string argument that we passed into `ValueError` upon initialization.

In Python 2.5 and earlier, the as keyword did not work for naming an exception. Instead a comma was used, so the previous example would look like except ValueError, e: This was changed in Python 3.0 to avoid confusion with the syntax for catching multiple types of exceptions (as in except ValueError, TypeError), and the change was backported to Python 2.6. The as keyword is therefore supported in most modern versions, but if you're working with an older interpreter, keep this syntax difference in mind, as it is bound to catch you.

We've seen several variations on the syntax for handling exceptions, but we still don't know how to execute code regardless of whether or not an exception has occurred. We also can't specify code that should be executed **only** if an exception does **not** occur. Two more keywords, `finally` and `else`, can provide the missing pieces. Neither one takes any extra arguments. The following example randomly picks an exception to throw and raises it. Then some not-so-complicated exception handling code is run that illustrates the newly introduced syntax:

```python
import random
some_exceptions = [ValueError, TypeError, IndexError, None]

try:
    choice = random.choice(some_exceptions)
    print("raising {}".format(choice))
    if choice:
        raise choice("An error")
except ValueError:
    print("Caught a ValueError")
except TypeError:
    print("Caught a TypeError")
except Exception as e:
    print("Caught some other error: %s" %
        ( e.__class__.__name__))
else:
    print("This code called if there is no exception")
finally:
    print("This cleanup code is always called")
```

If we run this example—which illustrates almost every conceivable exception handling scenario—a few times, we'll get different output each time, depending on which exception `random` chooses. Here are some example runs:

```
$ python finally_and_else.py
raising None
This code called if there is no exception
This cleanup code is always called


$ python finally_and_else.py
raising <class 'TypeError'>
Caught a TypeError
This cleanup code is always called
```

```
$ python finally_and_else.py
raising <class 'IndexError'>
Caught some other error: IndexError
This cleanup code is always called

$ python finally_and_else.py
raising <class 'ValueError'>
Caught a ValueError
This cleanup code is always called
```

Note how the `print` statement in the `finally` clause is executed no matter what. This is extremely useful, for example, when we need to clean up an open database connection, close an open file, or send a closing handshake over the network when our code has finished running, even if an exception has occurred. This can also be applied in interesting ways if we are inside a `try` clause when we `return` from a function; the `finally` handle will still be executed upon return.

Also pay attention to the output when no exception is raised; both the `else` and the `finally` clauses are executed. The `else` clause may seem redundant, as it appears that code that should be executed only when no exception is raised can just be placed after the entire `try...except` block. However, this code would still be executed in the case where an exception is caught and handled. We'll see more on this when we discuss using exceptions as flow control, shortly.

Any of the `except`, `else`, and `finally` clauses can be omitted after a `try` block (although, `else`, by itself is invalid). If you include more than one, the `except` clauses must come first, then the `else` clause, with the `finally` clause at the end. The order of the `except` clauses normally goes from most specific to most generic.

Exception hierarchy

We've already encountered many of the most common built-in exceptions, and you'll probably encounter the rest over the course of your regular Python development. As we noticed above, most exceptions are subclasses of the `Exception` class. But this is not true of all exceptions. `Exception` itself actually inherits from a class called `BaseException` (In fact, all exceptions **must** extend the `BaseException` class or one of its subclasses). There are two key exceptions, `SystemExit` and `KeyboardInterrupt`, that derive directly from `BaseException` instead of `Exception`.

`SystemExit` is an exception that is raised whenever the program exits naturally, typically because we called the `sys.exit` function somewhere in our code (for example, because the user selected an exit menu item, clicked the "close" button on a window, or entered a command to shut down a server). The exception is designed to allow us to clean up code before the program ultimately exits, so we generally don't need to handle it explicitly (because cleanup code happens inside a `finally` clause, right?). If we do handle it, we would normally re-raise the exception, since catching it would stop the program from exiting. There are, of course, situations where we might **want** to stop the program exiting, for example if there are unsaved changes and we want to prompt the user if they really want to exit. Usually, if we handle `SystemExit` at all, it's because we want to do something special with it or are anticipating it directly. We especially don't want it to be accidentally caught in generic clauses that catch all normal exceptions. This is why it derives directly from `BaseException`.

The `KeyboardInterrupt` exception is common in command-line programs. It is thrown when the user explicitly interrupts program execution with an OS-dependent key combination (normally *Ctrl* + *C*). This is a standard way for the user to deliberately interrupt a running program, and like `SystemExit`, it should almost always respond by terminating the program. Also like `SystemExit`, it should handle any cleanup tasks inside `finally` blocks.

Here is a class diagram that fully illustrates the exception hierarchy:

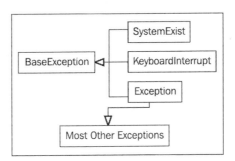

When we use the `except:` clause without specifying any type of exception, it will catch all subclasses of `BaseException`, which is to say, it will catch all exceptions, including the two "special" ones. Generally, we don't want to catch them, so, it is unwise to use the `except:` statement without any arguments. If you want to catch all exceptions **other** than the two we just discussed, explicitly catch `Exception`. As we discussed earlier, make sure this is the last `except` clause if you're trying to catch other more specific exceptions separately.

Further, if you do want to catch all exceptions, I suggest using the syntax `except BaseException:` instead of a raw `except:` This helps explicitly tell the readers of your code that you really meant to handle the special case exceptions.

Defining our own exceptions

Often, when we want to raise an exception, we find that none of the built-in exceptions are quite what we need. Luckily, it's very easy to define new exceptions of our own. The name of the class is usually designed to communicate what went wrong, and we can provide arbitrary arguments in the initializer to add additional information.

All we have to do is inherit from the `Exception` class. We don't even have to add any content to the class! We can, of course, extend `BaseException` directly, but then it will not be caught by generic `except Exception` clauses.

Without further ado, here's a simple exception we might use in a banking application:

```python
class InvalidWithdrawal(Exception):
    pass


raise InvalidWithdrawal("You don't have $50 in your account")
```

The last line illustrates how to raise the newly defined exception. We are able to pass an arbitrary number of arguments (often a string message, but any useful object can be stored) into the exception. The `Exception __init__` method is designed to accept any arguments and store them as a tuple in an attribute named `args`. This makes exceptions easier to define without needing to override `__init__`.

Of course, if we **do** want to customize the initializer, we are free to do so. Here's an exception whose initializer demands the current balance and the amount the user wanted to withdraw. In addition, it adds a method to calculate how much over the withdrawal was:

```python
class InvalidWithdrawal(Exception):
    def __init__(self, balance, amount):
        super().__init__("account doesn't have ${}".format(
            amount))
        self.amount = amount
        self.balance = balance

    def overage(self):
        return self.amount - self.balance

raise InvalidWithdrawal(25, 50)
```

The `raise` statement at the end illustrates how to construct the exception. As you can see, we can do anything with an exception that we would do with other objects. We could catch an exception and pass it around as a working object, although it is more common to include a reference to the working object as an attribute on an exception and pass that around instead.

Here's how we would handle an `InvalidWithdrawal` if one was raised:

```
try:
    raise InvalidWithdrawal(25, 50)
except InvalidWithdrawal as e:
    print("I'm sorry, but your withdrawal is "
            "more than your balance by "
            "${}".format(e.overage()))
```

Here we see a valid use of the `as` keyword. By convention, most Python coders name the exception variable e, although, as usual, you are free to call it ex, `exception`, or `aunt_sally` if you prefer.

Now that we have full control over exception definitions, including initializer, attributes, and methods, and we can access an exception instance when it is being handled, we have absolute power over the information passed with an exception.

There are many reasons for defining our own exceptions. It is often useful to add information to the exception or log it in some way. But the utility of custom exceptions truly comes to light when creating a framework, library, or API that is intended for access by other users. In that case, be careful to ensure your code is raising exceptions that make sense to the client programmer, are easy to handle, and clearly describe what went wrong so they can fix it (if it is a bug in their code) or handle it (if it's a situation they need to be made aware of).

Exceptions aren't exceptional

Novice programmers tend to think of exceptions as only useful for "exceptional circumstances". However, the definition of "exceptional circumstances" can be vague and subject to interpretation. Consider the following two functions:

```
def divide_with_exception(number, divisor):
    try:
        print("{} / {} = {}".format(
            number, divisor, number / divisor * 1.0))
    except ZeroDivisionError:
        print("You can't divide by zero")
```

```
def divide_with_if(number, divisor):
    if divisor == 0:
        print("You can't divide by zero")
    else:
        print("{} / {} = {}".format(
            number, divisor, number / divisor * 1.0))
```

These two functions behave identically. If `divisor` is zero, an error message is printed, otherwise, a message printing the result of division is displayed. Clearly, we could avoid a `ZeroDivisionError` ever being thrown by testing for it with an `if` statement. Similarly, we can avoid an `IndexError` by explicitly checking whether or not the parameter is within the confines of the list, and a `KeyError` by checking if the key is in a dictionary.

But we shouldn't do this. For one thing, we might write an `if` statement that checks if the index is lower than the parameters of the list, but forget to check negative values (remember, Python lists support negative indexing; -1 refers to the last element in the list). Eventually we would discover this and have to find all the places where we were checking code. But if we'd simply caught the `IndexError` and handled it, our code would just work.

In short, use exceptions for exceptional circumstances, even if those circumstances are only a little bit exceptional.

Turning this argument around, we can see that exception syntax is also effective for flow control. Like an `if` statement, exceptions can be used for decision making, branching, and message passing.

Imagine an inventory application for a company that sells widgets and gadgets. When a customer makes a purchase, the item can either be available, in which case the item is removed from inventory and the number of items left is returned, or it might be out of stock. Now, being out of stock is a perfectly normal thing to happen in an inventory application. It is certainly not an exceptional circumstance. But what do we return if it's out of stock? A string saying "out of stock"? A negative number? In both cases, the calling method would have to check whether the return value is a positive integer, or something else to determine if it is out of stock. That seems a bit messy. Instead, we can raise an `OutOfStockException` and use the `try` statement to direct program flow control. Make sense?

In addition, we want to make sure we don't sell the same item to two different customers, or sell an item that isn't in stock yet. One way to facilitate this is to lock each type of item to ensure only one person can update it at a time. The user must lock the item, manipulate the item (purchase, add stock, count items left...), and then unlock the item. Here's a non-functional `Inventory` object with docstrings that describes what some of the methods should do:

```
class Inventory:
    def lock(self, item_type):
        '''Select the type of item that is going to
        be manipulated. This method will lock the
        item so nobody else can manipulate the
        inventory until it's returned. This prevents
        selling the same item to two different
        customers.'''
        pass

    def unlock(self, item_type):
        '''Release the given type so that other
        customers can access it.'''
        pass

    def purchase(self, item_type):
        '''If the item is not locked, raise an
        exception. If the itemtype  does not exist,
        raise an exception. If the item is currently
        out of stock, raise an exception. If the item
        is available, subtract one item and return
        the number of items left.'''
        pass
```

We could hand this object prototype to a developer and have them implement the methods to do exactly as they say while we work on the code that needs to make a purchase. We'll use Python's robust exception handling to consider different branches depending on how the purchase was made:

```
item_type = 'widget'
inv = Inventory()
inv.lock(item_type)
try:
    num_left = inv.purchase(item_type)
except InvalidItemType:
    print("Sorry, we don't sell {}".format(item_type))
```

```
except OutOfStock:
    print("Sorry, that item is out of stock.")
else:
    print("Purchase complete. There are "
            "{} {}s left".format(num_left, item_type))
finally:
    inv.unlock()
```

Pay attention to how all the possible exception handling clauses are used to ensure the correct actions happen at the correct time. Even though OutOfStock is not a terribly exceptional circumstance, we are able to use an exception to handle it suitably. This same code could be written with an if...elif...else structure, but it wouldn't be as easy to read or maintain.

We can also use exceptions to pass messages between different methods. For example, if we wanted to inform the customer as to what date the item is expected to be in stock again, we could ensure our OutOfStock object requires a back_in_stock parameter when it is constructed. Then when we handle the exception we can check that value and provide additional information to the customer. The information attached to the object can be easily passed between two different parts of the program. The exception could even provide a method that instructs the inventory object to reorder or backorder an item.

Using exceptions for flow control can make for some handy program designs. The important thing to bring from this discussion is that exceptions are not a bad thing that we should try to avoid. Having an exception occur does not say, "you should have prevented this exceptional circumstance from happening". Rather, it is just a powerful way to communicate information between two sections of code that may not be directly calling each other.

Case study

We've been looking at the use and handling of exceptions at a fairly low level of detail; syntax and definitions. This case study will help tie it all in with our previous chapters so we can see how exceptions should be used in the larger context of objects, inheritance, and modules.

Today, we'll be designing a simple, central authentication and authorization system. The entire system will be placed in one module, and other code will be able to query that module object for authentication and authorization purposes. We should admit, from the start, that we aren't security experts, and that the system we are designing may be full of security holes. It will be sufficient, however, for a basic login and permission system that other code can interact with. Later, if that other code needs to be made more secure, we can have a security or cryptography expert review or rewrite our module, without changing the API.

Authentication is the process of ensuring a user is really the person they say they are. We'll follow the lead of common web systems today, which use a username and private password combination. Other methods of authentication include voice recognition, fingerprint or retinal scanners, and identification cards.

Authorization, on the other hand, is all about determining whether a given (authenticated) user is permitted to perform a specific action. We'll create a basic permission list system that stores a list of the specific people allowed to perform each action.

In addition, we'll add some administrative features to allow new users to be added to the system. For brevity, we'll leave out editing of passwords or changing of permissions once they've been added, but these (highly necessary) features can certainly be added in the future.

There's a simple analysis; now let's proceed with design. We're obviously going to need a User class that stores the username and an encrypted password. This class will also allow a user to log in by checking whether an entered password is valid. We probably won't need a Permission class, as those are just strings mapped to a list of users using a dictionary. We should have a central Authenticator class that handles user management and logging in or out. The last piece of the puzzle is an Authorizor class that deals with permissions and checking whether a user can perform an activity. We'll provide a single instance of each of these classes in the auth module so that other modules can use this central mechanism for all their authentication and authorization needs. Of course, if they want to instantiate private instances of these classes, for non-central authorization activities, they are free to do so.

We'll also be defining several exceptions as we go along. We'll start with a special AuthException base class that accepts a username and optional user object as parameters; most of our self-defined exceptions will inherit from this one.

Let's build the User class first; it seems simple enough. A new user can be initialized with a username and password. The password will be stored encrypted to reduce the chances of its being stolen. Our purpose is to study exceptions, not to secure a system. You have been warned! We'll also need a check_password method to test if a supplied password is the correct one. Here is the class in full:

```
import hashlib

class User:
    def __init__(self, username, password):
        '''Create a new user object. The password
        will be encrypted before storing.'''
        self.username = username
```

```
        self.password = self._encrypt_pw(password)
        self.is_logged_in = False

    def _encrypt_pw(self, password):
        '''Encrypt the password with the username and return
        the sha digest.'''
        hash_string = (self.username + password)
        hash_string = hash_string.encode("utf8")
        return hashlib.sha256(hash_string).hexdigest()

    def check_password(self, password):
        '''Return True if the password is valid for this
        user, false otherwise.'''
        encrypted = self._encrypt_pw(password)
        return encrypted == self.password
```

Since the code for encrypting a password is required in both __init__ and
check_password, we pull it out to its own method. That way, it only needs to be
changed in one place if someone realizes it is insecure and needs improvement. This
class could easily be extended to include mandatory or optional personal details such
as names, contact information, and birth dates.

Before we write code to add users (which will happen in the as-yet undefined
Authenticator class), we should examine some use cases. If all goes well, we can
add a user with a username and password; the User object is created and inserted
into a dictionary. But in what ways can all not go well? Well, clearly, we don't want
to add a user if that username already exists in the dictionary. Otherwise we'd
overwrite an existing user's data and the new user might have access to that user's
privileges. So we'll need a UsernameAlreadyExists exception. Also, for security's
sake, we should probably raise an exception if the password is too short. Both of
these exceptions will extend AuthException, which we mentioned earlier. So,
before writing the Authenticator, let's define these three exception classes.

```
    class AuthException(Exception):
        def __init__(self, username, user=None):
            super().__init__(username, user)
            self.username = username
            self.user = user

    class UsernameAlreadyExists(AuthException):
        pass

    class PasswordTooShort(AuthException):
        pass
```

The AuthException requires a username and has an optional user parameter. This second parameter should be an instance of the User class associated with that username. The two specific exceptions we're defining simply need to inform the calling class of an exceptional circumstance, so we don't need to add any extra methods to them.

Now, let's start on the Authenticator class. It can simply be a mapping of usernames to user objects, so we'll start with a dictionary in the initialization function. The method for adding a user needs to check the two conditions (password length and previously existing users) before creating a new User instance and adding it to the dictionary:

```
class Authenticator:
    def __init__(self):
        '''Construct an authenticator to manage
        users logging in and out.'''
        self.users = {}

    def add_user(self, username, password):
        if username in self.users:
            raise UsernameAlreadyExists(username)
        if len(password) < 6:
            raise PasswordTooShort(username)
        self.users[username] = User(username, password)
```

We could, of course, extend the password validation to raise exceptions for passwords that are too easy to crack in other ways, if we desired.

Now let's prepare the login method. If we weren't thinking about exceptions just now, we might just want the method to return True or False, depending on whether the login was successful or not. But we **are** thinking about exceptions, and this could be a good place to use them for a not-so-exceptional circumstance. We could raise different exceptions, for example, if the username does not exist or the password does not match. This will allow anyone trying to log a user in to elegantly handle the situation using a try/except/else clause. So first we add these new exceptions:

```
class InvalidUsername(AuthException):
    pass

class InvalidPassword(AuthException):
    pass
```

Then we can define a simple `login` method to our `Authenticator` class that raises these exceptions if necessary. If not, it flags the `user` as logged in and returns:

```
def login(self, username, password):
    try:
        user = self.users[username]
    except KeyError:
        raise InvalidUsername(username)

    if not user.check_password(password):
        raise InvalidPassword(username, user)

    user.is_logged_in = True
    return True
```

Notice how the `KeyError` is handled. This could have been handled using `if username not in self.users:` instead, but we choose to handle the exception directly. We end up eating up this first exception and raising a brand new one of our own that fits the user facing API better.

We can also add a method to check if a particular username is logged in. Deciding whether to use an exception here is trickier, should we raise an exception if the username does not exist? Should we raise an exception if the user is not logged in?

To answer these questions, we need to think about how the method would be accessed. Most often, this method will be used to answer the yes/no question, "Should I allow them access to <something>?" The answer will either be, "yes, the username is valid and they are logged in", or, "no, the username is not valid or they are not logged in". Therefore, a Boolean return value is sufficient. There is no need to use exceptions here, just for the sake of using an exception.

```
def is_logged_in(self, username):
    if username in self.users:
        return self.users[username].is_logged_in
    return False
```

Finally, we can add a default authenticator instance to our module so that client code can access it easily using `auth.authenticator`:

```
authenticator = Authenticator()
```

This line goes at the module level, outside any class definition, so the authenticator variable can be accessed as `auth.authenticator`. Now we can start on the `Authorizor` class, which maps permissions to users. The `Authorizor` should not permit a user access to a permission if they are not logged in, so they'll need a reference to a specific authenticator. We'll also need to set up the permission dictionary upon initialization:

```
class Authorizor:
    def __init__(self, authenticator):
        self.authenticator = authenticator
        self.permissions = {}
```

Now we can write methods to add new permissions and to set up which users are associated with each permission.

```
def add_permission(self, perm_name):
    '''Create a new permission that users
    can be added to'''
    try:
        perm_set = self.permissions[perm_name]
    except KeyError:
        self.permissions[perm_name] = set()
    else:
        raise PermissionError("Permission Exists")

def permit_user(self, perm_name, username):
    '''Grant the given permission to the user'''
    try:
        perm_set = self.permissions[perm_name]
    except KeyError:
        raise PermissionError("Permission does not exist")
    else:
        if username not in self.authenticator.users:
            raise InvalidUsername(username)
        perm_set.add(username)
```

The first method allows us to create a new permission, unless it already exists, in which case, an exception is raised. The second allows us to add a username to a permission, unless either the permission or the username doesn't yet exist.

We use a `set` instead of a `list` for usernames, so that even if you grant a user permission more than once, the nature of sets means the user is only in the set once. Sets are sequences, like lists, but unlike lists, they are unordered, and store unique values. No matter how many times we add a value to a set, it will only be stored in the set once.

A `PermissionError` is raised in both methods. This new error doesn't require a username, so we'll make it extend `Exception` directly, instead of our custom `AuthException`:

```
class PermissionError(Exception):
    pass
```

Finally, we can add a method to check whether a user has a specific `permission` or not. In order for them to be granted access, they have to be both logged into the authenticator and in the set of people who have been granted access to that privilege. If either of these conditions is not met, an exception is raised:

```
def check_permission(self, perm_name, username):
    if not self.authenticator.is_logged_in(username):
        raise NotLoggedInError(username)
    try:
        perm_set = self.permissions[perm_name]
    except KeyError:
        raise PermissionError("Permission does not exist")
    else:
        if username not in perm_set:
            raise NotPermittedError(username)
        else:
            return True
```

There are two new exceptions in here; they both take usernames, so we'll define them as subclasses of `AuthException`:

```
class NotLoggedInError(AuthException):
    pass


class NotPermittedError(AuthException):
    pass
```

Finally, we can add a "default" `authorizor` to go with our default authenticator:

```
authorizor = Authorizor(authenticator)
```

And that completes a basic, but complete authentication/authorization system. We can test the system at the Python prompt, checking to see if a user, `joe`, is permitted to do tasks in the paint department:

```
>>> import auth
>>> auth.authenticator.add_user("joe", "joepassword")
>>> auth.authorizor.add_permission("paint")
>>> auth.authorizor.check_permission("paint", "joe")
```

```
Traceback (most recent call last):
  File "<stdin>", line 1, in <module>
  File "auth.py", line 109, in check_permission
    raise NotLoggedInError(username)
auth.NotLoggedInError: joe
>>> auth.authenticator.is_logged_in("joe")
False
>>> auth.authenticator.login("joe", "joepassword")
True
>>> auth.authorizor.check_permission("paint", "joe")
Traceback (most recent call last):
  File "<stdin>", line 1, in <module>
  File "auth.py", line 116, in check_permission
    raise NotPermittedError(username)
auth.NotPermittedError: joe
>>> auth.authorizor.check_permission("mix", "joe")
Traceback (most recent call last):
  File "auth.py", line 111, in check_permission
    perm_set = self.permissions[perm_name]
KeyError: 'mix'
```

During handling of the above exception, another exception occurred:

```
Traceback (most recent call last):
  File "<stdin>", line 1, in <module>
  File "auth.py", line 113, in check_permission
    raise PermissionError("Permission does not exist")
auth.PermissionError: Permission does not exist
>>> auth.authorizor.permit_user("mix", "joe")
Traceback (most recent call last):
  File "auth.py", line 99, in permit_user
    perm_set = self.permissions[perm_name]
KeyError: 'mix'
```

During handling of the above exception, another exception occurred:

```
Traceback (most recent call last):
  File "<stdin>", line 1, in <module>
  File "auth.py", line 101, in permit_user
    raise PermissionError("Permission does not exist")
auth.PermissionError: Permission does not exist
>>> auth.authorizor.permit_user("paint", "joe")
>>> auth.authorizor.check_permission("paint", "joe")
True
```

The above output shows all of our code and most of our exceptions in action, but to really understand the API we've defined, we should write some exception handling code that actually uses it. Here's a basic menu interface that allows certain users to change or test a program:

```python
import auth

# Set up a test user and permission
auth.authenticator.add_user("joe", "joepassword")
auth.authorizor.add_permission("test program")
auth.authorizor.add_permission("change program")
auth.authorizor.permit_user("test program", "joe")

class Editor:
    def __init__(self):
        self.username = None
        self.menu_map = {
                "login": self.login,
                "test": self.test,
                "change": self.change,
                "quit": self.quit
            }

    def login(self):
        logged_in = False
        while not logged_in:
            username = input("username: ")
            password = input("password: ")
            try:
                logged_in = auth.authenticator.login(
                        username, password)
            except auth.InvalidUsername:
                print("Sorry, that username does not exist")
```

```
        except auth.InvalidPassword:
            print("Sorry, incorrect password")
        else:
            self.username = username

    def is_permitted(self, permission):
        try:
            auth.authorizor.check_permission(
                permission, self.username)
        except auth.NotLoggedInError as e:
            print("{} is not logged in".format(e.username))
            return False
        except auth.NotPermittedError as e:
            print("{} cannot {}".format(
                e.username, permission))
            return False
        else:
            return True

    def test(self):
        if self.is_permitted("test program"):
            print("Testing program now...")

    def change(self):
        if self.is_permitted("change program"):
            print("Changing program now...")

    def quit(self):
        raise SystemExit()

    def menu(self):
        try:
            answer = ""
            while True:
                print("""
Please enter a command:
\tlogin\tLogin
\ttest\tTest the program
\tchange\tChange the program
\tquit\tQuit
""")
                answer = input("enter a command: ").lower()
                try:
                    func = self.menu_map[answer]
```

```
        except KeyError:
            print("{} is not a valid option".format(
                answer))
        else:
            func()
    finally:
        print("Thank you for testing the auth module")


Editor().menu()
```

This rather long example is actually very simple. The `is_permitted` method is probably the most interesting; this is a mostly internal method that is called by both `test` and `change` to ensure the user is permitted access before continuing. Of course, those two methods are stubs, but we aren't writing an editor here, we're illustrating the use of exceptions and exception handlers by testing an authentication and authorization framework!

Exercises

If you've never dealt with exceptions before, the first thing you need to do is look at old Python code you've written and notice if there are places you should have been handling exceptions. How would you handle them? Do you need to handle them at all? Sometimes letting the exception propagate to the console is the best thing to do. Sometimes you can recover from the error and allow the program to continue. Sometimes you can only reformat the error into something the user can understand and display it to them.

Some common places to look are file I/O (is it possible your code will try to read a file that doesn't exist?), mathematical expressions (is it possible that a value you are dividing by is zero?) list indices (is the list empty?) and dictionaries (does the key exist?). Ask yourself if you should ignore the problem, handle it by checking values first, or handle it with an exception. Pay special attention to areas where you might have used `finally` and `else` to ensure the correct code is executed under all conditions.

Now write some new code. Think of a program that requires authentication and authorization, and try writing some code that uses the `auth` module we built in the case study. Feel free to modify the module if it's not flexible enough. Try to handle all the exceptions in a sensible way. If you're having trouble coming up with something that requires authentication, try adding authorization to the notepad example from *Chapter 2*. Or add authorization to the `auth` module itself—it's not a terribly useful module if just anybody can start adding permissions! Maybe require an administrator username and password before allowing privileges to be added or changed.

Finally, try to think of places in your code where you can raise exceptions. It can be in code you've written or are working on; or write a new project as an exercise. You'll probably have the best luck designing a small framework or API that is meant to be used by other people; exceptions are a terrific communication tool between your code and someone else's. Remember to design and document any self-raised exceptions as part of the API, or they won't know if or how to handle them!

Summary

In this chapter, we went into the gritty details of raising, handling, defining, and manipulating exceptions. Exceptions are a powerful way to communicate unusual circumstances or error conditions without requiring a calling function to explicitly check return values. Specifically, we covered:

- Built-in exceptions and raising exceptions
- Several ways to handle specific exceptions
- Defining new exceptions
- Using exceptions for unexceptional circumstances

In the next chapter, everything we've studied so far will come together as we discuss how object-oriented programming principles and structures should best be applied in Python applications.

5
When to Use Object-oriented Programming

In the previous chapters, we've covered many of the defining features of Object-oriented Programming. We now know the principles and paradigms of Object-oriented Design, and we've covered the syntax of Object-oriented Programming in Python.

Yet, things are still hazy when it comes to knowing how and when to apply these principles and syntax. Here, we'll discuss some of the more useful applications of the knowledge we've gained, while in *Chapter 7*, we'll cover something just as important: when not to use them! In this chapter we'll cover:

- How to recognize objects
- Data and behaviors, once again
- Wrapping data in behavior using properties
- Restricting data using behavior
- The Don't Repeat Yourself principle
- Recognizing code that is the same

Treat objects as objects

This may seem obvious, but you should generally give separate objects in your problem domain a special class in your code. We've seen examples of this in the case studies in previous chapters; the process is generally to identify objects in the problem and then model their data and behaviors.

Identifying objects is a very important task in object-oriented analysis and programming. But it isn't always as easy as counting the nouns in a short paragraph, as we've been doing. Remember, objects are things that have both data and behavior. If we are working with only data, we are often better off storing it in a list, set, dictionary, or some other Python data structure (which we'll be covering thoroughly in the next chapter). On the other hand, if we are working with only behavior, with no stored data, a simple function is more suitable.

An object, however, has both data and behavior. Most Python programmers use built-in data structures unless (or until) there is an obvious need to define a class. This is a good thing; there is no reason to add an extra level of abstraction if it doesn't help organize our code. Sometimes, though, the "obvious" need is not so obvious.

A Python programmer often starts by storing data in a few variables. As our program expands, we will later find that we are passing the same set of related variables to different functions. This is the time to think about grouping both variables and functions into a class. If we are designing a program to model polygons in two-dimensional space, we might start with each polygon being represented as a list of points. The points would be modeled as two-tuples (x,y) describing where that point is located. This is all data, stored in two nested data structures (specifically, a list of tuples):

```
square = [(1,1), (1,2), (2,2), (2,1)]
```

Now, if we want to calculate the distance around the perimeter of the polygon, we simply need to sum the distances between the two points, but to do that, we need a function to calculate the distance between two points. Here are two such functions:

```
import math

def distance(p1, p2):
    return math.sqrt((p1[0]-p2[0])**2 + (p1[1]-p2[1])**2)

def perimeter(polygon):
    perimeter = 0
    points = polygon + [polygon[0]]
    for i in range(len(polygon)):
        perimeter += distance(points[i], points[i+1])
    return perimeter
```

Now, as object-oriented programmers, we clearly recognize that a polygon class could encapsulate the list of points (data) and the `perimeter` function (behavior). Further, a point class, such as we defined in *Chapter 2* might encapsulate the x and y coordinates and the `distance` method. But should we do this?

For the previous code, maybe, maybe not. We've been studying object-oriented principles long enough that we can now write the object-oriented version in record time:

```python
import math

class Point:
    def __init__(self, x, y):
        self.x = x
        self.y = y

    def distance(self, p2):
        return math.sqrt((self.x-p2.x)**2 + (self.y-p2.y)**2)

class Polygon:
    def __init__(self):
        self.vertices = []

    def add_point(self, point):
        self.vertices.append((point))

    def perimeter(self):
        perimeter = 0
        points = self.vertices + [self.vertices[0]]
        for i in range(len(self.vertices)):
            perimeter += points[i].distance(points[i+1])
        return perimeter
```

As you can see from the highlighted sections, there is twice as much code here as there was in our earlier version, although we can argue that the add_point method is not strictly necessary.

Now, to understand the difference a little better, let's compare the two APIs in use. Here's how to calculate the perimeter of a square using the object-oriented code:

```python
>>> square = Polygon()
>>> square.add_point(Point(1,1))
>>> square.add_point(Point(1,2))
>>> square.add_point(Point(2,2))
>>> square.add_point(Point(2,1))
>>> square.perimeter()
4.0
```

That's fairly succinct and easy to read, you might think, but let's compare it to the function-based code:

```
>>> square = [(1,1), (1,2), (2,2), (2,1)]
>>> perimeter(square)
4.0
```

Hmm, maybe the object-oriented API isn't so compact! On the other hand, I'd argue that it was easier to **read** than the function example: How do we know what the list of tuples is supposed to represent in the second version? How do we remember what kind of object (a list of two-tuples? That's not intuitive!) we're supposed to pass into the perimeter function? We would need a lot of external documentation to explain how these functions should be used.

In contrast, the object-oriented code is relatively self documenting, we just have to look at the list of methods and their parameters to know what the object does and how to use it. By the time we wrote all the documentation for the functional version, it would probably be longer than the object-oriented code.

Besides, code length is a horrible indicator of code complexity. Some programmers (thankfully, not many of them are Python coders) get hung up on complicated, "one liners", that do incredible amounts of work in one line of code. One line of code that even the original author isn't able to read the next day, that is. Always focus on making your code easier to read and easier to use, not shorter.

As a quick exercise, can you think of any ways to make the object-oriented Polygon as easy to use as the functional implementation? Pause a moment and think about it.

Really, all we have to do is alter our Polygon API so that it can be constructed with multiple points. Let's give it an initializer that accepts a list of Point objects. In fact, let's allow it to accept tuples too, and we can construct the Point objects ourselves, if needed:

```
def __init__(self, points = []):
    self.vertices = []
    for point in points:
        if isinstance(point, tuple):
            point = Point(*point)
        self.vertices.append(point)
```

This example simply goes through the list and ensures that any tuples are converted to points. If the object is not a tuple, we leave it as is, assuming that it is either a Point already, or an unknown duck typed object that can act like a Point.

As we can see, it's not always easy to identify when an object should really be represented as a self-defined class. If we have new functions that accept a polygon argument, such as `area(polygon)` or `point_in_polygon(polygon, x, y)`, the benefits of the object-oriented code become increasingly obvious. Likewise, if we add other attributes to the polygon, such as `color` or `texture`, it makes more and more sense to encapsulate that data into a class.

The distinction is a design decision, but in general, the more complicated a set of data is, the more likely it is to have functions specific to that data, and the more useful it is to use a class with attributes and methods instead.

When making this decision, it also pays to consider how the class will be used. If we're only trying to calculate the perimeter of one polygon in the context of a much greater problem, using a function will probably be quickest to code and easiest to use "one time only". On the other hand, if our program needs to manipulate numerous polygons in a wide variety of ways (calculate perimeter, area, intersection with other polygons, and more), we have most certainly identified an object; one that needs to be extremely versatile.

Pay additional attention to the interaction **between** objects. Look for inheritance relationships; inheritance is impossible to model elegantly without classes, so make sure to use them. Look for the other types of relationships we discussed in *Chapter 1*: association and composition. Composition can, technically, be modeled using only data structures; for example, we can have a list of dictionaries holding tuple values, but it is often less complicated to create an object, especially if there is behavior associated with the data.

[Don't rush to use an object just because you can use an object, but *never* neglect to create a class when you need to use a class.]

Using properties to add behavior to class data

Throughout this book, we've been focusing on the separation of behavior and data. This is very important in object-oriented programming, but we're about to see that, in Python, the distinction can be eerily blurry. Python is very good at blurring distinctions; it doesn't exactly help us to "think outside the box". Rather, it teaches us that the box is in our own head; "there is no box".

Before we get into the details, let's discuss some bad object-oriented theory. Many object-oriented languages (Java is the most guilty) teach us to never access attributes directly. They teach us to write attribute access like this:

```
class Color:
    def __init__(self, rgb_value, name):
        self._rgb_value = rgb_value
        self._name = name

    def set_name(self, name):
        self._name = name

    def get_name(self):
        return self._name
```

The variables are prefixed with an underscore to suggest that they are private (in other languages it would actually force them to be private). Then the get and set methods provide access to each variable. This class would be used in practice as follows:

```
>>> c = Color("#ff0000", "bright red")
>>> c.get_name()
'bright red'
>>> c.set_name("red")
>>> c.get_name()
'red'
```

This is not nearly as readable as the direct access version that Python favors:

```
class Color:
    def __init__(self, rgb_value, name):
        self.rgb_value = rgb_value
        self.name = name

c = Color("#ff0000", "bright red")
print(c.name)
c.name = "red"
```

So why would anyone recommend the method-based syntax? Their reasoning is that someday we may want to add extra code when a value is set or retrieved. For example, we could decide to cache a value and return the cached value, or we might want to validate that the value is a suitable input. In code, we could decide to change the set_name() method as follows:

```
def set_name(self, name):
    if not name:
        raise Exception("Invalid Name")
    self._name = name
```

Now, in Java and similar languages, if we had written our original code to do direct attribute access, and then later changed it to a method like the above, we'd have a problem: Anyone who had written code that accessed the attribute directly would now have to access the method; if they don't change the access style, their code will be broken. The mantra in these languages is that we should never make public members private. This doesn't make much sense in Python since there isn't any concept of private members!

Indeed, the situation in Python is much better. We can use the Python `property` keyword to make methods look like a class attribute. If we originally wrote our code to use direct member access, we can later add methods to get and set the name without changing the interface. Let's see how it looks:

```python
class Color:
    def __init__(self, rgb_value, name):
        self.rgb_value = rgb_value
        self._name = name

    def _set_name(self, name):
        if not name:
            raise Exception("Invalid Name")
        self._name = name

    def _get_name(self):
        return self._name

    name = property(_get_name, _set_name)
```

If we had started with the earlier non-method-based class, which set the name attribute directly, we could later change the code to look like the above. We first change the name attribute into a (semi-) private _name attribute. Then we add two more (semi-) private methods to get and set that variable, doing our validation when we set it.

Finally, we have the `property` declaration at the bottom. This is the magic. It creates a new attribute on the Color class called name, which now replaces the previous name attribute. It sets this attribute to be a property, which calls the two methods we just created whenever the property is accessed or changed. This new version of the Color class can be used exactly the same way as the previous version, yet it now does validation when we set the name:

```python
>>> c = Color("#0000ff", "bright red")
>>> print(c.name)
bright red
```

```
>>> c.name = "red"
>>> print(c.name)
red
>>> c.name = ""
Traceback (most recent call last):
  File "<stdin>", line 1, in <module>
  File "setting_name_property.py", line 8, in _set_name
    raise Exception("Invalid Name")
Exception: Invalid Name
```

So if we'd previously written code to access the name attribute, and then changed it to use our property object, the previous code would still work, unless it was sending an empty property value, which is the behavior we wanted to forbid in the first place. Success!

Bear in mind that even with the name property, the previous code is not 100% safe. People can still access the _name attribute directly and set it to an empty string if they wanted to. But if they access a variable we've explicitly marked with an underscore to suggest it is private, they're the ones that have to deal with the consequences, not us.

How it works

So, what exactly is that property object doing? Think of the property function as returning an object that proxies any requests to set or access the attribute value through the methods we have specified. The property keyword is like a constructor for such an object.

This property constructor can actually accept two additional arguments, a deletion function and a docstring for the property. The delete function is rarely supplied in practice, but it can be useful for logging that a value has been deleted, or possibly to veto deleting if we have reason to do so. The docstring is just a string describing what the property does, no different from the docstrings we discussed in *Chapter 2*. If we do not supply this parameter, the docstring will instead be copied from the docstring for the first argument: the getter method.

Here is a silly example that simply states whenever any of the methods are called:

```
class Silly:
    def _get_silly(self):
        print("You are getting silly")
        return self._silly
    def _set_silly(self, value):
        print("You are making silly {}".format(value))
```

```
        self._silly = value
    def _del_silly(self):
        print("Whoah, you killed silly!")
        del self._silly

    silly = property(_get_silly, _set_silly,
            _del_silly, "This is a silly property")
```

If we actually use this class, it does indeed print out the correct strings when we ask it to:

```
>>> s = Silly()
>>> s.silly = "funny"
You are making silly funny
>>> s.silly
You are getting silly
'funny'
>>> del s.silly
Whoah, you killed silly!
```

Further, if we look at the help file for the `Silly` class (by issuing `help(silly)` at the interpreter prompt), it shows us the custom docstring for our `silly` attribute:

```
Help on class Silly in module __main__:

class Silly(builtins.object)
 |  Data descriptors defined here:
 |
 |  __dict__
 |      dictionary for instance variables (if defined)
 |
 |  __weakref__
 |      list of weak references to the object (if defined)
 |
 |  silly
 |      This is a silly property
```

Once again, everything is working as we planned. In practice, properties are normally only defined with the first two parameters; the getter and setter functions. The docstring is defined as a normal docstring on the getter and copied into the property, while the deletion function is left empty because object attributes are rarely deleted. If a coder does try to delete one that doesn't have a deletion function specified, however, it will raise an exception, so if there is any chance of a legitimate reason to delete our property, we should supply that function.

Decorators: another way to create properties

(If you've never used Python decorators before, you might want to skip this section and come back to it after we've discussed the decorator pattern in *Chapter 8*.)

Decorators were introduced in Python 2.4 as a way to modify functions dynamically by passing them as arguments to other functions, which eventually return a new function. We won't be covering decorators in-depth at this time, but the basic syntax is easy to grasp. If you've never used them before, you can still follow along.

Applying a decorator can be as simple as prefixing the function name with an @ symbol, and placing the result just before the definition of the function that is being decorated. The property function itself can be used with decorator syntax to turn a get function into a property:

```
class Foo:
    @property
    def foo(self):
        return "bar"
```

This applies `property` as a decorator, and is equivalent to applying it as `foo = property(foo)`. The main difference, from a readability perspective, is that we get to mark the `foo` function as a property at the top of the method, instead of after it is defined, where it can be easily overlooked.

Going one step further, we can specify a setter function for the new property as follows:

```
class Foo:
    @property
    def foo(self):
        return self._foo

    @foo.setter
    def foo(self, value):
        self._foo = value
```

This syntax looks a little odd. First we decorate the `foo` method as a getter. Then we decorate a new method with exactly the same name with the setter **attribute** of the original decorated `foo` method! Remember, the `property` function returns an object; this object is automatically set up to have a `setter` attribute, and this attribute can be applied as a decorator to other functions. Using the same name for the get and set methods is not required, but it does help group the multiple methods that create one property together.

We can, of course, also specify a deletion function with `@foo.deleter`. We cannot specify a docstring using property decorators, so we need to rely on the property copying the docstring from the initial getter method.

Here's our previous `Silly` class rewritten to use `property` as a decorator:

```
class Silly:
    @property
    def silly(self):
        "This is a silly property"
        print("You are getting silly")
        return self._silly

    @silly.setter
    def silly(self, value):
        print("You are making silly {}".format(value))
        self._silly = value

    @silly.deleter
    def silly(self):
        print("Whoah, you killed silly!")
        del self._silly
```

This class operates *exactly* the same as our earlier version, including the help text. You can use whichever syntax you feel is more readable and elegant.

When should we use properties?

With the **property** keyword smearing the division between behavior and data, it can be confusing to know which one to choose. The example use case we saw earlier is one of the most common uses of properties: we have some data on a class that we later want to add behavior to. There are also other factors to take into account when deciding to use a property.

Technically, in Python, data, properties, and methods are all attributes on a class. The fact that a method is callable does not distinguish it from other types of attributes; indeed, we'll see in *Chapter 7* that it is possible to create normal objects that are callable, and also that functions and methods are themselves normal objects.

The fact that methods are just callable attributes, and properties are just customizable attributes can help us in our decision. Methods should only represent *actions*; things that can be done to or performed by the object. When you call a method, even with only one argument, it should *do* something. Methods are generally verbs.

That leaves us to decide between standard data attributes and properties. In general, always use a standard attribute until you need to control access to that property in some way. In either case, your attribute should be a noun. The only difference between an attribute and a property is that we can invoke custom actions automatically when a property is retrieved, set, or deleted.

Let's try a more realistic example. A common need for custom behavior is caching a value that is difficult to calculate or expensive to look up (requiring, for example, a network request or database query). The goal is to store the value locally to avoid repeated calls to the expensive calculation.

We can do this with a custom getter on the property. The first time the value is retrieved, we perform the lookup or calculation. Then we could locally cache the value as a private attribute on our object (or in dedicated caching software), and the next time the value is requested, we return the stored data. Here's how we might cache a webpage:

```
from urllib.request import urlopen

class WebPage:
    def __init__(self, url):
        self.url = url
        self._content = None

    @property
    def content(self):
        if not self._content:
            print("Retrieving New Page...")
            self._content = urlopen(self.url).read()
        return self._content
```

We can test this code to see that the page is only retrieved once:

```
>>> import time
>>> webpage = WebPage("http://ccphillips.net/")
>>> now = time.time()
>>> content1 = webpage.content
Retrieving New Page...
>>> time.time() - now
22.43316888809204
>>> now = time.time()
>>> content2 = webpage.content
>>> time.time() - now
1.9266459941864014
>>> content2 == content1
True
```

On my awful satellite connection it takes twenty seconds the first time I load the content, but the second time, I get the result in two seconds (which is really just the amount of time it took to type the lines into the interpreter).

Custom getters are also useful for attributes that need to be calculated on the fly, based on other object attributes. For example, we might want to calculate the average for a list of integers:

```python
class AverageList(list):
    @property
    def average(self):
        return sum(self) / len(self)
```

This very simple class inherits from `list`, so we get list-like behavior for free. We just add a property to the class, and presto, our list can have an average:

```python
>>> a = AverageList([1,2,3,4])
>>> a.average
2.5
```

Of course, we could have made this a method instead, but then we should call it `calculate_average()`, since methods represent actions. But a property called `average` is more suitable; both easier to type, and easier to read.

Custom setters are useful for validation, as we've already seen, but they can also be used to proxy a value to another location. For example, we could add a content setter to the `WebPage` class that automatically logs into our web server and uploads a new page whenever the value is set.

Managing objects

We've been focused on objects and their attributes and methods. Now, we'll take a look at designing higher-level objects; the kinds of objects that manage other objects. The objects that tie everything together.

The difference between these objects and most of the examples we've seen so far is that our examples tend to represent concrete ideas. Management objects are more like office managers; they don't do the actual "visible" work out on the floor, but without them, there would be no communication between departments and nobody would know what they are supposed to do. Analogously, the attributes on a management class tend to refer to other objects that do the "visible" work; the behaviors on such a class delegate to those other classes at the right time, and pass messages between them.

As an example, we'll write a program that does a find and replace action for text files stored in a compressed ZIP file. We'll need objects to represent the ZIP file and each individual text file (luckily, we don't have to write these classes, they're available in the Python Standard Library). The manager object will be responsible for ensuring three steps occur in order:

1. Unzipping the compressed file.
2. Performing the find and replace action.
3. Zipping up the new files.

The class is initialized with the `.zip` filename and search and replace strings. We create a temporary directory to store the unzipped files in, so that the folder stays clean. We also add a useful helper method for internal use that helps identify an individual filename inside that directory:

```python
import sys
import os
import shutil
import zipfile

class ZipReplace:
    def __init__(self, filename, search_string,
            replace_string):
        self.filename = filename
        self.search_string = search_string
        self.replace_string = replace_string
        self.temp_directory = "unzipped-{}".format(
            filename)

    def _full_filename(self, filename):
        return os.path.join(self.temp_directory, filename)
```

Then we create an overall "manager" method for each of the three steps. This method delegates responsibility to other methods. Obviously, we could do all three steps in one method, or indeed, in one script without ever creating an object. There are several advantages to separating the three steps:

- **Readability**: The code for each step is in a self-contained unit that is easy to read and understand. The method names describe what the method does, and no additional documentation is required to understand what is going on.

- **Extensibility**: If a subclass wanted to use compressed TAR files instead of ZIP files, it could override the `zip` and `unzip` methods without having to duplicate the `find_replace` method.

- **Partitioning**: An external class could create an instance of this class and call the find and replace method directly on some folder without having to `zip` the content.

The delegation method is the first in the code below; the rest of the methods are included for completeness:

```python
def zip_find_replace(self):
    self.unzip_files()
    self.find_replace()
    self.zip_files()

def unzip_files(self):
    os.mkdir(self.temp_directory)
    zip = zipfile.ZipFile(self.filename)
    try:
        zip.extractall(self.temp_directory)
    finally:
        zip.close()

def find_replace(self):
    for filename in os.listdir(self.temp_directory):
        with open(self._full_filename(filename)) as file:
            contents = file.read()
        contents = contents.replace(
            self.search_string, self.replace_string)
        with open(
            self._full_filename(filename), "w") as file:
            file.write(contents)

def zip_files(self):
    file = zipfile.ZipFile(self.filename, 'w')
    for filename in os.listdir(self.temp_directory):
        file.write(
            self._full_filename(filename), filename)
    shutil.rmtree(self.temp_directory)

if __name__ == "__main__":
    ZipReplace(*sys.argv[1:4]).zip_find_replace()
```

For brevity, the code for zipping and unzipping files is sparsely documented. Our current focus is on object-oriented design; if you are interested in the inner details of the `zipfile` module, refer to the documentation in the standard library, either online at http://docs.python.org/library/zipfile.html or by typing `import zipfile ; help(zipfile)` into your interactive interpreter. Note that this example only searches the top-level files in a ZIP file; if there are any folders in the unzipped content, they will not be scanned, nor will any files inside those folders.

The last two lines in the code allow us to run the example from the command line by passing the ZIP filename, search string, and replace string as arguments:

```
python zipsearch.py hello.zip hello hi
```

Of course, this object does not have to be created from the command line; it could be imported from another module (to perform batch ZIP file processing) or accessed as part of a GUI interface or even a higher-level management object that knows what to do with ZIP files (for example to retrieve them from an FTP server or back them up to an external disk).

As programs become more and more complex, the objects being modeled become less and less like physical objects. Properties are other abstract objects and methods are actions that change the state of those abstract objects. But at the heart of every object, no matter how complex, is a set of concrete properties and well-defined behaviors.

Removing duplicate code

Often the code in management style classes such as ZipReplace is quite generic and can be applied in many different ways. It is possible to use either composition or inheritance to help keep this code in one place, thus eliminating duplicate code. Before we look at any examples of this, let's discuss a tiny bit of theory. Specifically: why is duplicate code a bad thing?

There are several reasons, but they all boil down to readability and maintainability. When we're writing a new piece of code that is similar to an earlier piece, the easiest thing to do is copy the old code and change whatever needs to change (variable names, logic, comments) to make it work in the new location. Alternatively, if we're writing new code that seems similar, but not identical to code elsewhere in the project, the easiest thing to do is write fresh code with similar behavior, rather than figure out how to extract the overlapping functionality.

But as soon as someone has to read and understand the code and they come across duplicate blocks, they are faced with a dilemma. Code that might have made sense suddenly has to be understood. How is one section different from the other? How are they the same? Under what conditions is one section called? When do we call the other? You might argue that you're the only one reading your code, but if you don't touch that code for eight months it will be as incomprehensible to you as to a fresh coder. When we're trying to read two similar pieces of code, we have to understand why they're different, as well as how they're different. This wastes the reader's time; code should always be written to be readable first.

I once had to try to understand someone's code that had three identical copies of the same three hundred lines of very poorly written code. I had been working with the code for a month before I realized that the three "identical" versions were actually performing slightly different tax calculations. Some of the subtle differences were intentional, but there were also obvious areas where someone had updated a calculation in one function without updating the other two. The number of subtle, incomprehensible bugs in the code could not be counted.

Reading such duplicate code can be tiresome, but code maintenance is an even greater torment. As the preceding story suggests, keeping two similar pieces of code up to date can be a nightmare. We have to remember to update both sections whenever we update one of them, and we have to remember how the multiple sections differ so we can modify our changes when we are editing each of them. If we forget to update both sections, we will end up with extremely annoying bugs that usually manifest themselves as, "but I fixed that already, why is it still happening?"

The result is that people who are reading or maintaining our code have to spend astronomical amounts of time understanding and testing it compared to if we had written the code in a non-repetitive manner in the first place. It's even more frustrating when we are the ones doing the maintenance. The time we save by copy-pasting existing code is lost the very first time we have to maintain it. Code is both read and maintained many more times and much more often than it is written. Comprehensible code should always be paramount.

This is why programmers, especially Python programmers (who tend to value elegant code more than average), follow what is known as the **Don't Repeat Yourself**, or **DRY** principle. DRY code is maintainable code. My advice to beginning programmers is to never use the copy and paste feature of their editor. To intermediate programmers, I suggest they think thrice before they hit *Ctrl + C*.

But what should we do instead of code duplication? The simplest solution is often to move the code into a function that accepts parameters to account for whatever sections are different. This isn't a terribly object-oriented solution, but it is frequently sufficient. For example, if we have two pieces of code that unzip a ZIP file into two different directories, we can easily write a function that accepts a parameter for the directory to which it should be unzipped instead. This may make the function itself slightly more difficult to read, but a good function name and docstring can easily make up for that, and any code that invokes the function will be easier to read.

That's certainly enough theory! The moral of the story is: always make the effort to refactor your code to be easier to read instead of writing bad code that is only easier to write.

In practice

Let's explore two ways we can reuse existing code. After writing our code to replace strings in a ZIP file full of text files, we are later contracted to scale all the images in a ZIP file to 640x480. Looks like we could use a very similar paradigm to what we used in ZipReplace. The first impulse, obviously, would be to save a copy of that file and change the find_replace method to scale_image or something similar. But, that's just not cool. What if someday we want to change the unzip and zip methods to also open TAR files? Or maybe we want to use a guaranteed unique directory name for temporary files. In either case, we'd have to change it in two different places!

We'll start by demonstrating an inheritance-based solution to this problem. First we'll modify our original ZipReplace class into a superclass for processing generic ZIP files:

```python
import os
import shutil
import zipfile

class ZipProcessor:
    def __init__(self, zipname):
        self.zipname = zipname
        self.temp_directory = "unzipped-{}".format(
            zipname[:-4])

    def _full_filename(self, filename):
        return os.path.join(self.temp_directory, filename)

    def process_zip(self):
        self.unzip_files()
        self.process_files()
        self.zip_files()

    def unzip_files(self):
        os.mkdir(self.temp_directory)
        zip = zipfile.ZipFile(self.zipname)
        try:
            zip.extractall(self.temp_directory)
        finally:
            zip.close()

    def zip_files(self):
        file = zipfile.ZipFile(self.zipname, 'w')
        for filename in os.listdir(self.temp_directory):
            file.write(self._full_filename(
                filename), filename)
        shutil.rmtree(self.temp_directory)
```

We changed the `filename` property to `zipfile` to avoid confusion with the `filename` local variables inside the various methods. This helps make the code more readable even though it isn't actually a change in design. We also dropped the two parameters to `__init__` (`search_string` and `replace_string`) that were specific to `ZipReplace`. Then we renamed the `zip_find_replace` method to `process_zip` and made it call an (as yet undefined) `process_files` method instead of `find_replace`; these name changes help demonstrate the more generalized nature of our new class. Notice that we have removed the `find_replace` method altogether; that code is specific to `ZipReplace` and has no business here.

This new `ZipProcessor` class doesn't actually define a `process_files` method; so if we ran it directly, it would raise an exception. Since it actually isn't meant to be run directly, we also removed the main call at the bottom of the original script.

Now, before we move on to our image processing app, let's fix up our original `zipsearch` to make use of this parent class:

```python
from zip_processor import ZipProcessor
import sys
import os


class ZipReplace(ZipProcessor):
    def __init__(self, filename, search_string,
            replace_string):
        super().__init__(filename)
        self.search_string = search_string
        self.replace_string = replace_string

    def process_files(self):
        '''perform a search and replace on all files
        in the temporary directory'''
        for filename in os.listdir(self.temp_directory):
            with open(self._full_filename(filename)) as file:
                contents = file.read()
            contents = contents.replace(
                    self.search_string, self.replace_string)
            with open(
                self._full_filename(filename), "w") as file:
                file.write(contents)

if __name__ == "__main__":
    ZipReplace(*sys.argv[1:4]).process_zip()
```

This code is a bit shorter than the original version, since it inherits its ZIP processing abilities from the parent class. We first import the base class we just wrote and make `ZipReplace` extend that class. Then we use `super()` to initialize the parent class. The `find_replace` method is still here, but we renamed it to `process_files` so the parent class can call it. Because this name isn't as descriptive as the old one, we added a docstring to describe what it is doing.

Now, that was quite a bit of work, considering that all we have now is a program that is functionally no different from the one we started with! But having done that work, it is now much easier for us to write other classes that operate on files in a ZIP archive, such as our photo scaler. Further, if we ever want to improve the zip functionality, we can do it for all classes by changing only the one `ZipProcessor` base class. Maintenance will be much more effective.

See how simple it is, now to create a photo scaling class that takes advantage of the `ZipProcessor` functionality. (Note: this class requires the third-party **pygame** library to be installed. You can download it from `http://www.pygame.org/`.)

```
from zip_processor import ZipProcessor
import os
import sys
from pygame import image
from pygame.transform import scale

class ScaleZip(ZipProcessor):

    def process_files(self):
        '''Scale each image in the directory to 640x480'''
        for filename in os.listdir(self.temp_directory):
            im = image.load(self._full_filename(filename))
            scaled = scale(im, (640,480))
            image.save(scaled, self._full_filename(filename))

if __name__ == "__main__":
    ScaleZip(*sys.argv[1:4]).process_zip()
```

All that work we did earlier paid off! Look how simple this class is! All we do is open each file (assuming that it is an image; it will unceremoniously crash if the file cannot be opened), scale it, and save it back. The `ZipProcessor` takes care of the zipping and unzipping without any extra work on our part.

Or we can use composition

Now, let's try solving the same problem using a composition-based solution. Even though we're completely changing paradigms, from inheritance to composition, we only have to make a minor modification to our `ZipProcessor` class:

```python
import os
import shutil
import zipfile


class ZipProcessor:
    def __init__(self, zipname, processor):
        self.zipname = zipname
        self.temp_directory = "unzipped-{}".format(
            zipname[:-4])
        self.processor = processor

    def _full_filename(self, filename):
        return os.path.join(self.temp_directory, filename)

    def process_zip(self):
        self.unzip_files()
        self.processor.process(self)
        self.zip_files()

    def unzip_files(self):
        os.mkdir(self.temp_directory)
        zip = zipfile.ZipFile(self.zipname)
        try:
            zip.extractall(self.temp_directory)
        finally:
            zip.close()

    def zip_files(self):
        file = zipfile.ZipFile(self.zipname, 'w')
        for filename in os.listdir(self.temp_directory):
            file.write(self._full_filename(filename), filename)
        shutil.rmtree(self.temp_directory)
```

All we did was change the initializer to accept a `processor` object. The `process_zip` function now calls a method on that `processor` object; the method called accepts a reference to the `ZipProcessor` itself. Now we can change our `ZipReplace` class to be a suitable `processor` object that no longer uses inheritance:

```python
from zip_processor import ZipProcessor
import sys
import os


class ZipReplace:
    def __init__(self, search_string,
            replace_string):
        self.search_string = search_string
        self.replace_string = replace_string

    def process(self, zipprocessor):
        '''perform a search and replace on all files in the
        temporary directory'''
        for filename in os.listdir(
                zipprocessor.temp_directory):
            with open(
                zipprocessor._full_filename(filename)) as file:
                contents = file.read()
            contents = contents.replace(
                self.search_string, self.replace_string)
            with open(zipprocessor._full_filename(
                    filename), "w") as file:
                file.write(contents)

if __name__ == "__main__":
    zipreplace = ZipReplace(*sys.argv[2:4])
    ZipProcessor(sys.argv[1], zipreplace).process_zip()
```

We didn't actually change much here; the class no longer inherits from `ZipProcessor`, and when we process the files, we accept a `zipprocessor` object that gives us the function to calculate `_full_filename`. In the bottom two lines, when we run from the command line, we first construct a `ZipReplace` object. This is then passed into the `ZipProcessor` constructor so the two objects can communicate.

This design is a terrific separation of interests. Now we have a `ZipProcessor` that can accept any object that has a `process` method to do the actual processing. Further, we have a `ZipReplace` that can be passed to any method, function, or object that wants to call its `process` function; it is no longer tied to the ZIP processing code through an inheritance relationship; it could now be applied with equal ease to a local or network filesystem, for example, or to a different kind of compressed file such as a RAR archive.

Any inheritance relationship can be modeled as a composition relationship (change the "is a" to a "has a parent") instead, but that does not mean it always should be. And the reverse is not true, most composition relationships cannot be (properly) modeled as inheritance.

Case study

For this case study, we'll try to delve further into the question, "when should I choose an object versus a built-in type?" We'll be modeling a `Document` class that might be used in a text editor or word processor. What objects, functions, or properties should it have?

We might start with a `str` for the `Document` contents, but strings aren't mutable. A mutable object is one that can be changed; but a `str` is immutable, we can't insert a character into it or remove one without creating a brand new string object. That's leaving a lot of `str` objects for Python's garbage collector to clean up behind us. So, instead of a string, we'll use a list of characters, which we can modify at will. In addition, a `Document` would need to know the current cursor position within the list, and should also store a filename for the document.

Now, what methods should it have? There are a lot of things we might want to do to a text document, including inserting and deleting characters, cut, copy, paste, and saving or closing the document. It looks like there are copious amounts of both data and behavior, so it makes sense to put all this stuff into its own `Document` class.

The question is, should this class be composed of a bunch of basic Python objects such as `str` filenames, `int` cursor positions, and a `list` of characters? Or should some or all of those things be specially defined objects in their own right? What about individual lines and characters, do they need to have classes of their own?

We'll answer these questions as we go, but let's just design the simplest possible `Document` class first and see what it can do:

```python
class Document:
    def __init__(self):
        self.characters = []
        self.cursor = 0
        self.filename = ''

    def insert(self, character):
        self.characters.insert(self.cursor, character)
        self.cursor += 1

    def delete(self):
```

```
        del self.characters[self.cursor]

    def save(self):
        f = open(self.filename, 'w')
        f.write(''.join(self.characters))
        f.close()

    def forward(self):
        self.cursor += 1

    def back(self):
        self.cursor -= 1
```

This simple class allows us full control over editing a basic document. Have a look at it in action:

```
>>> doc = Document()
>>> doc.filename = "test_document"
>>> doc.insert('h')
>>> doc.insert('e')
>>> doc.insert('l')
>>> doc.insert('l')
>>> doc.insert('o')
>>> "".join(doc.characters)
'hello'
>>> doc.back()
>>> doc.delete()
>>> doc.insert('p')
>>> "".join(doc.characters)
'hellp'
```

Looks like it's working. We could connect a keyboard's letter and arrow keys to these methods and the document would track everything just fine.

But what if we want to connect more than just arrow keys. What if we want to connect the *Home* and *End* keys as well? We could add more methods to the Document class that search forward or backwards for newline characters (in Python, a newline character, or \n represents the end of one line and the beginning of a new one) in the string and jump to them, but if we did that for every possible movement action (move by words, move by sentences, *Page Up*, *Page Down*, end of line, beginning of whitespace, and more), the class would be huge. Maybe it would be better to put those methods on a separate object. What we can do is turn the cursor attribute into an object that is aware of its position and can manipulate that position. We can move the forward and back methods to that class, and add a couple more for the *Home* and *End* keys:

```python
class Cursor:
    def __init__(self, document):
        self.document = document
        self.position = 0

    def forward(self):
        self.position += 1

    def back(self):
        self.position -= 1

    def home(self):
        while self.document.characters[
                self.position-1] != '\n':
            self.position -= 1
            if self.position == 0:
                # Got to beginning of file before newline
                break

    def end(self):
        while self.position < len(self.document.characters
                ) and self.document.characters[
                    self.position] != '\n':
            self.position += 1
```

This class takes the document as an initialization parameter so the methods have access to the contents of the document's character list. It then provides simple methods for moving backwards and forwards, as before, and for moving to the home and end positions.

> This code is not very safe. You can very easily move past the ending position, and if you try to go home on an empty file it will crash. These examples are kept short to make them readable, that doesn't mean they are defensive! You can improve the error checking of this code as an exercise; it might be a great opportunity to expand your exception handling skills.

The Document class itself is hardly changed, except for removing the two methods that were moved to the Cursor class:

```python
class Document:
    def __init__(self):
        self.characters = []
        self.cursor = Cursor(self)
        self.filename = ''

    def insert(self, character):
        self.characters.insert(self.cursor.position,
                character)
        self.cursor.forward()

    def delete(self):
        del self.characters[self.cursor.position]

    def save(self):
        f = open(self.filename, 'w')
        f.write(''.join(self.characters))
        f.close()
```

We simply updated anything that accessed the old cursor integer to use the new object instead. We can test that the home method is really moving to the newline character.

```python
>>> d = Document()
>>> d.insert('h')
>>> d.insert('e')
>>> d.insert('l')
>>> d.insert('l')
>>> d.insert('o')
>>> d.insert('\n')
>>> d.insert('w')
>>> d.insert('o')
>>> d.insert('r')
>>> d.insert('l')
>>> d.insert('d')
>>> d.cursor.home()
>>> d.insert("*")
>>> print("".join(d.characters))
hello
*world
```

Now, since we've been using that string `join` function a lot (to concatenate the characters so we can see the actual document contents), we can add a property to the `Document` class to give us the complete string:

```
@property
def string(self):
    return "".join(self.characters)
```

This makes our testing a little simpler:

```
>>> print(d.string)
hello
world
```

This framework is easy enough to extend to create a complete text editor document. Now, let's make it work for rich text; text that can have **bold**, <u>underlined</u>, or *italic* characters. There are two ways we could process this; the first is to insert "fake" characters into our character list that act like instructions such as "bold characters until you find a stop bold character". The second is to add information to each character indicating what formatting it should have. While the former method is probably more common, we'll implement the latter solution. To do that, we're obviously going to need a class for characters. This class will have an attribute representing the character, as well as three boolean attributes representing whether it is bold, italic, or underlined.

Hmm, Wait! Is this character class going to have any methods? If not, maybe we should use one of the many Python data structures instead; a tuple or named tuple would probably be sufficient. Are there any actions that we would want to do to, or invoke on a character?

Well, clearly, we might want to do things with characters, such as delete or copy them, but those are things that need to be handled at the `Document` level, since they are really modifying the list of characters. Are there things that need to be done to individual characters?

Actually, now that we're thinking about what a `Character` actually **is**... what is it? Would it be safe to say that a `Character` is a string? Maybe we should use an inheritance relationship here? Then we can take advantage of the numerous methods that `str` instances come with.

What sorts of methods are we talking about? There's `startswith`, `strip`, `find`, `lower`, and many more. Most of these methods expect to be working on strings that contain more than one character. In contrast, if `Character` were to subclass `str`, we'd probably be wise to override `__init__` to raise an exception if a multi-character string were supplied. Since all those methods we'd get for free wouldn't really apply to our `Character` class, it turns out we shouldn't use inheritance, after all.

This leaves us at our first question; should `Character` even be a class? There is a very important special method on the `object` class that we can take advantage of to represent our characters. This method, called __str__ (two underscores, like __init__), is used in string manipulation functions like `print` and the `str` constructor to convert any class to a string. The default implementation does some boring stuff like printing the name of the module and class and its address in memory. But if we override it, we can make it print whatever we like. For our implementation, we can make it prefix characters with special characters to represent whether they are bold, italic, or underlined. So we will create a class to represent a character, and here it is:

```
class Character:
    def __init__(self, character,
            bold=False, italic=False, underline=False):
        assert len(character) == 1
        self.character = character
        self.bold = bold
        self.italic = italic
        self.underline = underline

    def __str__(self):
        bold = "*" if self.bold else ''
        italic = "/" if self.italic else ''
        underline = "_" if self.underline else ''
        return bold + italic + underline + self.character
```

This class allows us to create characters and prefix them with a special character when the `str()` function is applied to them. Nothing too exciting there. We only have to make a few minor modifications to the `Document` and `Cursor` classes to work with this class. In the `Document` class, we add these two lines at the beginning of the insert method:

```
def insert(self, character):
    if not hasattr(character, 'character'):
        character = Character(character)
```

This is a rather strange bit of code. Its basic purpose is to check if the character being passed in is a `Character` or a `str`. If it is a string, it is wrapped in a `Character` class so all objects in the list are `Character` objects. However, it is entirely possible that someone using our code would want to use a class that is neither `Character` nor string, using duck typing. If the object has a character attribute, we assume it is a "Character-like" object. But if it does not, we assume it is a "str-like" object and wrap it in a `Character`. This helps the program take advantage of duck typing as well as polymorphism; as long as an object has a character attribute, it can be used in the `Document`. This could be very useful, for example, if we wanted to make a programmer's editor with syntax highlighting: we'd need extra data on the character, such as what type of token the character belongs to.

In addition, we need to modify the string property on Document to accept the new Character values. All we need to do is call str() on each character before we join it:

```
@property
def string(self):
    return "".join((str(c) for c in self.characters))
```

This code uses a generator expression, which we'll discuss in the next chapter. It's simply a shortcut to perform a specific action on all the objects in a sequence.

Finally we also need to check Character.character, instead of just the string character we were storing before, in the home and end functions when we're looking to see if it matches a newline.

```
def home(self):
    while self.document.characters[
            self.position-1].character != '\n':
        self.position -= 1
        if self.position == 0:
            # Got to beginning of file before newline
            break

def end(self):
    while self.position < len(
            self.document.characters) and \
            self.document.characters[
                self.position
            ].character != '\n':
        self.position += 1
```

This completes the formatting of characters. We can test it to see that it works:

```
>>> d = Document()
>>> d.insert('h')
>>> d.insert('e')
>>> d.insert(Character('l', bold=True))
>>> d.insert(Character('l', bold=True))
>>> d.insert('o')
>>> d.insert('\n')
>>> d.insert(Character('w', italic=True))
>>> d.insert(Character('o', italic=True))
>>> d.insert(Character('r', underline=True))
>>> d.insert('l')
>>> d.insert('d')
>>> print(d.string)
```

```
he*l*lo
/w/o_rld
>>> d.cursor.home()
>>> d.delete()
>>> d.insert('W')
>>> print(d.string)
he*l*lo
W/o_rld
>>> d.characters[0].underline = True
>>> print(d.string)
_he*l*lo
W/o_rld
>>>
```

As expected, whenever we print the string, each bold character is preceded by a *, each italic character by a /, and each underlined character by a _. All our functions seem to work, and we can modify characters in the list after the fact. We have a working rich text document object that could be plugged into a user interface and hooked up with a keyboard for input and a screen for output. Naturally, we'd want to display real bold, italic, and underlined characters on the screen, instead of using our __str__ method, but it was sufficient for the basic testing we demanded of it.

Exercises

We've looked at various ways that objects, data, and methods can interact with each other in an object-oriented Python program. As usual, your first thoughts should be how you can apply these principles to your own work. Do you have any messy scripts lying around that could be rewritten using an object-oriented manager? Look through some of your old code and look for methods that are not actions. If the name isn't a verb, try rewriting it as a property.

Think about code you've written in any language. Does it break the DRY principle? Is there any duplicate code? Did you copy and paste code? Did you write two versions of similar pieces of code because you didn't feel like understanding the original code? Go back over some of your recent code now and see if you can refactor the duplicate code using inheritance or composition. Try to pick a project you're still interested in maintaining; not code so old that you never want to touch it again. It helps keep your interest up when you do the improvements!

Now, look back over some of the examples we saw in this chapter. Start with the cached webpage example which uses a property to cache the retrieved data. An obvious problem with this example is that the cache is never refreshed. Add a timeout to the getter for the property, and only return the cached page if the page has been requested before the timeout has expired. You can use the `time` module (`time.time() - an_old_time` returns the number of seconds that have elapsed since `an_old_time`) to determine whether the cache has expired.

Now look at the composition and inheritance based versions of `ZipProcessor`. We wrote an inheritance-based `ScaleZipper`, but didn't port it to the composite `ZipProcessor`. Try writing the composite `ScaleZipper` and compare the two pieces of code. Which version do you find easier to use? Which is more elegant? What is easier to read? These are subjective questions; the answer varies for each of us. Knowing the answer, however, is important; if you find you prefer inheritance over composition, you have to pay attention that you don't overuse inheritance in your daily coding. If you prefer composition, make sure you don't miss opportunities to create an elegant inheritance-based solution.

Finally, add some error handlers to the various classes we created in the case study. They should ensure single characters are entered, that you don't try to move the cursor past the end or beginning of the file, that you don't delete a character that doesn't exist, and that you don't save a file without a filename. Try to think of as many edge cases as you can, and account for them. Consider different ways to handle them; should you raise an exception when the user tries to move past the end of the file, or just stay on the last character?

Pay attention, in your daily coding, to the copy and paste commands. Every time you use them in your editor, consider whether it would be a good idea to improve your program's organization so that you only have one version of the code you are about to copy.

Summary

In this chapter, we focused on identifying objects, especially objects that are not immediately apparent; objects that manage and control. In particular, we covered:

- Why objects should have both data and behavior
- How properties blur the distinction between data and behavior
- The DRY principle and the follies of duplicate code
- Inheritance and composition for reducing code duplication

In the next chapter we'll cover several of the built-in Python data structures and objects, focusing on their object-oriented properties and how they can be extended or adapted.

6
Python Data Structures

In our examples so far, we've already seen many of the built-in Python data structures in action. You've probably covered many of them in introductory books or tutorials. In this chapter, we'll be discussing the object-oriented features of these data structures, when they should be used instead of a regular class, and when they should not be used. In particular we'll be covering:

- Tuples
- Dictionaries
- Lists and sets
- How and why to extend built-in objects

Empty objects

Let's start with the most basic Python built-in, one that we've seen many times already, the one that we've extended in every class we have created: the `object`. Technically, we can instantiate an object without writing a subclass:

```
>>> o = object()
>>> o.x = 5
Traceback (most recent call last):
  File "<stdin>", line 1, in <module>
AttributeError: 'object' object has no attribute 'x'
```

Unfortunately, as you can see, it's not possible to set any attributes on an `object` that was instantiated directly. This isn't because the Python developers wanted to force us to write our own classes, or anything so sinister. No, they simply wanted to save memory; a lot of memory. When Python allows an object to have arbitrary attributes, it takes a certain amount of system memory to keep track of what attributes each object has, for storing both the attribute name and its value. Even if no attributes are stored, a certain amount of memory is allocated for *potential* new attributes. Given the dozens, hundreds, or thousands of objects (every class extends object) in a typical Python program, this small amount of memory would quickly become a large amount of memory. So Python disables arbitrary properties on `object`, and several other built-ins, by default.

It is possible to restrict arbitrary properties on our own classes using **slots**. Slots are beyond the scope of this book, but you now have a search term if you are looking for more information. In normal use, there isn't much benefit to using slots, but if you're writing an object that will be duplicated thousands of times throughout the system, they can help save memory, just as they do for `object`.

It is, however, trivial to create an empty object class of our own; we saw it in our earliest example:

```
class MyObject:
    pass
```

And, as we've also seen, it's possible to set attributes on such classes:

```
>>> m = MyObject()
>>> m.x = "hello"
>>> m.x
'hello'
```

Clearly, if we wanted to group properties together, we could store them in an empty object like this. But we don't normally want to do this. There are other built-ins designed for storing data, and we'll be looking at them very soon. As has been stressed throughout this book, classes and objects should only be used when you want to specify both data and behaviors. The main reason to write an empty class is when we want to quickly block something out and we know we're going to have to come back and add behavior to it later. It is much easier to adapt behaviors to a class than it is to replace a data structure with an object and change all references to it. It is important to decide from the outset if the data is just data, or if it is an object in disguise. Once that design decision is made, the rest of the design typically falls into place.

Tuples and named tuples

Tuples are objects that can store a specific number of other objects in order. They are immutable, so we can't add, remove, or replace objects on the fly. This may seem like a massive restriction, but the truth is, if you need to modify a tuple, you're using the wrong data type (a list would be more suitable). The primary benefit of tuples' immutability is that we can use them as keys in dictionaries, and in other locations where an object requires a hash value.

Tuples are used to store data; behavior cannot be stored in a tuple. If we require behavior to manipulate a tuple, we have to pass the tuple into a function (or method on another object) that performs the action.

Tuples should generally store values that are somehow different from each other. For example, we would not put three stock symbols in a tuple, but we might create a tuple of stock symbol, current price, high, and low for the day. The primary purpose of a tuple is to aggregate different pieces of data together into one container. Indeed, a tuple can be the easiest tool to replace the "object with no data" idiom from the previous section.

We can create a tuple by separating the values with a comma. Usually tuples are wrapped in parentheses to make them easy to read and to group them from other parts of an expression, but this is not always mandatory. The following two assignments are identical (they record a stock, the current price, the high, and the low for a rather profitable company):

```
>>> stock = "GOOG", 613.30, 625.86, 610.50
>>> stock2 = ("GOOG", 613.30, 625.86, 610.50)
```

If we're grouping a tuple inside of some other object, such as a function call, list comprehension, or generator, the parentheses are required. Otherwise it would be impossible for the interpreter to know if it is a tuple or another parameter. For example, the following function accepts a tuple and a date, and returns a tuple of the date and the middle value between the stock's high and low value:

```
import datetime
def middle(stock, date):
    symbol, current, high, low = stock
    return (((high + low) /2), date)

mid_value, date = middle(("GOOG", 613.30, 625.86, 610.50),
        datetime.date(2010, 1, 6))
```

The tuple is created directly inside the function call by separating the values with commas and enclosing the entire tuple in parenthesis. The tuple is followed by a comma to separate it from the second argument.

This example also illustrates tuple **unpacking**. The first line inside the function unpacks the stock parameter into four different variables. The tuple has to be exactly the same length as the number of variables, or it will raise an exception. We can also see an example of tuple unpacking on the last line, where the tuple returned inside the function is unpacked into two values, `mid_value`, and `date`. Granted, this is a strange thing to do, since we supplied the date to the function in the first place, but it gave us a chance to see unpacking at work.

Unpacking is a very useful feature in Python. We can group variables together to make storing and passing them around simpler, but the moment we need to access all of them, we can unpack them into separate variables. Of course, sometimes we only need access to one of the variables in the tuple. We can use the same syntax that we have used for other sequence types (lists and strings for example) to access an individual value:

```
>>> stock = "GOOG", 613.30, 625.86, 610.50
>>> high = stock[2]
>>> high
625.86
```

We can even use slice notation to extract larger pieces of tuples:

```
>>> stock[1:3]
(613.3, 625.86)
```

These examples, while illustrating how useful tuples can be, also demonstrate one of their major disadvantages: readability. How does someone reading this code know what is in the second position of a specific tuple? They can guess, from the name of the variable we assigned it to, that it is a `high` of some sort, but if we had just accessed the tuple value in a calculation without assigning it, there would be no such indication. They would have to paw through the code to find where the tuple was declared before they could discover what it does. Accessing tuple members directly is fine in some circumstances, but don't make a habit of it. Such so-called "magic numbers" (numbers that seem to come out of thin air with no apparent meaning within the code) are the source of many coding errors and hours of frustrated debugging. Try to use tuples only when you know that all the values are going to be useful at once and it's normally going to be unpacked when it is accessed. If you have to access a member directly or using a slice, and the purpose of that value is not immediately obvious, at least include a comment explaining where it came from.

Named tuples

So, what do we do when we want to group values together, but know we're frequently going to need to access them individually? Well, we could use an empty object, as discussed in the previous section (but that is rarely useful unless we anticipate adding behavior later), or we could use a dictionary (most useful if we don't know exactly how many or which specific data will be stored), as we'll cover in the next section.

If, however, we do not need to add behavior to the object, and we know in advance what attributes we need to store, we can use a named tuple. Named tuples are tuples with attitude. Named tuples are objects without behavior. Named tuples are a great way to group data together, especially read-only data.

Constructing a named tuple takes a bit more work than a normal tuple. First we have to import `namedtuple`, as it is not in the namespace by default. Then we describe the named tuple by giving it a name and outlining its attributes. This returns a class-like object that we can instantiate with the required values as many times as we want:

```
from collections import namedtuple
Stock = namedtuple("Stock", "symbol current high low")
stock = Stock("GOOG", 613.30, high=625.86, low=610.50)
```

The `namedtuple` constructor accepts two arguments. The first is an identifier for the named tuple. The second is a string of space-separated attributes that the named tuple can have. The first attribute should be listed, followed by a space, then the second attribute, then another space, and so on. The result is an object that can be used to instantiate other objects. This new object can be called just like a normal class. The constructor must have exactly the right number of arguments; these can be passed in order, or as keyword arguments, but all attributes must be specified. We can create as many instances of this "class" as we like, with different values for each.

The resulting named tuple can then be packed and unpacked like a normal tuple, but we can also access individual attributes on it as if it were a class:

```
>>> stock.high
625.86
>>> symbol, current, high, low = stock
>>> current
613.3
```

 Remember that constructing named tuples is a two-step process. First, use `collections.namedtuple` to create a class, and then create instances of that class.

Named tuples are perfect for many "data only" representations, but they are not ideal for all situations. Like tuples and strings, named tuples are immutable, so we cannot modify an attribute once it has been set. For example, the current value of our stock has gone down since we started this discussion, but we can't set the new value:

```
>>> stock.current = 609.27
Traceback (most recent call last):
  File "<stdin>", line 1, in <module>
AttributeError: can't set attribute
```

If we need to be able to change stored data, a dictionary may be what we need instead.

Dictionaries

Dictionaries are incredibly useful objects that allow us to map objects directly to other objects. An empty object with attributes to it is a sort of dictionary; the names of the properties map to the property values. This is actually closer to the truth than it sounds; internally, objects normally represent attributes as a dictionary, where the values are properties or methods on the objects. Even the attributes on a module are stored, internally, in a dictionary.

Dictionaries are extremely efficient at looking up a value, given a specific lookup object that maps to that value. They should always be used when you want to find one object based on another object. The object that is being stored is called the **value**; the object that is being used as an index is called the **key**. We've already seen dictionary syntax in some of our previous examples, but for completeness, we'll go over it again. Dictionaries can be created either using the dict() constructor, or using the {} syntax shortcut. In practice the latter format is almost always used. We can pre-populate a dictionary by separating the keys from the values using a colon, and separating the key value pairs using a comma.

For example, in a stock application, we would most often want to look up prices by the stock symbol. We can create a dictionary that uses stock symbols as keys, and tuples of current, high, and low as values like this:

```
stocks = {"GOOG": (613.30, 625.86, 610.50),
          "MSFT": (30.25, 30.70, 30.19)}
```

As we've seen in previous examples, we can then look up values in the dictionary by requesting a key inside square brackets. If the key is not in the dictionary, it will raise an exception:

```
>>> stocks["GOOG"]
(613.3, 625.86, 610.5)
>>> stocks["RIM"]
Traceback (most recent call last):
  File "<stdin>", line 1, in <module>
KeyError: 'RIM'
```

We can, of course, catch the KeyError and handle it. But we have other options. Remember, dictionaries are objects, even if their primary purpose is to hold other objects. As such, they have several behaviors associated with them. One of the most useful of these methods is the get method; it accepts a key as the first parameter and an optional default value if the key doesn't exist:

```
>>> print(stocks.get("RIM"))
None
>>> stocks.get("RIM", "NOT FOUND")
'NOT FOUND'
```

For even more control, we can use the setdefault method. If the key is in the dictionary, this method behaves just like get; it returns the value for that key. Otherwise, if the key is not in the dictionary, it will not only return the default value we supply in the method call (just like get does), it will also set the key to the same value. Another way to think of it is that setdefault sets a value in the dictionary only if that value has not previously been set. Then it returns the value in the dictionary, either the one that was already there, or the newly provided default value.

```
>>> stocks.setdefault("GOOG", "INVALID")
(613.3, 625.86, 610.5)
>>> stocks.setdefault("RIM", (67.38, 68.48, 67.28))
(67.38, 68.48, 67.28)
>>> stocks["RIM"]
(67.38, 68.48, 67.28)
```

The GOOG stock was already in the dictionary, so when we tried to setdefault it to an invalid value, it just returned the value already in the dictionary. RIM was not in the dictionary, so setdefault returned the default value and set the new value in the dictionary for us. We then check that the new stock is, indeed, in the dictionary.

Three other very useful dictionary methods are `keys()`, `values()`, and `items()`. The first two return an iterator over all the keys and all the values in the dictionary. We can use these like lists or in `for` loops if we want to process all the keys or values. The `items()` method is probably the most useful; it returns an iterator over tuples of (key, value) pairs for every item in the dictionary. This works great with tuple unpacking in a `for` loop to loop over associated keys and values. This example does just that to print each stock in the dictionary with its current value:

```
>>> for stock, values in stocks.items():
...     print("{} last value is {}".format(stock, values[0]))
...
GOOG last value is 613.3
RIM last value is 67.38
MSFT last value is 30.25
```

Each key/value tuple is unpacked into two variables named `stock` and `values` (we could use any variable names we wanted, but these both seem appropriate) and then printed in a formatted string.

Notice that the stocks do not show up in the same order in which they were inserted. Dictionaries, due to the efficient algorithm (known as hashing) that is used to make key lookup so fast, are inherently unsorted.

So, there are numerous ways to retrieve data from a dictionary once it has been instantiated; we can use square brackets as index syntax, the `get` method, the `setdefault` method, or iterate over the `items` method, among others.

Finally, as you probably already know, we can set a value in a dictionary using the same indexing syntax we use to retrieve a value:

```
>>> stocks["GOOG"] = (597.63, 610.00, 596.28)
>>> stocks['GOOG']
(597.63, 610.0, 596.28)
```

Google's price is lower today, so I've updated the tuple value in the dictionary. We can use this index syntax to set a value for any key, regardless of whether the key is in the dictionary. If it is in the dictionary, the old value will be replaced with the new one; otherwise, a new key/value pair will be created.

We've been using strings as dictionary keys, so far but we aren't limited to string keys. It is common to use strings as keys, especially when we're storing data in a dictionary to gather it together (instead of using an object with named properties). But we can also use tuples, numbers, or even objects we've defined ourselves as dictionary keys. We can even use different types of keys in a single dictionary:

```python
random_keys = {}
random_keys["astring"] = "somestring"
random_keys[5] = "aninteger"
random_keys[25.2] = "floats work too"
random_keys[("abc", 123)] = "so do tuples"

class AnObject:
    def __init__(self, avalue):
        self.avalue = avalue

my_object = AnObject(14)
random_keys[my_object] = "We can even store objects"
my_object.avalue = 12
try:
    random_keys[[1,2,3]] = "we can't store lists though"
except:
    print("unable to store list\n")

for key, value in random_keys.items():
    print("{} has value {}".format(key, value))
```

This code shows several different types of keys we can supply to a dictionary. It also shows one type of object that cannot be used. We've already used lists extensively, and we'll be seeing many more details of them in the next section. Because lists can change at any time (by adding or removing items, for example), they cannot hash to a specific value. Objects that are **hashable** basically have a defined algorithm that converts the object into an integer value for rapid lookup. This hash is what is actually used to look up values in a dictionary. Strings map to integers based on the characters in the string, while tuples combine hashes of the items inside the tuple, for example. Any two objects that are somehow considered equal (like strings with the same characters or tuples with the same values) should have the same hash value, and the hash value for an object should never ever change. Lists, however, can have their contents changed, which would change their hash value (two lists should only be equal if their contents are the same). Because of this, they can't be used as dictionary keys. For the same reason, dictionaries cannot be used as keys into other dictionaries.

In contrast, there are no limits on the types of objects that can be used as dictionary values. We can use a string key that maps to a list value, for example, or we can have a nested dictionary as a value in another dictionary.

When should we use dictionaries?

Dictionaries are extremely versatile and have numerous uses. There are two major ways that dictionaries can be used. The first is dictionaries where all the keys represent different instances of similar objects; for example, our stock dictionary. This is an indexing system. We use the stock symbol as an index to the values. The values could even have been complicated self-defined objects that made buy and sell decisions or set a stop-loss, rather than simple tuples.

The second design is dictionaries where each key represents some aspect of a single object; in this case, we'd probably use a separate dictionary for each object, and they'd all have similar (though often not identical) sets of keys. This latter situation may have overlapped with named tuples; named tuples should typically be used when we know exactly what attributes the data must store, and we know that all pieces of the data must be supplied at once (when the item is constructed). Further, named tuples are only useful when we know this data will not change. For other instances, if we need to build the dictionary keys over a period of time, or each dictionary may have slightly (or widely) varying sets of keys, or we need to change values frequently, a dictionary is much better.

Using defaultdict

We've seen how to use `setdefault` to set a default value if a key doesn't exist, but this can get a bit monotonous if we need to set a default value every time we look up a value. For example, if we're writing code that counts the number of times a letter occurs in a given sentence, we could do this:

```
def letter_frequency(sentence):
    frequencies = {}
    for letter in sentence:
        frequency = frequencies.setdefault(letter, 0)
        frequencies[letter] = frequency + 1
    return frequencies
```

Every time we access the dictionary, we need to check that it has a value already, and, if not, set it to zero. When something like this needs to be done every time an empty key is requested, we can use a different version of the dictionary, called `defaultdict`:

```
from collections import defaultdict
def letter_frequency(sentence):
    frequencies = defaultdict(int)
    for letter in sentence:
        frequencies[letter] += 1
    return frequencies
```

This code looks like it couldn't possibly work. The `defaultdict` class accepts a function in its constructor; whenever a key is accessed that is not already in the dictionary, it calls that function, with no parameters, to create a default value.

In this case, the function it calls is `int`, which is actually the constructor for an integer object. Normally integers are created simply by typing an integer number into our code, and if we do create one using the `int` constructor, we pass it the item we want to create (for example, to convert a string of digits into an integer). But if we call `int` without any arguments, it returns, conveniently, the number zero. In this code, if the letter doesn't exist in the `defaultdict`, the number zero is returned when we access it. Then we add one to this number to indicate we've found another instance of that letter, and the next time we find one, we increment the value again.

The `defaultdict` class is useful for creating containers. If we want to create a dictionary of stock prices for the past 30 days, we could use a stock symbol as the key, and store the prices in a `list`; the first time we access the stock price, we would want it to create an empty list. Simply pass `list` into the `defaultdict` constructor, and it will be called every time an empty key is accessed. We can do similar things with sets or even empty dictionaries if we want to associate one with a key.

Of course, we can also write our own functions and pass them into the `defaultdict` constructor. Suppose we want to create a `defaultdict` where each new element contains a tuple of the number of items inserted into the dictionary at that time and an empty list to hold other things. Nobody knows why we would want to create such an object, but let's have a look:

```
from collections import defaultdict
num_items = 0
def tuple_counter():
    global num_items
    num_items += 1
    return (num_items, [])

d = defaultdict(tuple_counter)
```

When we run this code, we can access empty keys and insert into the list all in one statement:

```
>>> d = defaultdict(tuple_counter)
>>> d['a'][1].append("hello")
>>> d['b'][1].append('world')
>>> d
defaultdict(<function tuple_counter at 0x82f2c6c>,
{'a': (1, ['hello']), 'b': (2, ['world'])})
```

When we print the `dict` at the end, we see that the counter really was working.

This example, while succinctly demonstrating how to create our own function for `defaultdict`, is not actually very good code; using a global variable means that if we created four different `defaultdict` segments that each used a `tuple_counter`, it would count the number of entries in all dictionaries, rather than having a different count for each one. It would be better to create a class and pass a method on that class to `defaultdict`.

Lists

Lists are the least object-oriented of Python's data structures. While lists are, themselves, objects, there is a lot of syntax in Python to make using them as painless as possible. Unlike many other object-oriented languages, lists in Python are simply available. We don't need to import them and rarely need to call methods on them. We can loop over a list without explicitly requesting an iterator object, and we can construct a list (like a dictionary) with custom syntax. Further, list comprehensions and generator expressions turn them into a veritable Swiss-army knife of functionality.

We won't go into too much detail of the syntax; you've seen it in introductory tutorials across the web and previous examples in this book. You can't code Python very long without learning how to use lists! Instead, we'll be covering when lists should be used, and their nature as objects. If you don't know how to create or append to a list, how to retrieve items from a list, or what "slice notation" is, I direct you to the official Python tutorial, post-haste. It can be found online at:

```
http://docs.python.org/py3k/tutorial/
```

Lists, in Python, should normally be used when we want to store several instances of the "same" type of object; lists of strings or lists of numbers; most often, lists of objects we've defined ourselves. Lists should always be used when we want to store items in some kind of order. Often, this is the order in which they were inserted, but they can also be sorted by some criteria.

As we saw in the case study from the previous chapter, lists are also very useful when we need to modify the contents: insert to or delete from an arbitrary location of the list, or update a value within the list.

Like dictionaries, Python lists use an extremely efficient and well-tuned internal data structure so we can worry about what we're storing, rather than how we're storing it. Many object-oriented languages provide different data structures for queues, stacks, linked lists, and array-based lists. Python does provide special instances of some of these classes, if optimizing access to **huge** sets of data is required. Normally, however, the list data structure can serve all these purposes at once, and the coder has complete control over how they access it.

Don't use lists for collecting different attributes of individual items. We do not want, for example, a list of the properties a particular shape has. Tuples, named tuples, dictionaries, and objects would all be more suitable for this purpose. In some languages, they might create a list in which each alternate item is a different type; for example, they might write `['a', 1, 'b', 3]` for our letter frequency list. They'd have to use a strange loop that accesses two elements in the list at once, or a modulus operator to determine which position was being accessed.

Don't do this in Python. We can group related items together using a dictionary, as we did in the previous section (if sort order doesn't matter), or using a list of tuples. Here's a rather convoluted example that demonstrates how we could do the frequency example using a list. It is much more complicated than the dictionary examples, and illustrates how much of an effect choosing the right (or wrong) data structure can have on the readability of our code.

```python
import string
CHARACTERS  = list(string.ascii_letters) + [" "]


def letter_frequency(sentence):
    frequencies = [(c, 0) for c in CHARACTERS]
    for letter in sentence:
        index = CHARACTERS.index(letter)
        frequencies[index] = (letter,frequencies[index][1]+1)
    return frequencies
```

This code starts with a list of possible characters. The `string.ascii_letters` attribute provides a string of all the letters, lower and upper case, in order. We convert this to a list, and then use list concatenation (the plus operator causes two lists to be merged into one) to add one more character, the space. These are the available characters in our frequency list (the code would break if we tried to add a letter that wasn't in the list, but an exception handler could solve this).

The first line inside the function uses a list comprehension to turn the CHARACTERS list into a list of tuples. List comprehensions are an important, non-object-oriented tool in Python; we'll be covering them in detail in the next chapter.

Then we loop over each of the characters in the sentence. We first look up the index of the character in the CHARACTERS list, which we know has the same index in our frequencies list, since we just created the second list from the first. We then update that index in the frequencies list by creating a new tuple, discarding the original one. Aside from the garbage collection and memory waste concerns, this is rather difficult to read!

The resulting code works, but is not nearly so elegant as the dictionary. The code has two advantages over the earlier dictionary example, however. The list stores zero frequencies for characters not in the sentence, and when we receive the list, it comes in sorted order. The output shows the difference:

```
>>> letter_frequency("the quick brown fox jumps over the lazy dog")
[('a', 1), ('b', 1), ('c', 1), ('d', 1), ('e', 3), ('f', 1), ('g', 1),
('h', 2), ('i', 1), ('j', 1), ('k', 1), ('l', 1), ('m', 1), ('n', 1),
('o', 4), ('p', 1), ('q', 1), ('r', 2), ('s', 1), ('t', 2), ('u', 2),
('v', 1), ('w', 1), ('x', 1), ('y', 1), ('z', 1), ('A', 0), ('B', 0),
('C', 0), ('D', 0), ('E', 0), ('F', 0), ('G', 0), ('H', 0), ('I', 0),
('J', 0), ('K', 0), ('L', 0), ('M', 0), ('N', 0), ('O', 0), ('P', 0),
('Q', 0), ('R', 0), ('S', 0), ('T', 0), ('U', 0), ('V', 0), ('W', 0),
('X', 0), ('Y', 0), ('Z', 0), (' ', 8)]
```

The dictionary version could be adapted to provide these advantages by pre-populating the dictionary with zero values for all available characters, and by sorting the keys on the returned dictionary whenever we need them in order.

Like dictionaries, lists are objects too, and they have several methods that can be invoked upon them. The most common is `append(element)`, which adds an element to the list. Similarly, `insert(index, element)` inserts an item at a specific position. The `count(element)` method tells us how many times an element appears in the list, and `index()` — as we saw in the previous example — tells us the index of an item in the list. The `reverse()` method does exactly what it says: turning the list around. The `sort()` method is also obvious, but it has some fairly complicated object-oriented behaviors, which we'll cover now.

Sorting lists

Without any parameters, `sort` will generally do the expected thing. If it's a list of strings, it will place them in alphabetical order. This operation is case sensitive, so all capital letters will be sorted before lower case letters, that is z comes before a. If it is a list of numbers, they will be sorted in numerical order. If a list of tuples is provided, the list is sorted by the first element in each tuple. If a mixture of unsortable items is supplied, the sort will raise a `TypeError` exception.

If we want to place objects we define ourselves into a list and make those objects sortable, we have to do a bit more work. The special method `__lt__`, which stands for "less than", should be defined on the class to make instances of that class comparable. The `sort` method on list will access this method on each object to determine where it goes in the list. This method should return `True` if our class is somehow less than the passed parameter, and `False` otherwise. Here's a rather silly class that can be sorted based on either a string or a number:

```
class WeirdSortee:
    def __init__(self, string, number, sort_num):
        self.string = string
        self.number = number
        self.sort_num = sort_num

    def __lt__(self, object):
        if self.sort_num:
            return self.number < object.number
        return self.string < object.string

    def __repr__(self):
        return"{}:{}".format(self.string, self.number)
```

The `__repr__` method makes it easy to see the two values when we print a list. This `__lt__` implementation compares the object to another instance of the same class (or any duck typed object that has `string`, `number`, and `sort_num` attributes; it will fail if those attributes are missing). The following output illustrates this class in action, when it comes to sorting:

```
>>> a = WeirdSortee('a', 4, True)
>>> b = WeirdSortee('b', 3, True)
>>> c = WeirdSortee('c', 2, True)
>>> d = WeirdSortee('d', 1, True)
>>> l = [a,b,c,d]
>>> l
```

```
[a:4, b:3, c:2, d:1]
>>> l.sort()
>>> l
[d:1, c:2, b:3, a:4]
>>> for i in l:
...     i.sort_num = False
...
>>> l.sort()
>>> l
[a:4, b:3, c:2, d:1]
```

The first time we call `sort`, it sorts by numbers, because `sort_num` is `True` on all the objects being compared. The second time, it sorts by letters. The `__lt__` method is the only one we need to implement to enable sorting. Technically, however, if it is implemented, the class should normally also implement the similar `__gt__`, `__eq__`, `__ne__`, `__ge__`, and `__le__` methods, so that all of the `<`, `>`, `==`, `!=`, `>=`, and `<=` operators also work properly.

The `sort` method can also take an optional `key` argument. This argument is a function that can transform each object in a list into an object that can be somehow compared. This is useful if we have a tuple of values and want to sort on the second item in the tuple rather than the first (which is the default for sorting tuples):

```
>>> x = [(1,'c'), (2,'a'), (3, 'b')]
>>> x.sort()
>>> x
[(1, 'c'), (2, 'a'), (3, 'b')]
>>> x.sort(key=lambda i: i[1])
>>> x
[(2, 'a'), (3, 'b'), (1, 'c')]
```

The `lambda` keyword in the command line creates a function that takes a tuple as input and uses sequence lookups to return the item with index 1 (that is the second item in the tuple).

As another example, we can also use the `key` parameter to make a sort case insensitive. To do this, we simply need to compare the all lowercase versions of strings, so we can pass the built-in `str.lower` function as the key function:

```
>>> l = ["hello", "HELP", "Helo"]
>>> l.sort()
>>> l
```

```
['HELP', 'Helo', 'hello']
>>> l.sort(key=str.lower)
>>> l
['hello', 'Helo', 'HELP']
```

Remember, even though `lower` is a method on string objects, it is also a function that can accept a single argument, `self`. In other words, `str.lower(item)` is equivalent to `item.lower()`. When we pass this function as a key, it performs the comparison on lowercase values instead of doing the default case-sensitive comparison.

Sets

Lists are extremely versatile tools that suit most container object applications. But they are not useful when we want to ensure objects in the list are unique. For example, a song library may contain many songs by the same artist. If we want to sort through the library and create a list of all the artists, we would have to check the list to see if we've added the artist already before we add them again.

This is where sets come in. Sets come from mathematics, where they represent an unordered group of (usually) unique numbers. We can add a number to a set five times, but it will show up in the set only once.

In Python, sets can hold any hashable object, not just numbers. Hashable objects are the same objects that can be used as keys in dictionaries, so again, lists and dictionaries are out. Like mathematical sets, they can store only one copy of each object. So if we're trying to create a list of song artists, we can create a set of string names and simply add them to the set. This example starts with a list of (song, artist) tuples and creates a set of the artists:

```
song_library = [("Phantom Of The Opera", "Sarah Brightman"),
        ("Knocking On Heaven's Door", "Guns N' Roses"),
        ("Captain Nemo", "Sarah Brightman"),
        ("Patterns In The Ivy", "Opeth"),
        ("November Rain", "Guns N' Roses"),
        ("Beautiful", "Sarah Brightman"),
        ("Mal's Song", "Vixy and Tony")]

artists = set()
for song, artist in song_library:
    artists.add(artist)

print(artists)
```

There is no built-in syntax for an empty set as there is for lists and dictionaries; we create a set using the `set()` constructor. However, we can use the curly braces of dictionary syntax to create a set, so long as the set contains values. If we use colons to separate pairs of values, it's a dictionary, as in `{'key': 'value', 'key2': 'value2'}`. If we just separate values with commas, it's a set, as in `{'value', 'value2'}`. Items can be added individually to the set using its `add` method. If we run this script, we see that the set works as advertised:

```
{'Sarah Brightman', "Guns N' Roses", 'Vixy and Tony', 'Opeth'}
```

If you're paying attention to the output, you'll notice that the items are not printed in the order they were added to the sets. Sets, like dictionaries, are unordered. They both use an underlying hash-based data structure for efficiency. Because they are unordered, sets cannot have items looked up by index. The primary purpose of a set is to divide the world into two groups: "things that are in the set", and, "things that are not in the set". It is easy to check if an item is in the set or to loop over the items in a set, but if we want to sort or order them, we'll have to convert the set to a list. This output shows all three of these activities:

```
>>> "Opeth" in artists
True
>>> for artist in artists:
...         print("{} plays good music".format(artist))
...
Sarah Brightman plays good music
Guns N' Roses plays good music
Vixy and Tony play good music
Opeth plays good music
>>> alphabetical = list(artists)
>>> alphabetical.sort()
>>> alphabetical
["Guns N' Roses", 'Opeth', 'Sarah Brightman', 'Vixy and Tony']
```

While the primary **feature** of a set is uniqueness, that is not its primary **purpose**. Sets are most useful when two or more of them are used in combination. Most of the methods on the set type operate on other sets, allowing us to efficiently combine or compare the items in two or more sets. These methods have strange names if you're not familiar with mathematical sets, since they use the same terminology used in mathematics. We'll start with three methods that return the same result regardless of which is the calling set and which is the called set.

The `union` method is the most common and easiest to understand. It takes a second set as a parameter and returns a new set that contains all elements that are in **either** of the two sets; if an element is in both original sets, it will, of course, only show up once in the new set. Union is like a logical `or` operation, indeed, the `|` operator can be used to get the same effect, if you don't like calling methods.

Conversely, the `intersection` method accepts a second set and returns a new set that contains only those elements that are in **both** sets. It is like a logical `and` operation, and can also be referenced using the `&` operator.

Finally, the `symmetric_difference` method tells us what's left; it is the set of objects that are in one set or the other, but not both. The following example illustrates these methods by comparing some artists from my song library to those in my sister's:

```python
my_artists = {"Sarah Brightman", "Guns N' Roses",
        "Opeth", "Vixy and Tony"}

auburns_artists = {"Nickelback", "Guns N' Roses",
        "Savage Garden"}

print("All: {}".format(my_artists.union(auburns_artists)))
print("Both: {}".format(auburns_artists.intersection(my_artists)))
print("Either but not both: {}".format(
    my_artists.symmetric_difference(auburns_artists)))
```

If we run this code, we see that these three methods do what the print statements suggest they will do:

```
All: {'Sarah Brightman', "Guns N' Roses", 'Vixy and Tony',
'Savage Garden', 'Opeth', 'Nickelback'}
Both: {"Guns N' Roses"}
Either but not both: {'Savage Garden', 'Opeth', 'Nickelback',
'Sarah Brightman', 'Vixy and Tony'}
```

These methods all return the same result regardless of which set calls the other. We can say `my_artists.union(auburns_artists)` or `auburns_artists.union(my_artists)` and get the same result. There are also methods that return different results depending on who is the caller and who is the argument.

These methods include `issubset` and `issuperset`, which are the inverse of each other. Both return a boolean. The `issubset` method returns `True`, if all of the items in the calling set are also in the set passed as an argument. The `issuperset` method returns `True`, if all of the items in the argument are also in the calling set. Thus `s.issubset(t)` and `t.issuperset(s)` are identical. They will both return `True` if `t` contains all the elements in `s`.

Finally, the `difference` method returns all the elements that are in the calling set, but not in the set passed as an argument; this is like half a `symmetric_difference`. The difference method can also be represented by the - operator. The following code illustrates these methods in action:

```
my_artists = {"Sarah Brightman", "Guns N' Roses",
        "Opeth", "Vixy and Tony"}

bands = {"Guns N' Roses", "Opeth"}

print("my_artists is to bands:")
print("issuperset: {}".format(my_artists.issuperset(bands)))
print("issubset: {}".format(my_artists.issubset(bands)))
print("difference: {}".format(my_artists.difference(bands)))
print("*"*20)
print("bands is to my_artists:")
print("issuperset: {}".format(bands.issuperset(my_artists)))
print("issubset: {}".format(bands.issubset(my_artists)))
print("difference: {}".format(bands.difference(my_artists)))
```

This code simply prints out the response of each method when called from one set on the other. Running it gives us the following output:

```
my_artists is to bands:
issuperset: True
issubset: False
difference: {'Sarah Brightman', 'Vixy and Tony'}
********************
bands is to my_artists:
issuperset: False
issubset: True
difference: set()
```

The `difference` method, in the second case, returns an empty set, since there are no items in `bands` that are not in `my_artists`.

The union, intersection, and difference methods can all take multiple sets as arguments; they will return, as we might expect, the set that is created when the operation is called on all the parameters.

So the methods on sets clearly suggest that sets are meant to operate on other sets, and that they are not just containers. If we have data coming in from two different sources and need to quickly combine them in some way, to determine where the data overlaps, or is different, we can use set operations to efficiently compare them. Or if we have data incoming that may contain duplicates of data that has already been processed, we can use sets to compare the two and process only the new data.

Extending built-ins

We discussed briefly in *Chapter 3* how built-in data types can be extended using inheritance. Now, we'll go into more detail as to when we would want to do that.

When we have a built-in container object that we want to add functionality to, we have two options. We can either create a new object, which holds that container as an attribute (composition), or we can subclass the built-in object and add or adapt methods on it to do what we want (inheritance).

Composition is usually the best alternative if all we want to do is use the container to store some objects using that container's features. That way, it's easy to pass that data structure into other methods and they will know how to interact with it. But we need to use inheritance if we want to change the way the container actually works. For example, if we want to ensure every item in a list is a string with exactly five characters, we need to extend list and override the append() method to raise an exception for invalid input. We'd also have to override __setitem__(self, index, value), a special method on lists that is called whenever we use the x[index] = "value" syntax.

That's right, all that special non-object-oriented looking syntax we've been looking at for accessing lists, dictionary keys, looping over containers, and similar tasks is actually "syntactic sugar" that maps to an object-oriented paradigm underneath. We might ask the Python designers why they did this, when common perception suggests that object-oriented programming is **always** better. That question is easy to answer. In the following hypothetical examples, which is easier to read, as a programmer? Which requires less typing?:

```
c = a + b
c = a.add(b)

l[0] = 5
l.setitem(0, 5)
```

```
d[key] = value
d.setitem(key, value)

for x in alist:
    #do something with x
it = alist.iterator()
while it.has_next():
    x = it.next()
    #do something with x
```

The highlighted sections show what object-oriented code might look like (in practice, these methods actually exist as special double-underscore methods on associated objects). Python programmers agree that the non-object-oriented syntax is easier to read and to write. Non-Python programmers say that syntax like this means Python is not object-oriented. That, however, is hogwash. All of the above Python syntaxes map to object-oriented methods underneath the hood. These methods have special names (with double-underscores before and after) to remind us that there is a better syntax out there. However, we now have the means to override these behaviors. For example, we can make a special integer that always returns 0 when we add two of them together:

```
class SillyInt(int):
    def __add__(self, num):
        return 0
```

This is a very strange thing to do, granted, but it illustrates perfectly the object-oriented principles in action. And now we have an argument when people tell us Python isn't truly object-oriented. It's just object-oriented that has been made easy to work with. Check out the above class in action:

```
>>> a = SillyInt(1)
>>> b = SillyInt(2)
>>> a + b
0
```

The awesome thing about the __add__ method is that we can add it to any class we write, and if we use the + operator on instances of that class, it will be called. This is how string, tuple, and list concatenation works.

This is true of all the special methods. If we want to use x in myobj syntax, we can override __contains__. If we want to use myobj[i] = value syntax, we implement __setitem__ and if we want to use something = myobj[i], we implement __getitem__.

There are thirty-three of these special methods on the `list` class. We can use the `dir` function to see all of them:

```
>>> dir(list)
```

```
['__add__', '__class__', '__contains__', '__delattr__','__delitem__', '__
doc__', '__eq__', '__format__', '__ge__', '__getattribute__', '__getitem_
_', '__gt__', '__hash__', '__iadd__', '__imul__', '__init__', '__iter__',
'__le__', '__len__', '__lt__', '__mul__', '__ne__', '__new__', '__reduce_
_', '__reduce_ex__', '__repr__', '__reversed__', '__rmul__', '__setattr__
', '__setitem__', '__sizeof__', '__str__', '__subclasshook__', 'append',
'count', 'extend', 'index', 'insert', 'pop', 'remove', 'reverse', 'sort'
```

Further, if we want any additional information on how any of these methods works, we can use the `help` function:

```
>>> help(list.__add__)
Help on wrapper_descriptor:

__add__(...)
    x.__add__(y) <==> x+y
```

The plus operator on lists concatenates two lists. We don't have room to discuss all of the available special functions in this book, but you are now able to explore all this functionality with `dir` and `help`. The official online Python reference (http://docs.python.org/) has plenty of useful information as well. Focus, especially, on the abstract base classes discussed in the collections module.

So to get back to the earlier point about when we would want to use composition versus inheritance: if we need to somehow change any of the methods on the class, including the special methods we definitely need to use inheritance. If we used composition, we could write methods that do the validation or alterations and ask the caller to use those methods, but there is nothing stopping them from accessing the property directly (no private members, remember?). They could insert an item into our list that does not have five characters, and that might confuse other methods in the list.

Often, the need to extend a built-in data type is an indication that we're using the wrong sort of data type. It is not always the case, but if you're suddenly looking to extend a built-in, carefully consider whether or not a different data structure would be more suitable.

As a last example, let's consider what it takes to create a dictionary that remembers the order in which keys were inserted. One way (likely not the best way) to do this is to keep an ordered list of keys that is stored in a specially derived subclass of dict. Then we can override the methods keys, values, __iter__, and items to return everything in order. Of course, we'll also have to override __setitem__ and setdefault to keep our list up to date. There are likely to be a few other methods in the output of dir(dict) that need overriding to keep the list and dictionary consistent (clear and __delitem__ come to mind, to track when items are removed), but we won't worry about them for this example.

So we'll be extending dict and adding a list of ordered keys. Trivial enough, but where do we create the actual list? We could include it in the __init__ method, which would work just fine, but we have no guarantees that any subclass will call that initializer. Remember the __new__ method we discussed in *Chapter 2*? I said it was generally only useful in very special cases. This is one of those special cases. We know __new__ will be called exactly once, and we can create a list on the new instance that will always be available to our class. With that in mind, here is our entire sorted dictionary:

```python
from collections import KeysView, ItemsView, ValuesView
class DictSorted(dict):
    def __new__(*args, **kwargs):
        new_dict = dict.__new__(*args, **kwargs)
        new_dict.ordered_keys = []
        return new_dict

    def __setitem__(self, key, value):
        '''self[key] = value syntax'''
        if key not in self.ordered_keys:
            self.ordered_keys.append(key)
        super().__setitem__(key, value)

    def setdefault(self, key, value):
        if key not in self.ordered_keys:
            self.ordered_keys.append(key)
        return super().setdefault(key, value)

    def keys(self):
        return KeysView(self)

    def values(self):
        return ValuesView(self)

    def items(self):
```

```
        return ItemsView(self)

    def __iter__(self):
        '''for x in self syntax'''
        return self.ordered_keys.__iter__()
```

The __new__ method simply creates a new dictionary and then puts an empty list on that object. We don't override __init__, as the default implementation works (actually, this is only true if we initialize an empty DictSorted object, which is standard behavior. If we want to support other variations of the dict constructor, which accept dictionaries or lists of tuples, we'd need to fix __init__ to also update our ordered_keys). The two methods for setting items are very similar; they both update the list of keys, but only if the item hasn't been added before. We don't want duplicates in the list, but we can't use a set here; it's unordered!

The keys, items, and values methods all return views onto the dictionary. The collections library provides three read-only View objects onto the dictionary; they use the __iter__ method to loop over the keys, and then use __getitem__ (which we didn't need to override) to retrieve the values. So we only need to define our custom __iter__ method to make these three views work. You would think the superclass would do to create these views properly using polymorphism, but if we don't override these three methods, they don't return properly ordered views.

Finally, the __iter__ method is the really special one; it ensures that if we loop over the dictionary's keys (using for...in syntax), it will return the values in the correct order. It simply does this by returning the __iter__ of the ordered_keys list, which returns the same iterator object that would be used if we used for...in on the list instead. Since ordered_keys is a list of all available keys (due to the way we overrode other methods), this is the correct iterator object for the dictionary as well.

Let's look at a few of these methods in action, compared to a normal dictionary:

```
>>> ds = DictSorted()
>>> d = {}
>>> ds['a'] = 1
>>> ds['b'] = 2
>>> ds.setdefault('c', 3)
3
>>> d['a'] = 1
>>> d['b'] = 2
>>> d.setdefault('c', 3)
3
>>> for k,v in ds.items():
```

```
...        print(k,v)
...
a 1
b 2
c 3
>>> for k,v in d.items():
...        print(k,v)
...
a 1
c 3
b 2
```

Ah, our dictionary is sorted and the normal dictionary is not. Hurray!

 If you wanted to use this class in production, you'd have to override several other methods to ensure the keys are up-to-date in all cases. However, you don't need to do this; the functionality this class provides is already available in Python, using the OrderedDict object in the collections module. Try importing the class from collections, and use help(OrderedDict) to find out more about it.

Case study

To tie everything together, we'll be writing a simple link collector, which will visit a website and collect every link on every page it finds in that site. Before we start, though, we'll need some test data to work with. Simply write some HTML files to work with that contain links to each other and to other sites on the internet, something like this:

```html
<html>
    <body>
        <a href="contact.html">Contact us</a>
        <a href="blog.html">Blog</a>
        <a href="esme.html">My Dog</a>
        <a href="/hobbies.html">Some hobbies</a>
        <a href="/contact.html">Contact AGAIN</a>
        <a href="http://www.archlinux.org/">Favorite OS</a>
    </body>
</html>
```

Name one of the files `index.html` so it shows up first when pages are served. Make sure the other files exist, and keep things complicated so there is lots of linking between them. The examples for this chapter include a directory called `case_study_serve` (one of the lamest personal websites in existence!) if you'd rather not set them up yourself.

Now, start a simple web server by entering the directory containing all these files and run the following command:

```
python3 -m http.server
```

This will start a server running on port 8000; you can see the pages you made by visiting `http://localhost:8000/` in your web browser.

 I doubt anyone can get a website up and running with less work! Never let it be said, "you can't do that easily with Python".

The goal will be to pass our collector the base URL for the site (in this case: `http://localhost:8000/`), and have it create a list containing every unique link on the site. We'll need to take into account three types of URLs (links to external sites, which start with `http://`, absolute internal links, which start with a `/`, and relative links, for everything else). We also need to be aware that pages may link to each other in a loop; we need to be sure we don't process the same page multiple times, or it may never end. With all this uniqueness going on, it sounds like we're going to need some sets.

Before we get into that, let's start with the basics. What code do we need to connect to a page and parse all the links from that page?:

```python
from urllib.request import urlopen
from urllib.parse import urlparse
import re
import sys
LINK_REGEX = re.compile(
        "<a [^>]*href=['\"]([^'\"]+)['\"][^>]*>")

class LinkCollector:
    def __init__(self, url):
        self.url = "http://" + urlparse(url).netloc

    def collect_links(self, path="/"):
        full_url = self.url + path
        page = str(urlopen(full_url).read())
        links = LINK_REGEX.findall(page)
```

```
        print(links)

    if __name__ == "__main__":
        LinkCollector(sys.argv[1]).collect_links()
```

This is a short piece of code, considering what it's doing. It connects to the server in the argument passed on the command line, downloads the page, and extracts all the links on that page. The `__init__` method uses the `urlparse` function to extract just the hostname from the URL; so even if we pass in `http://localhost:8000/some/page.html` it will still operate on the top-level of the host, `http://localhost:8000/`. This makes sense, because we want to collect all the links on the site.

The `collect_links` method connects to and downloads the specified page from the server, and uses a regular expression to find all the links in the page. Regular expressions are an extremely powerful string processing tool. Unfortunately, they have a steep learning curve; if you haven't used them before, I strongly recommend studying any of the entire books or websites on the topic. If you don't think they're worth knowing, try writing the above code without them.

The example above stops in the middle of the `collect_links` method to print the value of `links`. This is a common way to test a program as we're writing it: stop and output the value to ensure it is the value we expect. Here's what it outputs for our example:

```
['contact.html', 'blog.html', 'esme.html', '/hobbies.html',
'/contact.html', 'http://www.archlinux.org/']
```

So now we have a collection of all the links in the first page. What should we do with it? We can't just pop the links into a set to remove duplicates, because links may be relative or absolute. For example `contact.html` and `/contact.html` point to the same page. No, the first thing we should do is normalize all the links to their full URL, including hostname and relative path. We can do this by adding a `normalize_url` method to our object:

```
        def normalize_url(self, path, link):
            if link.startswith("http://"):
                return link
            elif link.startswith("/"):
                return self.url + link
            else:
                return self.url + path.rpartition('/'
                        )[0] + '/' + link
```

This method converts all URLs to complete URLs with protocol and hostname. Now the two contact pages have the same value and we can store them in a set. We'll have to modify `__init__` to create the set, and `collect_links` to put all the links into it.

Then we'll have to visit all the non-external links and collect them too. But wait a minute, if we do that, how do we keep from revisiting a link when we encounter the same page twice? It looks like we're actually going to need two sets, a set of collected links, and a set of visited links. This suggests that we were wise to choose a set to represent our data; we know that sets are most useful when we're manipulating more than one of them. Let's set these up:

```python
class LinkCollector:
    def __init__(self, url):
        self.url = "http://+" + urlparse(url).netloc
        self.collected_links = set()
        self.visited_links = set()

    def collect_links(self, path="/"):
        full_url = self.url + path
        self.visited_links.add(full_url)
        page = str(urlopen(full_url).read())
        links = LINK_REGEX.findall(page)
        links = {self.normalize_url(path, link
            ) for link in links}
        self.collected_links = links.union(
                self.collected_links)
        unvisited_links = links.difference(
                self.visited_links)
        print(links, self.visited_links,
                self.collected_links, unvisited_links)
```

The line that creates the normalized list of links uses a set comprehension, no different from a list comprehension, except that it creates a set out of the values. We'll be covering these babies in detail in the next chapter. Once again, the method stops to print out the current values, so we can verify we don't have our sets confused, and that `difference` really was the method we wanted to call to collect `unvisited_links`. We can then add a few lines of code that loop over all the unvisited links and adds them to the collection as well:

```python
for link in unvisited_links:
    if link.startswith(self.url):
        self.collect_links(urlparse(link).path)
```

The `if` statement ensures that we are only collecting links from the one website; we don't want to go off and collect all the links from all the pages on the internet (unless we're Google or the Internet Archive!). If we modify the main code at the bottom of the program to output the collected links, we can see it seems to have collected them all:

```python
if __name__ == "__main__":
    collector = LinkCollector(sys.argv[1])
    collector.collect_links()
    for link in collector.collected_links:
        print(link)
```

It displays all the links we've collected, and only once; even though many of the pages in my example linked to each other multiple times:

```
$ python3 link_collector.py http://localhost:8000

http://localhost:8000/

http://en.wikipedia.org/wiki/Cavalier_King_Charles_Spaniel

http://masterhelenwu.com

http://archlinux.me/dusty/

http://localhost:8000/blog.html

http://ccphillips.net/

http://localhost:8000/contact.html

http://localhost:8000/taichi.html

http://www.archlinux.org/

http://localhost:8000/esme.html

http://localhost:8000/hobbies.html
```

Even though it collected links **to** external pages, it didn't go off collecting links **from** any of the external pages we linked to. This is a great little program if we want to collect all the links in a site. But it doesn't give me all the information I might need to build a site map; it tells me which pages I have, but it doesn't tell me which pages link to other pages. If we want to do that instead, we're going to have to make some modifications.

The first thing we should do is look at our data structures. The set of collected links doesn't work anymore; we want to know which links were linked to from which pages. The first thing we could do, then, is turn that set into a dictionary of sets for each page we visit. The dictionary keys will represent the exact same data that is currently in the set. The values will be sets of all the links on that page. Here are the changes:

```python
from urllib.request import urlopen
from urllib.parse import urlparse
import re
import sys
LINK_REGEX = re.compile(
        "<a [^>]*href=['\"]([^'\"]+)['\"][^>]*>")


class LinkCollector:
    def __init__(self, url):
        self.url = "http://%s" % urlparse(url).netloc
        self.collected_links = {}
        self.visited_links = set()

    def collect_links(self, path="/"):
        full_url = self.url + path
        self.visited_links.add(full_url)
        page = str(urlopen(full_url).read())
        links = LINK_REGEX.findall(page)
        links = {self.normalize_url(path, link
            ) for link in links}
        self.collected_links[full_url] = links
        for link in links:
            self.collected_links.setdefault(link, set())
        unvisited_links = links.difference(
                self.visited_links)
        for link in unvisited_links:
            if link.startswith(self.url):
                self.collect_links(urlparse(link).path)

    def normalize_url(self, path, link):
        if link.startswith("http://"):
            return link
        elif link.startswith("/"):
            return self.url + link
        else:
            return self.url + path.rpartition('/'
                    )[0] + '/' + link
```

```
if __name__ == "__main__":
    collector = LinkCollector(sys.argv[1])
    collector.collect_links()
    for link, item in collector.collected_links.items():
        print("{}: {}".format(link, item))
```

It is a surprisingly small change; the line that originally created a union of two sets has been replaced with three lines that update the dictionary. The first of these simply tells the dictionary what the collected links for that page are. The second creates an empty set for any items in the dictionary that have not already been added to the dictionary, using `setdefault`. The result is a dictionary that contains all the links as its keys, mapped to sets of links for all the internal links, and empty sets for the external links.

Exercises

The best way to learn how to choose the correct data structure is to do it wrong a few times. Take some code you've recently written, or write some new code that uses a list. Try rewriting it using some different data structures. Which ones make more sense? Which don't? Which have the most elegant code?

Try this with a few different pairs of data structures. You can look at examples you've done for previous chapter exercises. Are there objects with methods where you could have used a `namedtuple` or a `dict` instead? Attempt both and see. Are there dictionaries that could have been sets because you don't really access the values? Do you have lists that check for duplicates? Would a set suffice? Or maybe several sets?

If you want some specific examples to work with, try adapting the link collector to also save the title used for each link. Perhaps you can generate a site map in HTML that lists all the pages on the site, and contains a list of links to other pages, named with the same link titles.

Have you written any container objects recently that you could improve by inheriting a built-in and overriding some of the "special" double-underscore methods? You may have to do some research (using `dir` and `help`, or the Python library reference) to find out which methods need overriding. Are you sure inheritance is the correct tool to apply; could a composition-based solution be more effective? Try both (if it's possible) before you decide. Try to find different situations where each method is better than the other.

If you were familiar with the various Python data structures and their uses before you started this chapter, you may have been bored. But if that is the case, there's a good chance you use data structures too much! Look at some of your old code and rewrite it to use more self-made objects. Carefully consider the alternatives, and try them all out; which one makes for the most readable and maintainable system?

Always critically evaluate your code and design decisions. Make a habit of reviewing old code and take note if your understanding of "good design" has changed since you've written it. Software design has a large aesthetic component, and like painters, we all have to find the style that suits us best.

Summary

We've covered several built-in data structures and attempted to understand how to choose one for specific applications. Sometimes the best thing we can do is create a new class of objects, but often, one of the built-ins provides exactly what we need. When it doesn't, we can always use inheritance or composition to adapt them to our needs. In particular, we covered:

- Tuples and named tuples
- Dictionaries and default dictionaries
- Lists and sets
- Overriding special variables on built-ins

In the next chapter we'll discuss how to integrate the object-oriented and not-so-object-oriented aspects of Python. Along the way, we'll discover that it's more object-oriented than it looks at first sight!

7
Python Object-oriented Shortcuts

Now let's look at some aspects of Python that appear more reminiscent of structural or functional programming than object-oriented programming. Although object-oriented programming is the most popular kid on the block these days, the old paradigms still offer useful tools. Most of these tools are really syntactic sugar over an underlying object-oriented implementation; we can think of them as a further abstraction layer built on top of the (already abstracted) object-oriented paradigm. In this chapter we'll be covering:

- Built-in functions that take care of common tasks in one call
- List, set, and dictionary comprehensions
- Generators
- An alternative to method overloading
- Functions as objects

Python built-in functions

There are numerous functions in Python that perform a task or calculate a result on certain objects without being methods on the class. Their purpose is to abstract common calculations that apply to many types of classes. This is applied duck typing; these functions accept objects with certain attributes or methods that satisfy a given interface, and are able to perform generic tasks on the object.

Len

The simplest example is the len() function. This function counts the number of items in some kind of container object such as a dictionary or list. For example:

```
>>> len([1,2,3,4])
4
```

Why don't these objects have a length property instead of having to call a function on them? Technically, they do. Most objects that len() will apply to have a method called __len__() that returns the same value. So len(myobj) seems to call myobj.__len__().

Why should we use the function instead of the method? Obviously the method is a special method with double-underscores suggesting that we shouldn't call it directly. There must be an explanation for this. The Python developers don't make such design decisions lightly.

The main reason is efficiency. When we call __len__ on an object, the object has to look the method up in its namespace, and, if the special __getattribute__ method (which is called every time an attribute or method on an object is accessed) is defined on that object, it has to be called as well. Further __getattribute__ for that particular method may have been written to do something nasty like refusing to give us access to special methods such as __len__! The len function doesn't encounter any of this. It actually calls the __len__ function on the underlying class, so len(myobj) maps to MyObj.__len__(myobj).

Another reason is maintainability. In the future, the Python developers may want to change len() so that it can calculate the length of objects that don't have a __len__, for example by counting the number of items returned in an iterator. They'll only have to change one function instead of countless __len__ methods across the board.

Reversed

The reversed() function takes any sequence as input, and returns a copy of that sequence in reverse order. It is normally used in for loops when we want to loop over items from back to front.

Similar to len, reversed calls the __reversed__() function on the **class** for the parameter. If that method does not exist, reversed builds the reversed sequence itself using calls to __len__ and __getitem__. We only need to override __reversed__ if we want to somehow customize or optimize the process:

```
normal_list=[1,2,3,4,5]

class CustomSequence():
    def __len__(self):
        return 5

    def __getitem__(self, index):
        return "x{0}".format(index)

class FunkyBackwards(CustomSequence):
    def __reversed__(self):
        return "BACKWARDS!"

for seq in normal_list, CustomSequence(), FunkyBackwards():
    print("\n{}: ".format(seq.__class__.__name__), end="")
    for item in reversed(seq):
        print(item, end=", ")
```

The `for` loops at the end print the reversed versions of a normal list, and instances of the two custom sequences. The output shows that `reversed` works on all three of them, but has very different results when we define __reversed__ ourselves:

```
list: 5, 4, 3, 2, 1,
CustomSequence: x4, x3, x2, x1, x0,
FunkyBackwards: B, A, C, K, W, A, R, D, S, !,
```

 Note: the above two classes aren't very good sequences, as they don't define a proper version of __iter__ so a forward `for` loop over them will never end.

Enumerate

Sometimes when we're looping over an iterable object in a `for` loop, we want access to the index (the current position in the list) of the current item being processed. The `for` loop doesn't provide us with indexes, but the `enumerate` function gives us something better: it creates a list of tuples, where the first object in each tuple is the index and the second is the original item.

This is useful if we want to use index numbers directly. Consider some simple code that outputs all the lines in a file with line numbers:

```python
import sys
filename = sys.argv[1]

with open(filename) as file:
    for index, line in enumerate(file):
        print("{0}: {1}".format(index+1, line), end='')
```

Running this code on itself as the input file shows how it works:

```
1: import sys
2: filename = sys.argv[1]
3:
4: with open(filename) as file:
5:     for index, line in enumerate(file):
6:         print("{0}: {1}".format(index+1, line), end='')
```

The enumerate function returns a list of tuples, our for loop splits each tuple into two values, and the print statement formats them together. It adds one to the index for each line number, since enumerate, like all sequences is zero based.

Zip

The zip function is one of the least object-oriented functions in Python's collection. It takes two or more sequences and creates a new sequence of tuples. Each tuple contains one element from each list.

This is easily explained by an example; let's look at parsing a text file. Text data is often stored in tab-delimited format, with a "header" row as the first line in the file, and each line below it describing data for a unique record. A simple contact list in tab-delimited format might look like this:

```
first     last    email
john      smith   jsmith@example.com
jane      doan    janed@example.com
david     neilson     dn@example.com
```

A simple parser for this file can use zip to create lists of tuples that map headers to values. These lists can be used to create a dictionary, a much easier object to work with in Python than a file!

```python
import sys
filename = sys.argv[1]
```

```
contacts = []
with open(filename) as file:
    header = file.readline().strip().split('\t')
    for line in file:
        line = line.strip().split('\t')
        contact_map = zip(header, line)
        contacts.append(dict(contact_map))

for contact in contacts:
    print("email: {email} -- {last}, {first}".format(
        **contact))
```

What's actually happening here? First we open the file, whose name is provided on the command line, and read the first line. We strip the trailing newline, and split what's left into a list of three elements. We pass `'\t'` into the strip method to indicate that the string should be split at tab characters. The resulting header list looks like `["first", "last", "email"]`.

Next, we loop over the remaining lines in the file (after the header). We split each line into three elements. Then, we use `zip` to create a sequence of tuples for each line. The first sequence would look like `[("first", "john"), ("last", "smith"), ("email", "jsmith@example.com")]`.

Pay attention to what `zip` is doing. The first list contains headers; the second contains values. The `zip` function created a tuple of header/value pairs for each matchup.

The `dict` constructor takes the list of tuples, and maps the first element to a key and the second to a value to create a dictionary. The result is added to a list.

At this point, we are free to use dictionaries to do all sorts of contact-related activities. For testing, we simply loop over the contacts and output them in a different format. The format line, as usual, takes variable arguments and keyword arguments. The use of `**contact` automatically converts the dictionary to a bunch of keyword arguments (we'll understand this syntax before the end of the chapter) Here's the output:

```
email: jsmith@example.com -- smith, john
email: janed@example.com -- doan, jane
email: dn@example.com -- neilson, david
```

If we provide `zip` with lists of different lengths, it will stop at the end of the shortest list. There aren't many useful applications of this feature, but `zip` will not raise an exception if that is the case. We can always check the list lengths and add empty values to the shorter list, if necessary.

The `zip` function is actually the inverse of itself. It can take multiple sequences and combine them into a single sequence of tuples. Because tuples are also sequences, we can "unzip" a zipped list of tuples by zipping it again. Huh? Have a look at this example:

```
>>> list_one = ['a', 'b', 'c']
>>> list_two = [1, 2, 3]
>>> zipped = zip(list_one, list_two)
>>> zipped = list(zipped)
>>> zipped
[('a', 1), ('b', 2), ('c', 3)]
>>> unzipped = zip(*zipped)
>>> list(unzipped)
[('a', 'b', 'c'), (1, 2, 3)]
```

First we `zip` the two lists and convert the result into a list of tuples. We can then use parameter unpacking to pass these individual sequences as arguments to the `zip` function. `zip` matches the first value in each tuple into one sequence and the second value into a second sequence; the result is the same two sequences we started with!

Other functions

Another key function is `sorted()`, which takes an iterable as input, and returns a list of the items in sorted order. It is very similar to the `sort()` method on lists, the difference being that it works on all iterables, not just lists.

Like `list.sort`, `sorted` accepts a `key` argument that allows us to provide a function to return a sort value for each input. It can also accept a `reverse` argument.

Three more functions that operate on sequences are `min`, `max`, and `sum`. These each take a sequence as input, and return the minimum or maximum value, or the sum of all values in the sequence. Naturally, `sum` only works if all values in the sequence are numbers. The `max` and `min` functions use the same kind of comparison mechanism as `sorted` and `list.sort`, and allow us to define a similar `key` function. For example, the following code uses `enumerate`, `max`, and `min` to return the indices of the values in a list with the maximum and minimum value:

```
def min_max_indexes(seq):
    minimum = min(enumerate(seq), key=lambda s: s[1])
    maximum = max(enumerate(seq), key=lambda s: s[1])
    return minimum[0], maximum[0]
```

The `enumerate` call converts the sequence into `(index, item)` tuples. The `lambda` function passed in as a `key` tells the function to search the second item in each tuple (the original item). The `minimum` and `maximum` variables are then set to the appropriate tuples returned by `enumerate`. The `return` statement takes the first value (the index from enumerate) of each tuple and returns the pair. The following interactive session shows how the returned values are, indeed, the indices of the minimum and maximum values:

```
>>> alist = [5,0,1,4,6,3]
>>> min_max_indexes(alist)
(1, 4)
>>> alist[1], alist[4]
(0, 6)
```

We've only touched on a few of the more important Python built-in functions. There are numerous others in the standard library, including:

- `all` and `any`, which accept an iterable and returns `True` if all, or any, of the items evaluate to true (that is a non-empty string or list, a non-zero number, an object that is not `None`, or the literal `True`).

- `eval`, `exec`, and `compile`, which execute string as code inside the interpreter.

- `hasattr`, `getattr`, `setattr`, and `delattr`, which allow attributes on an object to be manipulated as string names.

- And many more! See the interpreter help documentation for each of the functions listed in `dir(__builtins__)`.

Comprehensions

We've already seen a lot of Python's `for` loop. It allows us to loop over any object that supports the iterable protocol and do something specific with each of the elements in turn.

Supporting the iterable protocol simply means an object has an `__iter__` method that returns another object that supports the iterator protocol. Supporting the iterator protocol is a fancy way of saying it has a `__next__` method that either returns the next object in the sequence, or raises a `StopIteration` exception when all objects have been returned.

As you can see, the `for` statement, in spite of not looking terribly object-oriented, is actually a shortcut to some extremely object-oriented designs. Keep this in mind as we discuss comprehensions, as they, too, appear to be the polar opposite of an object-oriented tool. Yet, they use the same iteration protocol as `for` loops. They're just another kind of shortcut.

List comprehensions

List comprehensions are one of the most powerful tools in Python, so people tend to think of them as advanced. They're not. Indeed, I've taken the liberty of littering previous examples with comprehensions and assuming you'd understand them. While it's true that advanced programmers use comprehensions a lot, it's not because they're advanced, it's because they're trivial, and handle some of the most common operations in programming.

Let's have a look at one of those common operations, namely, converting a list of items into a list of related items. Specifically, let's assume we just read a list of strings from a file, and now we want to convert it to a list of integers; we know every item in the list is an integer, and we want to do some activity (say, calculate an average) on those numbers. Here's one simple way to approach it:

```python
input_strings = ['1', '5', '28', '131', '3']

output_integers = []
for num in input_strings:
    output_integers.append(int(num))
```

This works fine, it's only three lines of code. If you aren't used to comprehensions, you may not even think it looks ugly! Now, look at the same code using a list comprehension:

```python
input_strings = ['1', '5', '28', '131', '3']

output_integers = [int(num) for num in input_strings]
```

We're down to one line and we've dropped an `append` method call. Overall, it's pretty easy to tell what's going on, even if you're not used to comprehension syntax.

The square brackets show we're creating a list. Inside this list is a `for` loop that loops over each item in the input sequence. The only thing that may be confusing is what's happening between the list's opening brace and the start of the `for` loop. Whatever happens here is applied to **each** of the items in the input list. The item in question is referenced by the `num` variable from the loop. So it's converting each such item to an `int`.

That's all there is to a basic list comprehension. They are not so advanced, after all! Comprehensions are highly optimized; list comprehensions are far faster than `for` loops when we are looping over a huge number of items. If readability alone isn't a convincing reason to use them as much as possible, then speed should be.

Converting one list of items into a related list isn't the only thing we can do with a list comprehension. We can also choose to exclude certain values by adding an `if` statement inside the comprehension. Have a look:

```
output_ints = [int(n) for n in input_strings if len(n) < 3]
```

I shortened the name of the variable from `num` to `n` and the result variable to `output_ints` so it would still fit on one line. Other than that, all that's different between this example and the previous one is the `if len(n) < 3` part. This extra code excludes any strings with more than two characters. The `if` statement is applied before the `int` function, so it's testing the length of a string. Since our input strings are all integers at heart, it refers to any number over ninety-nine. Now **that** is all there is to list comprehensions! We use them to map input values to output values, applying a filter along the way to exclude any values that don't meet a specific condition.

Any iterable can be the input to a list comprehension; anything we can wrap in a `for` loop can also be placed inside a comprehension. For example, text files are iterable; each call to `__next__` on the file's iterator will return one line of the file. The contact file example we used earlier (to try out the `zip` function) can use a list comprehension instead:

```
import sys
filename = sys.argv[1]

with open(filename) as file:
    header = file.readline().strip().split('\t')
    contacts = [
            dict(
                zip(header, line.strip().split('\t'))
                ) for line in file
        ]
```

This time, I've added some whitespace to make it more readable (list comprehensions don't **have** to fit on one line). This example is doing the same thing as the previous version: creating a list of dictionaries from the zipped header and split lines for each line in the file.

Er, what? Don't worry if that code or explanation doesn't make sense; it's a bit confusing. One little list comprehension is doing a pile of work here, and the code is hard to understand, read, and ultimately, maintain. This example shows that list comprehensions aren't always the best solution; most programmers would agree that the earlier `for` loop is more readable than this version. Remember: the tools we are provided with should not be abused! Always pick the right tool for the job, and that job is writing maintainable code.

Set and dictionary comprehensions

Comprehensions aren't restricted to lists. We can use a similar syntax with braces to create sets and dictionaries as well. Let's start with sets. One way to create a set is to wrap a list comprehension in the `set()` constructor, which converts it to a set. But why waste memory on an intermediate list that gets discarded when we can create a set directly?

Here's an example that uses a named tuple to model author/title/genre triads, and then retrieves a set of all the authors that write in a specific genre:

```python
from collections import namedtuple

Book = namedtuple("Book", "author title genre")
books = [
        Book("Pratchett", "Nightwatch", "fantasy"),
        Book("Pratchett", "Thief Of Time", "fantasy"),
        Book("Le Guin", "The Dispossessed", "scifi"),
        Book("Le Guin", "A Wizard Of Earthsea", "fantasy"),
        Book("Turner", "The Thief", "fantasy"),
        Book("Phillips", "Preston Diamond", "western"),
        Book("Phillips", "Twice Upon A Time", "scifi"),
        ]

fantasy_authors = {
        b.author for b in books if b.genre == 'fantasy'}
```

That set comprehension sure is short in comparison to the set up required! If we'd used a list comprehension, of course, Terry Pratchett would have been listed twice. As it is, the nature of sets removes the duplicates and we end up with:

```
>>> fantasy_authors
{'Turner', 'Pratchett', 'Le Guin'}
```

We can introduce a colon to create a dictionary comprehension. This converts a sequence into a dictionary using `key : value` pairs. For example, it may be useful to quickly look up the author or genre in a dictionary if we know the title. We can use a dictionary comprehension to map titles to book objects:

```
fantasy_titles = {
        b.title: b for b in books if b.genre == 'fantasy'}
```

Now we have a dictionary and can look up books by title using the normal syntax.

In summary, comprehensions are not advanced Python, and they aren't "non-object-oriented" tools that should be avoided. They are simply a more concise and optimized syntax for creating a list, set, or dictionary from an existing sequence.

Generator expressions

Sometimes we want to process a new sequence without placing a new list, set, or dictionary into system memory. If we're just looping over items one at a time, and don't actually care about having a final container object created, creating that container is a waste of memory. When processing one item at a time, we only need the current object stored in memory at any one moment. But when we create a container, all the objects have to be stored in that container before we start processing them.

For example, consider a program that processes log files. A very simple log might contain information in this format:

```
Jan 26, 2010 11:25:25   DEBUG     This is a debugging message.
Jan 26, 2010 11:25:36   INFO      This is an information method.
Jan 26, 2010 11:25:46   WARNING   This is a warning. It could be
serious.
Jan 26, 2010 11:25:52   WARNING   Another warning sent.
Jan 26, 2010 11:25:59   INFO      Here's some information.
Jan 26, 2010 11:26:13   DEBUG     Debug messages are only useful if
you want to figure something out.
Jan 26, 2010 11:26:32   INFO      Information is usually harmless,
but helpful.
Jan 26, 2010 11:26:40   WARNING   Warnings should be heeded.
Jan 26, 2010 11:26:54   WARNING   Watch for warnings.
```

Log files for popular web servers, databases, or e-mail servers can contain many gigabytes of data. If we want to process each line in the log, we don't want to use a list comprehension on those lines; it would create a list containing every line in the file. This probably wouldn't fit in memory and could bring the computer to its knees, depending on the operating system.

If we used a `for` loop on the log file, we could process one line at a time before reading the next one into memory. Wouldn't be nice if we could use comprehension syntax to get the same effect?

This is where generator expressions come in. They use the same syntax as comprehensions, but they don't create a final container object. To create a generator expression, wrap the comprehension in `()` instead of `[]` or `{}`.

The following code parses a log file in the previously presented format, and outputs a new log file that contains only the `WARNING` lines:

```
import sys

inname = sys.argv[1]
outname = sys.argv[2]

with open(inname) as infile:
    with open(outname, "w") as outfile:
        warnings = (l for l in infile if 'WARNING' in l)
        for l in warnings:
            outfile.write(l)
```

This program takes the two filenames on the command line, uses a generator expression to filter out the warnings (in this case, it uses the `if` syntax, and leaves the line unmodified), and then outputs the warnings to another file. If we run it on our sample file, the output looks like this:

```
Jan 26, 2010 11:25:46   WARNING     This is a warning. It could be
serious.
Jan 26, 2010 11:25:52   WARNING     Another warning sent.
Jan 26, 2010 11:26:40   WARNING     Warnings should be heeded.
Jan 26, 2010 11:26:54   WARNING     Watch for warnings.
```

Of course, with such a short input file, we could have safely used a list comprehension, but if the file is millions of lines long, the generator expression will have a huge impact on both memory and speed.

Generator expressions can also be useful inside function calls. For example, we can call `sum`, `min`, or `max` on a generator expression instead of a list, since these functions process one object at a time. We're only interested in the result, not any intermediate container.

In general, a generator expression should be used whenever possible. If we don't actually need a list, set, or dictionary, but simply need to filter or convert items in a sequence, a generator expression will be most efficient. If we need to know the length of a list, or sort the result, remove duplicates, or create a dictionary, we'll have to use the comprehension syntax.

Generators

Generator expressions are actually a sort of comprehension too; they compress the more advanced (this time it really is more advanced!) generator syntax into one line. The greater generator syntax looks even less object-oriented than anything we've seen, but we'll discover that once again, it is a simple syntax shortcut to create a kind of object.

Let's take the log file example a little further. If we want to delete the WARNING column from our output file (since it's redundant; this file contains only warnings), we have several options, at various levels of readability. We can do it with a generator expression:

```
import sys
inname, outname = sys.argv[1:3]

with open(inname) as infile:
    with open(outname, "w") as outfile:
        warnings = (l.replace('\tWARNING', '')
                for l in infile if 'WARNING' in l)
        for l in warnings:
            outfile.write(l)
```

That's perfectly readable, though I wouldn't want to make the expression any more complicated than that. We could also do it with a normal `for` loop:

```
import sys
inname, outname = sys.argv[1:3]

with open(inname) as infile:
    with open(outname, "w") as outfile:
        for l in infile:
            if 'WARNING' in l:
                outfile.write(l.replace('\tWARNING', ''))
```

That's maintainable, but so many levels of indent in so few lines is kind of ugly. Now let's consider a truly object-oriented solution, without any shortcuts:

```
import sys
inname, outname = sys.argv[1:3]

class WarningFilter:
    def __init__(self, insequence):
        self.insequence = insequence
    def __iter__(self):
```

```
            return self
        def __next__(self):
            l = self.insequence.readline()
            while l and 'WARNING' not in l:
                l = self.insequence.readline()
            if not l:
                raise StopIteration
            return l.replace('\tWARNING', '')

with open(inname) as infile:
    with open(outname, "w") as outfile:
        filter = WarningFilter(infile)
        for l in filter:
            outfile.write(l)
```

No doubt about it: that is ugly and difficult to read. What is happening here? Well, we created an object that takes a file object as input, and then provides a __next__ method to allow it to work as an iterator in for loops. That method reads lines from the file, discarding them if they are not WARNING lines. When it encounters a WARNING line, it returns it, and the for loop will call __next__ again to get the next line. When we run out of lines, we raise StopIteration to tell the loop we're finished. It's pretty ugly compared to the other examples, but it's also powerful; now that we have a class in our hands, we can do whatever we want to it.

With that background behind us, we finally get to see generators in action. This next example does exactly the same thing as the previous one: it creates an object that allows us to loop over the input:

```
import sys
inname, outname = sys.argv[1:3]


def warnings_filter(insequence):
    for l in insequence:
        if 'WARNING' in l:
            yield l.replace('\tWARNING', '')

with open(inname) as infile:
    with open(outname, "w") as outfile:
        filter = warnings_filter(infile)
        for l in filter:
            outfile.write(l)
```

OK, that's pretty readable, maybe... at least it's short. But what on earth is going on here, it doesn't make sense. And what is yield, anyway?

Last question first: `yield` is the key to generators. When Python sees `yield` in a function, it takes that function and wraps it up in an object not unlike the one in our previous example. Think of the `yield` statement as similar to the `return` statement; it exits the function and returns a line. Unlike `return`, when the function is called again, it will start where it left off; on the line after the `yield` statement. In this example, there is no line after the `yield` statement, so it jumps to the next iteration of the `for` loop. Since the `yield` statement is inside an `if` statement, it only yields lines that contain WARNING.

While it looks like that function is simply looping over the lines, it is really creating an object; a generator object:

```
>>> print(warnings_filter([]))
<generator object warnings_filter at 0xb728c6bc>
```

I passed an empty list into the function to act as an iterator. All the function does is create and return a generator object. That object has __iter__ and __next__ methods on it, much like the one we created in the previous example. Whenever __next__ is called, the generator runs the function until it finds a `yield` statement. It then returns the value from `yield`, and the next time __next__ is called, it picks up where it left off.

This use of generators isn't that advanced, but if you don't realize the function is creating an object, it can seem magical. We can even have multiple calls to `yield` in a single function; it will simply pick up at the most recent `yield` and continue to the next one.

There is even more to generators than what we have covered. We can send values back into generators when calling `yield`, turning them into a dark art called coroutines. While technically objects, coroutines encourage us to think very differently from the object-oriented principles we've been discussing, and are beyond the scope of this book. Do a search if you are interested in learning more about them.

An alternative to method overloading

One prominent feature of many object-oriented programming languages is a tool called **method overloading**. Method overloading simply refers to having multiple methods with the same name that accept different sets of arguments. In statically typed languages, this is useful if we want to have a method that accepts either an integer or a string, for example. In non-object-oriented languages we might need two functions called `add_s` and `add_i` to accommodate such situations. In statically typed object-oriented languages, we'd need two methods, both called `add`, one that accepts strings, and one that accepts integers.

In Python, we only need one method, which accepts any type of object. It may have to do some testing on the object type (for example, if it is a string, convert it to an integer), but only one method is required.

However, method overloading is also useful when we want a method with the same name to accept different numbers or sets of arguments. For example, an e-mail message method might come in two versions, one of which accepts an argument for the from e-mail address. The other method might look up a default from address instead. Python doesn't permit multiple methods with the same name, but it does provide a different, equally flexible, interface.

We've seen some of the possible ways to send arguments to methods and functions in previous examples, but now we'll cover all the details. The simplest function accepts no arguments. We probably don't need an example, but here's one for completeness:

```
def no_args():
    pass
```

and here's how it's called:

```
no_args()
```

A function that does accept arguments will provide the names of those arguments in a comma-separated list. Only the name of each argument needs to be supplied.

When calling the function, these **positional** arguments must be specified in order, and none can be missed or skipped. This is the most common way we've specified arguments in our previous examples:

```
def mandatory_args(x, y, z):
    pass
```

and to call it:

```
mandatory_args("a string", a_variable, 5)
```

Any type of object can be passed as an argument: an object, a container, a primitive, even functions and classes. The above call shows a hard-coded string, an unknown variable, and an integer passed into the function.

Default arguments

If we want to make an argument optional, rather than creating a second method with a different set of arguments, we can specify a default value in a single method, using an equals sign. If the calling code does not supply this argument, it will be assigned a default value. However, the calling code can still choose to override the default by passing in a different value. Often, a default value of None, or an empty string or list is suitable.

Here's a function definition with default arguments:

```
def default_arguments(x, y, z, a="Some String", b=False):
    pass
```

The first three arguments are still mandatory and must be passed by the calling code. The last two parameters have default arguments supplied.

There are several ways we can call this function. We can supply all arguments in order, as though all the arguments were positional arguments.

```
kwargs("a string", variable, 8, "", True)
```

Or we can supply just the mandatory arguments in order, leaving the keyword arguments to be assigned their default values:

```
kwargs("a longer string", some_variable, 14)
```

We can also use the equals sign syntax when calling a function to provide values in a different order or to skip default values that we aren't interested in. For example, we can skip the first keyword arguments and supply the second one:

```
kwargs("a string", variable, 14, b=True)
```

Surprisingly, we can even use the equals sign syntax to mix up the order of positional arguments, so long as all of them are supplied.

```
>>> kwargs(y=1,z=2,x=3,a="hi")
3 1 2 hi False
```

With so many options, it may seem hard to pick one, but if you think of the positional arguments as an ordered list, and keyword arguments as sort of like a dictionary, you'll find that the correct layout tends to fall into place. If you need to require the caller to specify an argument, make it mandatory; if you have a sensible default, then make it a keyword argument. Choosing how to call the method normally takes care of itself, depending on which values need to be supplied, and which can be left at their defaults.

One thing to take note of with keyword arguments is that anything we provide as a default argument is evaluated when the function is first interpreted, not when it is called. This means we can't have dynamically generated default values. For example, the following code won't behave quite as expected:

```
number = 5
def funky_function(number=number):
    print(number)

number=6
funky_function(8)
funky_function()
print(number)
```

If we run this code, it outputs the number 8, first, but then it outputs the number 5 for the call with no arguments. We had set the variable to the number 6, as evidenced by the last line of output, but when the function is called, the number 5 is printed; the default value was calculated when the function was defined, not when it was called.

This is tricky with empty containers. For example, it is common to ask calling code to supply a list that our function is going to manipulate, but the list is optional. We'd like to make an empty list as a default argument. We can't do this; it will create only one list, when the code is first constructed:

```
>>> def hello(b=[]):
...      b.append('a')
...      print(b)
...
>>> hello()
['a']
>>> hello()
['a', 'a']
```

Whoops, that's not quite what we expected! The usual way to get around this is to make the default value None, and then use the idiom if argument is None: arg = [] inside the method. Pay close attention!

Variable argument lists

Default values alone do not allow us all the flexible benefits of method overloading. The thing that makes Python really slick is the ability to write methods that accept an arbitrary number of positional or keyword arguments without explicitly naming them. We can also pass arbitrary lists and dictionaries into such functions.

For example, a function to accept a link or list of links and download the web pages could use such variadic arguments, or **varargs**. Instead of accepting a single value that is expected to be a list of links, we can accept an arbitrary number of arguments, where each argument is a different link. We do this by specifying the * operator in the function definition:

```
def get_pages(*links):
    for link in links:
        #download the link with urllib
        print(link)
```

The *links says "I'll accept any number of arguments and put them all in a list of strings named links". If we supply only one argument, it'll be a list with one element, if we supply no arguments, it'll be an empty list. Thus, all these function calls are valid:

```
get_pages()
get_pages('http://www.archlinux.org')
get_pages('http://www.archlinux.org',
          'http://ccphillips.net/')
```

We can also accept arbitrary keyword arguments. These arrive into the function as a dictionary. They are specified with two asterisks (as in **kwargs) in the function declaration. This tool is commonly used in configuration setups. The following class allows us to specify a set of options with default values:

```
class Options:
    default_options = {
            'port': 21,
            'host': 'localhost',
            'username': None,
            'password': None,
            'debug': False,
            }
    def __init__(self, **kwargs):
        self.options = dict(Options.default_options)
        self.options.update(kwargs)

    def __getitem__(self, key):
        return self.options[key]
```

All the interesting stuff in this class happens in the __init__ method. We have a dictionary of default options and values at the class level. The first thing the __init__ method does is make a copy of this dictionary. We do that instead of modifying the dictionary directly in case we instantiate two separate sets of options. (Remember, class level variables are shared between instances of the class.) Then, __init__ uses the update method on the new dictionary to change any non-default values to those supplied as keyword arguments. The __getitem__ method simply allows us to use the new class using indexing syntax. Here's a session demonstrating the class in action:

```
>>> options = Options(username="dusty", password="drowssap",
        debug=True)
>>> options['debug']
True
>>> options['port']
21
>>> options['username']
'dusty'
```

We're able to access our options instance using dictionary indexing syntax, and the dictionary includes both default values and the ones we set using keyword arguments.

The keyword argument syntax can be dangerous, as it may break the "explicit is better than implicit" rule. In the above example, it's possible to pass arbitrary keyword arguments to the Options initializer to represent options that don't exist in the default dictionary. This may not be a bad thing, depending on the purpose of the class, but it makes it hard for someone using the class to discover what valid options are available. It also makes it easy to enter a confusing typo ("Debug" instead of "debug", for example) that adds two options where only one should have existed.

The above example is not that bad if we instruct the user of the class to only pass default options (we could even add some code to enforce this rule). The options are documented in the class definition so it'll be easy to look them up.

Keyword arguments are also very useful when we need to accept arbitrary arguments to pass to a second function, but we don't know what those arguments will be. We saw this in action in *Chapter 3*, when we were building support for multiple inheritance.

We can, of course, combine the variable argument and variable keyword argument syntax in one function call, and we can use normal positional and default arguments as well. The following example is somewhat contrived, but demonstrates the four types in action:

```
import shutil
import os.path
def augmented_move(target_folder, *filenames,
        verbose=False, **specific):
    '''Move all filenames into the target_folder, allowing
    specific treatment of certain files.'''

    def print_verbose(message, filename):
        '''print the message only if verbose is enabled'''
        if verbose:
            print(message.format(filename))

    for filename in filenames:
        target_path = os.path.join(target_folder, filename)
        if filename in specific:
            if specific[filename] == 'ignore':
                print_verbose("Ignoring {0}", filename)
            elif specific[filename] == 'copy':
                print_verbose("Copying {0}", filename)
                shutil.copyfile(filename, target_path)
        else:
            print_verbose("Moving {0}", filename)
            shutil.move(filename, target_path)
```

This example will process an arbitrary list of files. The first argument is a target folder, and the default behavior is to move all remaining non-keyword argument files into that folder. Then there is a keyword-only argument, verbose, which tells us whether to print information on each file processed. Finally, we can supply a dictionary containing actions to perform on specific filenames; the default behavior is to move the file, but if a valid string action has been specified in the keyword arguments, it can be ignored or copied instead. Notice the ordering of the parameters in the function; first the positional argument is specified, then the *filenames list, then any specific keyword-only arguments, and finally, a **specific dictionary to hold remaining keyword arguments.

We create an inner helper function, print_verbose, which will print messages only if the verbose key has been set. This function keeps code readable by encapsulating this functionality into a single location.

In common cases, this function would likely be called as:

```
>>> augmented_move("move_here", "one", "two")
```

This command would move the files one and two into the move_here directory, assuming they exist (There's no error checking or exception handling in the function, so it would fail spectacularly if the files or target directory didn't exist). The move would occur without any output, since verbose is False by default.

If we want to see the output, we can call it with:

```
>>> augmented_move("move_here", "three", verbose=True)
Moving three
```

This moves one file, named three, and tells us what it's doing. Notice that it is impossible to specify verbose as a positional argument in this example; we **must** pass a keyword argument. Otherwise Python would think it was another filename in the *filenames list.

If we want to copy or ignore some of the files in the list, instead of moving them, we can pass additional keyword arguments:

```
>>> augmented_move("move_here", "four", "five", "six",
        four="copy", five="ignore")
```

This will move the sixth file and copy the fourth, but won't display any output, since we didn't specify verbose. Of course, we can do that, too, and keyword arguments can be supplied in any order:

```
>>> augmented_move("move_here", "seven", "eight", "nine",
        seven="copy", verbose=True, eight="ignore")
Copying seven
Ignoring eight
Moving nine
```

Unpacking arguments

There's one more nifty trick involving variable arguments and keyword arguments. We've used it in some of our previous examples, but it's never too late for an explanation. Given a list or dictionary of values, we can pass those values into a function as if they were normal positional or keyword arguments. Have a look at this code:

```
def show_args(arg1, arg2, arg3="THREE"):
    print(arg1, arg2, arg3)
```

```
some_args = range(3)
more_args = {
        "arg1": "ONE",
        "arg2": "TWO"}

print("Unpacking a sequence:", end=" ")
show_args(*some_args)
print("Unpacking a dict:", end=" ")
show_args(**more_args)
```

Here's what it looks like when we run it:

```
Unpacking a sequence: 0 1 2
Unpacking a dict: ONE TWO THREE
```

The function accepts three arguments, one of which has a default value. But when we have a list of three arguments, we can use the * operator inside a function call to unpack it into the three arguments. If we have a dictionary of arguments, we can use the ** syntax to unpack it as a collection of keyword arguments.

This is most often useful when mapping information that has been collected from user input or from an outside source (an internet page, a text file) to a function or method call.

Remember our earlier example that used headers and lines in a text file to create a list of dictionaries with contact information? Instead of just adding the dictionaries to a list, we could use keyword unpacking to pass the arguments to the __init__ method on a specially built Contact object that accepts the same set of arguments. See if you can adapt the example to make this work.

Functions are objects too

Programming languages that over-emphasize object-oriented principles tend to frown on functions that are not methods. In such languages, you're expected to create an object to sort of wrap the single method involved. There are numerous situations where we'd like to pass around a small object that is simply called to perform an action. This is most frequently done in event-driven programming, such as graphical toolkits or asynchronous servers; we'll see some design patterns that use it in the next two chapters.

In Python, we don't need to wrap such methods in an object, because functions already are objects! We can set attributes on functions (though this isn't a common activity), and we can pass them around to be called at a later date. They even have a few special properties that can be accessed directly. Here's yet another contrived example:

```python
def my_function():
    print("The Function Was Called")
my_function.description = "A silly function"


def second_function():
    print("The second was called")
second_function.description = "A sillier function."


def another_function(function):
    print("The description:", end=" ")
    print(function.description)
    print("The name:", end=" ")
    print(function.__name__)
    print("The class:", end=" ")
    print(function.__class__)
    print("Now I'll call the function passed in")
    function()


another_function(my_function)
another_function(second_function)
```

If we run this code, we can see that we were able to pass two different functions into our third function, and get different output for each one:

```
The description: A silly function
The name: my_function
The class: <class 'function'>
Now I'll call the function passed in
The Function Was Called
The description: A sillier function.
The name: second_function
The class: <class 'function'>
Now I'll call the function passed in
The second was called
```

We set an attribute on the function, named description (not very good descriptions, admittedly). We were also able to see the function's __name__ attribute, and to access its class, demonstrating that the function really is an object with attributes. Then we called the function by using the callable syntax (the parentheses).

The fact that functions are top-level objects is most often used to pass them around to be executed at a later date, for example, when a certain condition has been satisfied. Let's build an event-driven timer that does just this:

```python
import datetime
import time

class TimedEvent:
    def __init__(self, endtime, callback):
        self.endtime = endtime
        self.callback = callback

    def ready(self):
        return self.endtime <= datetime.datetime.now()

class Timer:
    def __init__(self):
        self.events = []

    def call_after(self, delay, callback):
        end_time = datetime.datetime.now() + \
                datetime.timedelta(seconds=delay)

        self.events.append(TimedEvent(end_time, callback))

    def run(self):
        while True:
            ready_events = (e for e in self.events if e.ready())
            for event in ready_events:
                event.callback(self)
                self.events.remove(event)
            time.sleep(0.5)
```

In production, this code should definitely have extra documentation using docstrings! The `call_after` method should at least mention that the `delay` is in seconds and that the `callback` function should accept one argument: the timer doing the calling.

We have two classes here. The `TimedEvent` class is not really meant to be accessed by other classes; all it does is store an `endtime` and `callback`. We could even use a `tuple` or `namedtuple` here, but as it is convenient to give the object a behavior that tells us whether or not the event is ready to run, we use a class instead.

The Timer class simply stores a list of upcoming events. It has a call_after method to add a new event. This method accepts a delay parameter representing the number of seconds to wait before executing the callback, and the callback itself: a function to be executed at the correct time. This callback function should accept one argument.

The run method is very simple; it uses a generator expression to filter out any events whose time has come, and executes them in order. The timer loop then continues indefinitely, so it has to be interrupted with a keyboard interrupt (*Ctrl + C* or *Ctrl + Break*). We sleep for half a second after each iteration so as to not grind the system to a halt.

The important things to note here are the lines that touch callback functions. The function is passed around like any other object and the timer never knows or cares what the original name of the function is or where it was defined. When it's time to call the function, the timer simply applies the parenthesis syntax to the stored variable.

Here's a set of callbacks that test the timer:

```python
from timer import Timer
import datetime

def format_time(message, *args):
    now = datetime.datetime.now().strftime("%I:%M:%S")
    print(message.format(*args, now=now))

def one(timer):
    format_time("{now}: Called One")

def two(timer):
    format_time("{now}: Called Two")

def three(timer):
    format_time("{now}: Called Three")

class Repeater:
    def __init__(self):
        self.count = 0
    def repeater(self, timer):
        format_time("{now}: repeat {0}", self.count)
        timer.call_after(5, self.repeater)

timer = Timer()
timer.call_after(1, one)
```

```
timer.call_after(2, one)
timer.call_after(2, two)
timer.call_after(4, two)
timer.call_after(3, three)
timer.call_after(6, three)
repeater = Repeater()
timer.call_after(5, repeater.repeater)
format_time("{now}: Starting")
timer.run()
```

This example allows us to see how multiple callbacks interact with the timer. The first function is the `format_time` function. It uses the string `format` method to add the current time to the message, and illustrates variable arguments in action. The `format_time` method will accept any number of positional arguments, using variable argument syntax, which are then forwarded as positional arguments to the string's `format` method. After that we create three simple callback methods that simply output the current time and a short message telling us which callback has been fired.

The `Repeater` class demonstrates that methods can be used as callbacks too, since they are really just functions. It also shows why the `timer` argument to the callback functions is useful: we can add a new timed event to the timer from inside a presently running callback.

Then we simply create a timer and add several events to it that are called after different amounts of time. Then we start the timer running; the output shows that events are run in the expected order:

```
02:53:35: Starting
02:53:36: Called One
02:53:37: Called One
02:53:37: Called Two
02:53:38: Called Three
02:53:39: Called Two
02:53:40: repeat 0
02:53:41: Called Three
02:53:45: repeat 1
02:53:50: repeat 2
02:53:55: repeat 3
02:54:00: repeat 4
```

Using functions as attributes

One of the interesting effects of functions being objects is that they can be set as callable attributes on other objects. It is possible to add or change a function to an instantiated object:

```python
class A:
    def print(self):
        print("my class is A")

def fake_print():
    print("my class is not A")

a = A()
a.print()
a.print = fake_print
a.print()
```

This code creates a very simple class with a `print` method that doesn't tell us anything we don't know. Then we create a new function that tells us something we don't believe.

When we call `print` on an instance of the A class, it behaves as expected. If we then set the `print` method to point at a new function, it tells us something different:

```
my class is A
my class is not A
```

It is also possible to replace methods on classes, instead of objects, although in that case we have to add the `self` argument to the parameter list. This will change the method for all instances of that object, even ones that have already been instantiated.

Obviously, replacing methods like this can be very dangerous and confusing to maintain. Somebody reading the code will see that a method has been called, and look up that method on the original class. But the method on the original class is not the one that was called. Figuring out what really happened can become a very tricky debugging session.

It does have its uses though. Often, replacing or adding methods at run time (called **monkey-patching**) is used in automated testing. If testing a client-server application, we may not want to actually connect to the server when testing the client; that may result in accidental transfers of funds or embarrassing test e-mails being sent to real people. Instead, we can set up our test code to replace some of the key methods on the object that sends requests to the server, so it only records that the methods have been called.

Monkey-patching can also be used to fix bugs or add features in third-party code that we are interacting with and does not behave quite the way we need it to. It should, however, be applied sparingly, it's almost always a "messy hack". Sometimes, though, it is the only way to adapt an existing library to suit our needs.

Callable objects

Since functions are just objects that happen to respond to the call syntax, we start to wonder if it's possible to write objects that can be called yet aren't real functions. Yes, of course!

Any object can be turned into a callable, as easily as giving it a __call__ method that accepts the required arguments. Let's make our Repeater class from the timer example a little easier to use by making it a callable:

```
class Repeater:
    def __init__(self):
        self.count = 0
    def __call__(self, timer):
        format_time("{now}: repeat {0}", self.count)
        self.count += 1
        timer.call_after(5, self)

timer = Timer()
timer.call_after(5, Repeater())
format_time("{now}: Starting")
timer.run()
```

This example isn't much different from the earlier class; all we did was change the name of the repeater function to __call__ and pass the object itself as a callable. Note that when we make the call_after call, we pass the argument Repeater(). Those two parentheses are creating a new instance of the class, they are not explicitly calling the class. That happens later, inside the timer. If we want to execute the __call__ method on a newly instantiated object, we'd use a rather odd syntax: Repeater()(). The first set of parentheses constructs the object; the second set executes the __call__ method.

Case study

To tie together some of the principles presented in this chapter, let's build a mailing list manager. The manager will keep track of e-mail addresses categorized into named groups. When it's time to send a message, we can pick a group and send the message to all e-mail addresses assigned to that group.

Now, before we start working on this project, we ought to have a safe way to test it, without sending e-mails to a bunch of real people. Luckily, Python has our back here; like the test HTTP server, it has a built in **Simple Mail Transfer Protocol (SMTP)** server that we can instruct to capture any messages we send without actually sending them. We can run the server with the following command:

```
python -m smtpd -n -c DebuggingServer localhost:1025
```

Running this command at a command prompt will start an SMTP server running on port 1025 on the local machine. But we've instructed it to use the DebuggingServer class (it comes with the built-in SMTP module), which, instead of sending mails to the intended recipients, simply prints them on the terminal screen as it receives them. Neat, eh?

Now, before writing our mailing list, let's write some code that actually sends mail. Of course, Python supports this in the standard library too, but it's a bit of an odd interface, so we'll write a new function to wrap it all cleanly:

```python
import smtplib
from email.mime.text import MIMEText

def send_email(subject, message, from_addr, *to_addrs,
        host="localhost", port=1025, **headers):

    email = MIMEText(message)
    email['Subject'] = subject
    email['From'] = from_addr
    for header, value in headers.items():
        email[header] = value

    sender = smtplib.SMTP(host, port)
    for addr in to_addrs:
        del email['To']
        email['To'] = addr
        sender.sendmail(from_addr, addr, email.as_string())
    sender.quit()
```

We won't cover the code inside this method too thoroughly; the documentation in the standard library can give you all the information you need to use the `smtplib` and `email` modules effectively.

We've used both variable argument and keyword argument syntax in the function call; any unknown arguments are mapped to extra addresses to send to; any extra keyword arguments are mapped to e-mail headers.

The headers passed into the function represent auxiliary headers that can be attached to a method. Such headers might include Reply-To, Return-Path, or X-pretty-much-anything. Can you see a problem here?

Any valid identifier in Python cannot include the - character. In general, that character represents subtraction. So it's not possible to call a function with `Reply-To = my@email.com`. Perhaps we were too eager to use keyword arguments because they are a new tool we just learned this chapter?

We'll have to change the argument to a normal dictionary; this will work because any string can be used as a key in a dictionary. By default, we'd want this dictionary to be empty, but we can't make the default parameter an empty dictionary. No, we'll have to make the default argument None, and then set up the dictionary at the beginning of the method:

```
def send_email(subject, message, from_addr, *to_addrs,
        host="localhost", port=1025, headers=None):

    headers = {} if headers is None else headers
```

If we have our debugging SMTP server running in one terminal, we can test this code in a Python interpreter:

```
>>> send_email("A model subject", "The message contents",
 "from@example.com", "to1@example.com", "to2@example.com")
```

Then if we check the output from the debugging SMTP server, we get the following:

```
---------- MESSAGE FOLLOWS ----------
Content-Type: text/plain; charset="us-ascii"
MIME-Version: 1.0
Content-Transfer-Encoding: 7bit
Subject: A model subject
From: from@example.com
To: to1@example.com
X-Peer: 127.0.0.1

The message contents
```

```
------------ END MESSAGE ------------
---------- MESSAGE FOLLOWS ----------
Content-Type: text/plain; charset="us-ascii"
MIME-Version: 1.0
Content-Transfer-Encoding: 7bit
Subject: A model subject
From: from@example.com
To: to2@example.com
X-Peer: 127.0.0.1

The message contents
------------ END MESSAGE ------------
```

Excellent, it has "sent" our e-mail to the two correct addresses with subject and message contents included.

Now that we can send messages, let's work on the e-mail group management system. We'll need an object that somehow matches e-mail addresses with the groups they are in. Since this is a many-to-many relationship (any one e-mail address can be in multiple groups, any one group can be associated with multiple e-mail addresses), none of the data structures we've studied seem quite ideal. We could try a dictionary of group-names matched to a list of associated e-mail addresses, but that would duplicate e-mail addresses. We could also try a dictionary of e-mail addresses matched to groups, resulting in a duplication of groups. Neither seems optimal. Let's try this latter version, even though intuition tells me the groups to e-mail address solution would be more straightforward.

Since the values in our dictionary will always be collections of **unique** e-mail addresses, we should probably store them in a set. We can use `defaultdict` to ensure there is always a set available for each key:

```python
from collections import defaultdict
class MailingList:
    '''Manage groups of e-mail addresses for sending e-mails.'''
    def __init__(self):
        self.email_map = defaultdict(set)

    def add_to_group(self, email, group):
        self.email_map[email].add(group)
```

Now let's add a method that allows us to collect all the e-mail addresses in one or more groups. We can use a set comprehension to take care of this easily:

```python
def emails_in_groups(self, *groups):
    groups = set(groups)
    return {e for (e, g) in self.email_map.items()
            if g & groups}
```

OK, that set comprehension needs explaining, doesn't it? First look at what we're iterating over: `self.email_map.items()`. That method, of course, returns a tuple of key-value pairs for each item in the dictionary. The values are sets of strings representing the groups. We split these into two variables named `e` and `g`, short for e-mail and groups. We only return the key (the e-mail address) for each item though, since the desired output is a set of e-mail addresses.

The only thing left that may not make sense is the condition clause. This clause simply intersects the `groups` set with the set of groups associated with the e-mails. If the result is non-empty, the e-mail gets added, otherwise, it is discarded. The `g &`
`groups` syntax is a shortcut for `g.intersection(groups)`; the `set` class does this by implementing the special method `__and__` to call `intersection`.

Now, with these building blocks, we can trivially add a method to our `MailingList` class that sends e-mail to specific groups:

```python
def send_mailing(self, subject, message, from_addr,
        *groups, **kwargs):
    emails = self.emails_in_groups(*groups)
    send_email(subject, message, from_addr,
            *emails, **kwargs)
```

This function stresses on variable arguments. As input, it takes a list of groups as variable arguments, and optional keyword arguments as a dictionary. It doesn't care about the keyword arguments at all; it simply passes those arguments on to the `send_email` function we defined earlier. It then gets the list of e-mails for the specified groups, and passes those as variable arguments into `send_email`.

The program can be tested by ensuring the SMTP debugging server is running in one command prompt, and, in a second prompt, load the code using:

```
>>> python -i mailing_list.py
```

Create a `MailingList` object with:

```
>>> m = MailingList()
```

Then create a few fake e-mail addresses and groups, along the lines of:

```
>>> m.add_to_group("friend1@example.com", "friends")
>>> m.add_to_group("friend2@example.com", "friends")
>>> m.add_to_group("family1@example.com", "family")
>>> m.add_to_group("pro1@example.com", "professional")
```

Finally, use a command like this to send e-mails to specific groups:

```
>>> m.send_mailing("A Party",
"Friends and family only: a party", "me@example.com", "friends",
"family", headers={"Reply-To": "me2@example.com"})
```

E-mails to each of the addresses in the specified groups should show up in the console on the SMTP server.

Exercises

If you don't use comprehensions in your daily coding very often, the first thing you should do is search through some existing code and find some for loops. See if any of them can be trivially converted to a generator expression or a list, set, or dictionary comprehension.

Test the claim that list comprehensions are faster than for loops. This can be done with the built-in timeit module. Use the help documentation for the timeit. timeit function to find out how to use it. Basically, write two functions that do the same thing, one using a list comprehension, and one using a for loop. Pass each function into timeit.timeit, and compare the results. If you're feeling adventurous, compare generators and generator expressions as well. Testing code using timeit can become addictive, so bear in mind that code does not need to be hyper-fast unless it's being executed an immense number of times, such as on a huge input list or log file.

Try writing the case study using groups as dictionary keys and lists of e-mail addresses as the values. You'll likely be surprised at how little needs to be changed. If you're interested, try reworking it to accept first and last names as well as e-mail addresses. Then allow customizing e-mail messages (use str.format) to have the person's first or last name in each message.

Except the send_mailing method itself, the MailingList object is really quite generic. Consider what needs to be done to make it perform any generic activity on each e-mail address, instead of just sending mail. Hint: callback functions will be very useful.

Play around with generator functions. Start with basic iterators that require multiple values (mathematical sequences are canonical examples; the Fibonacci sequence is overused if you can't think of anything better). Try some more advanced generators that do things like take multiple input lists and somehow yield values that merge them. Generators can also be used on files; can you write a simple generator that shows those lines that are identical in two files?

Summary

We covered several very different topics in this chapter. Each represented an important non-object-oriented feature that is popular in Python. Just because we can use object-oriented principles does not always mean we should!

However, we also saw that "the Python way" often just provides a shortcut to traditional object-oriented syntax. Knowing the object-oriented principles underlying these tools allows us to use them effectively in our own classes.

We covered:

- Built-in functions
- Comprehensions and generators
- Function arguments, variable arguments, and keyword arguments
- Callback functions and callable objects

In the next chapter, we're going to study design patterns; building blocks that object-oriented programmers use to create maintainable applications. In many cases, we'll see that, as in this chapter, Python provides syntax for popular design patterns that we can use instead.

8
Python Design Patterns I

We've covered the basic building blocks of object-oriented programming. Now, we'll look at secondary structures that can be built from those blocks. These higher-level structures, called design patterns, can help organize complex systems. In the next two chapters, we'll be covering:

- What design patterns are
- Numerous specific patterns
- A canonical implementation of each pattern in Python
- Python syntax to replace certain patterns

Design patterns

When engineers and architects decide to build a bridge, or a tower, or a building, they follow certain principles to ensure structural integrity. There are various possible designs for bridges (suspension or cantilever for example), but if the engineer doesn't use one of the standard designs, and doesn't have a brilliant new design, it is likely the bridge he/she designs will collapse.

Design patterns are an attempt to bring this same formal definition for correctly designed structures to software engineering. There are many different design patterns to solve different general problems. People who create design patterns first identify a common problem faced by developers in a wide variety of situations. They then suggest what might be considered the ideal solution for that problem, in terms of object-oriented design.

We already have plenty of experience with one of the most common design patterns, the iterator. Canonically, the iterator pattern is meant to provide a common interface for looping over the items in a sequence. Separating the looping action from the sequence that is actually being looped over allows the looping code to be changed without interfering with either the code doing the looping, or the object being looped over. For example, two iterators may loop over the items in different directions, or in a sorted order. Further, it's possible to change the internal structure of an object, but still allow it to be looped over using a single iterator interface.

In typical design pattern parlance, an iterator is an object with a `next()` method and a `done()` method; the latter returns `True` if there are no items left in the sequence. In a programming language without built-in support for iterators, the iterator would be looped over like this:

```
while not iterator.done():
    item = iterator.next()
    # do something with the item
```

Of course, in Python, the method is named `__next__` instead, and we have the much more readable `for item in iterator` syntax to actually access the items. Rather than a `done` method, it raises `StopIteration` when completed. The same pattern is being applied, and it is still based on a design pattern solution, but Python has provided us with a more readable way to apply and access the pattern.

Knowing a design pattern and choosing to use it in our software does not, however, guarantee that we are creating a "correct" solution. In 1907, the Québec Bridge (to this day, the longest cantilever bridge in the world) collapsed before construction was completed because the engineers who designed it grossly underestimated the weight of the steel used to construct it. Similarly, in software development, we may incorrectly choose or apply a design pattern, and create software that "collapses" under normal operating situations or when stressed beyond its original design limits.

Any one design pattern proposes a set of objects interacting in a specific way to solve a general problem. The job of the programmer is to recognize when they are facing a specific version of that problem, and to adapt the general design in their solution.

In this chapter, we'll be reviewing several common patterns, and how they are implemented in Python. Python often provides an alternative syntax to make working with such problems simpler. We will cover both the "traditional" design, and the Python version for these patterns.

Decorator pattern

The decorator pattern allows us to "wrap" an object that provides core functionality with other objects that alter that functionality. Any object that uses the decorated object will interact with it in exactly the same way as if it were undecorated (that is, the interface of the decorated object is identical to the core object).

There are two primary uses of the decorator pattern:

- Enhancing the response of a component that is sending data to a second component
- Supporting multiple optional behaviors

The second option is often a suitable alternative to multiple inheritance. We can construct a core object, and then create a decorator around that core. Since the decorator object has the same interface as the core object, we can even wrap the new object in other decorators. Here's how it looks in UML:

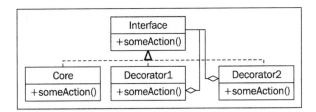

Here, **Core**, and all the decorators implement a specific **Interface**. The decorators maintain a reference to another instance of that **Interface**, via composition. When called, the decorator will do some added processing before or after calling its wrapped interface. The wrapped object may be another decorator, or the core functionality; multiple decorators may wrap each other, but the object in the "center" of all those decorators will provide core functionality.

Decorator example

Let's look at an example from network programming. We'll be using a TCP socket. The `socket.send()` method takes a string of input bytes and outputs them to the receiving socket at the other end. There are plenty of libraries that accept sockets and access this function to send data on the stream. Let's create such an object; it will be an interactive shell that waits for a connection from a client and then prompts the user for a string response:

```python
import socket

def respond(client):
    response = input("Enter a value: ")
    client.send(bytes(response, 'utf8'))
    client.close()

server = socket.socket(socket.AF_INET, socket.SOCK_STREAM)
server.bind(('localhost',2401))
server.listen(1)
try:
    while True:
        client, addr = server.accept()
        respond(client)
finally:
    server.close()
```

The `respond` function accepts a socket parameter and prompts for data to be sent as a reply, then sends it. After that, we construct a server socket and tell it to listen on port `2401` (I picked the port randomly) on the local computer. When a client connects, it calls the `respond` function, which requests data interactively and responds appropriately. The important thing to notice is that the `respond` function only cares about two methods of the socket interface: `send` and `close`. To test this, we can write a very simple client that connects to the same port and outputs the response before exiting:

```python
import socket

client = socket.socket(socket.AF_INET, socket.SOCK_STREAM)
client.connect(('localhost', 2401))
print("Received: {0}".format(client.recv(1024)))
client.close()
```

To use these programs:

1. Start the server in one terminal.

2. Open a second terminal window and run the client.

3. At the **Enter a value**: prompt in the server window, type a value and press enter.

4. The client will receive what you typed, print it to the console, and exit. Run the client a second time; the server will prompt for a second value.

Now, looking again at our server code, we see two sections. The `respond` function sends data into a socket object. The remaining script is responsible for creating that socket object. We'll create a pair of decorators that customize the socket behavior without having to extend or modify the socket itself.

Let's start with a "logging" decorator. This object will simply output any data being sent to the server's console before it sends it to the client:

```
class LogSocket:
    def __init__(self, socket):
        self.socket = socket

    def send(self, data):
        print("Sending {0} to {1}".format(
            data, self.socket.getpeername()[0]))
        self.socket.send(data)

    def close(self):
        self.socket.close()
```

This class decorates a socket object and presents the `send` and `close` interface to client sockets. A better decorator would also implement (and possibly customize) all of the socket methods. It should properly implement all of the arguments to `send`, (which actually accepts an optional flags argument) as well, but let's keep the example simple! Whenever `send` is called on this object, it logs the output to the screen before sending just like the original socket did.

We only have to change one line in our original code to use this decorator. Instead of calling `respond` with the socket, we call it with a decorated socket:

```
respond(LogSocket(client))
```

While that's quite simple, we have to ask ourselves why we didn't just extend the socket class and override the `send` method. We could call `super().send` to do the actual sending, after we logged it. This is a valid design.

When faced with a choice between decorators and inheritance, we should only use decorators if we need to modify the object dynamically, according to some condition. For example, we may only want to enable the logging decorator if the server is currently in debugging mode. Decorators also beat out multiple inheritance when we have multiple optional behaviors. As an example, we can write a second decorator that compresses data using `gzip` compression whenever `send` is called:

```python
import gzip
from io import BytesIO

class GzipSocket:
    def __init__(self, socket):
        self.socket = socket

    def send(self, data):
        buf = BytesIO()
        zipfile = gzip.GzipFile(fileobj=buf, mode="w")
        zipfile.write(data)
        zipfile.close()
        self.socket.send(buf.getvalue())

    def close(self):
        self.socket.close()
```

The `send` method in this version compresses the incoming data before sending it on to the client. We don't have room for the example, but it's possible to write a client that extracts the gzipped content.

Now that we have these two decorators, we can write code that dynamically switches between them when responding. This example is not complete, but it illustrates the logic we might follow to mix and match decorators:

```python
client, addr = server.accept()
if log_send:
    client = LoggingSocket(client)
if client.getpeername()[0] in compress_hosts:
    client = GzipSocket(client)
respond(client)
```

This code checks a hypothetical configuration variable named `log_send`. If it's enabled it wraps the socket in a `LoggingSocket` decorator. Similarly, it checks if the client that has connected is in a list of addresses known to accept compressed content. If so, it wraps the client in a `GzipSocket` decorator. Notice that none, either, or both of the decorators may be enabled, depending on the configuration and connecting client. Try writing this using multiple inheritance and see how confused you get!

Decorators in Python

The decorator pattern is useful in Python, but there are other options. For example, we may be able to use monkey-patching, which we discussed in *Chapter 7*, to get a similar effect. Single inheritance, where the "optional" calculations are done in one large method can be an option, and multiple inheritance should not be written off just because it's not suitable for the specific example seen previously!

In Python, it is very common to use this pattern on functions. As we saw in the previous chapter, functions are objects too. In fact, this is so common that Python provides a special syntax to make it easy to apply such decorators to functions.

For example, we can look at the logging example in a more general way. Instead of logging only send calls on sockets, we may find it helpful to log all calls to certain functions or methods. The following example implements a decorator that does just this:

```python
import time

def log_calls(func):
    def wrapper(*args, **kwargs):
        now = time.time()
        print("Calling {0} with {1} and {2}".format(
            func.__name__, args, kwargs))
        return_value = func(*args, **kwargs)
        print("Executed {0} in {1}ms".format(
            func.__name__, time.time() - now))
        return return_value
    return wrapper

def test1(a,b,c):
    print("\ttest1 called")

def test2(a,b):
    print("\ttest2 called")

def test3(a,b):
    print("\ttest3 called")
    time.sleep(1)

test1 = log_calls(test1)
test2 = log_calls(test2)
test3 = log_calls(test3)

test1(1,2,3)
test2(4,b=5)
test3(6,7)
```

This decorator function is very similar to the example we explored earlier; in those cases, the decorator took a socket-like object and created a socket-like object. This time, our decorator takes a function object and returns a new function object. This code is comprised of three separate tasks:

- A function, `log_calls` accepts a function.
- The function defines (internally) a new function, named `wrapper`, that does some extra calculations before calling the original function.
- This new function is returned, to replace the original function.

Three sample functions demonstrate the decorator in use. The third one even includes a sleep call to demonstrate the timing test. We pass each function into the decorator, which returns a new function. We assign this new function to the original variable name, effectively replacing the original function with a decorated one.

This syntax allows us to build up decorated function objects dynamically as we did with the socket example; if we had not replaced the name, we could even have kept decorated and non-decorated versions for different situations.

Often these decorators are general modifications that are applied permanently to different functions. In this situation, Python supports a special syntax to apply the decorator at the time the function is defined. We first saw it in action with the property decorator. Instead of applying the decorator function after the method definition, we can use the `@decorator` syntax to do it all at once:

```python
@log_calls
def test1(a,b,c):
    print("\ttest1 called")
```

The primary benefit of this syntax is that we can easily see that the function has been decorated at the time it is defined. If the decorator is applied later, someone reviewing the code may miss that the function has been altered at all. Answering a question like, "Why is my program logging function calls to the console?" can become much more difficult! Obviously, the syntax can only be applied to functions we define. If we need to decorate functions we didn't write, we have to use the earlier syntax.

There is more to the decorator syntax than we've seen here. We don't have room to cover the advanced topics here, so check the Python reference manual or other tutorials for more information. Decorators can be created as callable objects, not just functions that return functions. Classes can also be decorated; in that case, the decorator returns a new class instead of a new function. Finally, decorators can take arguments to customize them on a per-application basis.

Observer pattern

The observer pattern is useful for state monitoring and event handling situations. This pattern ensures a single core object can be monitored by an unknown, possibly expanding, array of "observer" objects. Whenever a value on the core object changes, it lets all the observer objects know that a change has occurred, by calling an `update()` method. Each observer may be responsible for different tasks whenever the core object changes; the core object doesn't know or care what those tasks are, and the observers don't typically know or care what other observers are doing. Here it is in UML:

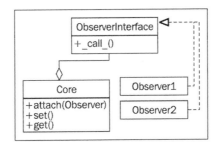

Observer example

The observer pattern could be useful in a redundant backup system. We can write a core object that maintains certain values, and then have one or more observers create serialized copies of that object. These copies might be stored in a database, on a remote host, or in a local file, for example. Let's implement the core object using properties:

```python
class Inventory:
    def __init__(self):
        self.observers = []
        self._product = None
        self._quantity = 0

    def attach(self, observer):
        self.observers.append(observer)

    @property
    def product(self):
        return self._product
    @product.setter
```

```
    def product(self, value):
        self._product = value
        self._update_observers()

    @property
    def quantity(self):
        return self._quantity
    @quantity.setter
    def quantity(self, value):
        self._quantity = value
        self._update_observers()

    def _update_observers(self):
        for observer in self.observers:
            observer()
```

This object has two properties that, when set, call the _update_observers method on itself. All this method does is loop over the available observers and let each one know that something has changed. In this case, we call the observer object directly; the object will have to implement __call__ to process the update. This would not be possible in many object-oriented programming languages, but it's a useful shortcut in Python that can help make our code more readable.

Now let's implement a simple observer object; this one will just print out some state to the console:

```
class ConsoleObserver:
    def __init__(self, inventory):
        self.inventory = inventory

    def __call__(self):
        print(self.inventory.product)
        print(self.inventory.quantity)
```

There's nothing terribly exciting here; the observed object is set up in the initializer, and when the observer is called, we do "something." We can test the observer in an interactive console:

```
>>> i = Inventory()
>>> c = ConsoleObserver(i)
>>> i.attach(c)
>>> i.product = "Widget"
Widget
0
>>> i.quantity = 5
Widget
5
```

After attaching the observer to the inventory object, whenever we change one of the two observed properties, the observer is called and its action is invoked. We can even add two different observer instances:

```
>>> i = Inventory()
>>> c1 = ConsoleObserver(i)
>>> c2 = ConsoleObserver(i)
>>> i.attach(c1)
>>> i.attach(c2)
>>> i.product = "Gadget"
Gadget
0
Gadget
0
```

This time when we change the product, there are two sets of output, one for each observer. The key idea here is that we can easily add totally different types of observers that back up the data in a file, database, or internet application at the same time.

The observer pattern detaches the code being observed from the code doing the observing. If we were not using this pattern, we would have had to put code in each of the properties to handle the different cases that might come up; logging to the console, updating a database or file, and so on. The code for each of these tasks would all be mixed in with the observed object. Maintaining it would be a nightmare, and adding new monitoring functionality at a later date would be painful.

Strategy pattern

The strategy pattern is a common demonstration of abstraction in object-oriented programming. The pattern implements different solutions to a single problem each in a different object. The client code can then choose the most appropriate implementation dynamically at runtime.

Typically, different algorithms have different trade-offs; one might be faster than another, but uses a lot more memory, while a third algorithm may be most suitable when multiple CPUs are present or a distributed system is provided. Here is the strategy pattern in UML:

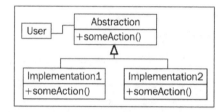

The **User** code connecting to the strategy pattern simply needs to know that it is dealing with the **Abstraction** interface. The actual implementation chosen will perform the same task, but in possibly very different ways; either way, the interface is identical.

Strategy example

The canonical example of the strategy pattern is sort routines; over the years, numerous algorithms have been invented for sorting a collection of objects; quick sort, merge sort, and heap sort are all fast sort algorithms with different features, each useful in its own right, depending on the size and type of inputs, how out of order they are, and the requirements of the system.

If we have client code that needs to sort a collection, we could pass it to an object with a sort() method. This object may be a QuickSorter or a MergeSorter object; but the result will be the same in either case: a sorted list. The strategy used to do the sorting is abstracted from the calling code, making it modular and replaceable.

Of course, in Python, we typically just call the sorted function or list.sort method and trust that it will do the sorting in a near-optimal fashion. So we really need to look at a better example, don't we?

Let's consider a desktop wallpaper manager. For starters, the strategy pattern might be used to load different image formats (JPEG, GIF, PNG, TIFF) from the hard drive and then display them. There are libraries that take care of this transparently for us, however, so let's move a bit higher up the stack. When an image is displayed on a desktop background, it can be adjusted to the screen size in different ways. For example, assuming the image is smaller than the screen, it can be tiled across the screen, centered on it, or scaled to fit. There are other, more complicated, strategies that can be used as well, such as scaling to the maximum height or width, combining it with a solid, semi-transparent, or gradient background color, or other manipulations. While we may want to add these strategies later, let's start with the basic ones.

Our strategy objects will take two inputs; the image to be displayed, and a tuple of the width and height of the screen. They will return a new image the size of the screen, with the image manipulated to fit according to the given strategy.

```python
from pygame import image
from pygame.transform import scale
from pygame import Surface

class TiledStrategy:
    def make_background(self, img_file, desktop_size):
        in_img = image.load(img_file)
        out_img = Surface(desktop_size)
        for x in range((out_img.get_width(
            ) // in_img.get_width()) + 1):
            for y in range((out_img.get_height(
                ) // in_img.get_height()) + 1):
                out_img.blit(in_img, (in_img.get_width() * x,
                    in_img.get_height() * y))
        return out_img

class CenteredStrategy:
    def make_background(self, img_file, desktop_size):
        in_img = image.load(img_file)
        out_img = Surface(desktop_size)
        out_img.fill((0,0,0))
        left = (out_img.get_width() - in_img.get_width()) / 2
        top = (out_img.get_height() - in_img.get_height()) / 2
        out_img.blit(in_img, (left, top))
        return out_img

class ScaledStrategy:
    def make_background(self, img_file, desktop_size):
        in_img = image.load(img_file)
        return scale(in_img, desktop_size)
```

Here we have three strategies, each using `pygame` to perform their task. Individual strategies have a `make_background` method that accepts the same set of parameters. Once selected, the appropriate strategy can be called to create a correctly sized version of the desktop image. `TiledStrategy` loops over the number of input images that would fit in the width and height of the image and copies it into each location, repeatedly. `CenteredStrategy` figures out how much space needs to be left on the four edges of the image to center it. `ScaledStrategy` simply forces the image to the output size (ignoring aspect ratio).

Consider how switching between these options would be implemented without the strategy pattern. We'd need to put all the code inside one great big method and use an awkward `if` statement to select the expected one. Every time we wanted to add a new strategy, we'd have to make the method even more ungainly.

Strategy in Python

The above canonical implementation of the strategy pattern, while very common in most object-oriented libraries, is rarely seen in Python programming. Can you see why?

That's right: these classes each represent objects that do nothing but provide a single function. We could just as easily call that function __call__ and make the object callable directly. Since there is no other data associated with the object, we can actually create a set of top-level functions and pass them around instead.

Opponents of design pattern philosophy will therefore say, "because Python has first-class functions, the strategy pattern is unnecessary". In truth, Python's first-class functions allow us to implement the strategy pattern in a more straightforward way. Knowing the pattern exists can still help us choose a correct design for our program; we simply implement it using different syntax. The strategy pattern, or a top-level function implementation of it, should be used when we need to allow client code or the end user to select between multiple implementations of the same interface.

State pattern

State pattern is structurally similar to strategy pattern, but its intent and purpose are very different. The goal of the state pattern is to represent state-transition systems: systems where it is obvious that an object can be in a specific state, and that certain activities may drive it to a different state.

To make this work, we need a manager, or context class that provides an interface for switching states. Internally, this class contains a pointer to the current state; each state knows what other states it is allowed to be in and will transition to those states depending on actions invoked upon it.

So we have two types of classes, the context class and multiple state classes. The context class maintains the current state, and forwards actions to the state classes. The state classes are typically hidden from any other objects that are calling the context; it acts like a black box that happens to perform state management internally. Here's how it looks in UML:

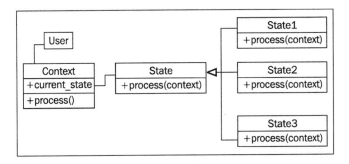

State example

To illustrate the state pattern, let's build an XML parsing tool. The context class will be the parser itself. It will take a string as input and place the tool in an initial parsing state. The various parsing states will eat characters, looking for a specific value, and when that value is found, change to a different state. The goal is to create a tree of node objects for each tag and its contents. To keep things manageable, we'll parse only a subset of XML; tags and tag names. We won't be able to handle attributes on tags. It will parse text content of tags, but won't attempt to parse "mixed" content, which has tags inside of text. Here is an example "simplified XML" file that we'll be able to parse:

```
<book>
    <author>Dusty Phillips</author>
    <publisher>Packt Publishing</publisher>
    <title>Python 3 Object Oriented Programming</title>
    <content>
        <chapter>
            <number>1</number>
            <title>Object Oriented Design</title>
        </chapter>
```

```
        <chapter>
            <number>2</number>
            <title>Objects In Python</title>
        </chapter>
    </content>
</book>
```

Before we look at the states and the parser, let's consider the output of this program. We know we want a tree of `Node` objects, but what does a `Node` look like? Well, clearly it'll need to know the name of the tag it is parsing, and since it's a tree, it should probably maintain a pointer to the parent node and a list of the node's children in order. Some nodes have a text value, but not all of them. Let's look at the `Node` class first:

```python
class Node:
    def __init__(self, tag_name, parent=None):
        self.parent = parent
        self.tag_name = tag_name
        self.children = []
        self.text=""

    def __str__(self):
        if self.text:
            return self.tag_name + ": " + self.text
        else:
            return self.tag_name
```

This class sets default attribute values upon initialization. The `__str__` method is supplied to help visualize the tree structure when we're finished.

Now, looking at the example document, we need to consider what states our parser can be in. Clearly it's going to start in a state where no nodes have yet been processed. We'll need a state for processing opening tags and closing tags. And when we're inside a tag with text contents, we'll have to process that as a separate state, too.

Switching states can be tricky; how do we know if the next node is an opening tag, a closing tag, or a text node.? We could put a little logic in each state to work that out, but it actually makes more sense to create a new state whose sole purpose is figuring out which state we'll be switching to next. If we call this transition state **ChildNode**, we end up with the following states:

- FirstTag
- ChildNode
- OpenTag
- CloseTag
- Text

The **FirstTag** state will switch to **ChildNode**, which is responsible for deciding which of the other three states to switch to; when those states are finished, they'll switch back to **ChildNode**. The following state-transition diagram shows the available state changes:

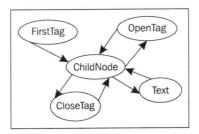

The states are responsible for taking "what's left of the string", processing as much of it as they know what to do with, and then telling the parser to take care of the rest of it. Let's construct the `Parser` class first:

```
class Parser:
    def __init__(self, parse_string):
        self.parse_string = parse_string
        self.root = None
        self.current_node = None

        self.state = FirstTag()

    def process(self, remaining_string):
        remaining = self.state.process(remaining_string, self)
        if remaining:
            self.process(remaining)

    def start(self):
        self.process(self.parse_string)
```

The initializer sets up a few variables on the class that the individual states will access. The `parse_string` is the text that we are trying to parse. The `root` node is the "top" node in the XML structure. The `current_node` is the one that we are currently adding children to.

The important feature of this parser is the `process` method, which accepts the remaining string, and passes it off to the current state. The parser (the `self` argument) is also passed into the state's process method so that the state can manipulate it. The state is expected to return the remainder of the unparsed string when it is finished processing. The parser then recursively calls the `process` method on this remaining string to construct the rest of the tree.

Now, let's have a look at the `FirstTag` state:

```python
class FirstTag:
    def process(self, remaining_string, parser):
        i_start_tag = remaining_string.find('<')
        i_end_tag = remaining_string.find('>')
        tag_name = remaining_string[i_start_tag+1:i_end_tag]
        root = Node(tag_name)
        parser.root = parser.current_node = root
        parser.state = ChildNode()
        return remaining_string[i_end_tag+1:]
```

This state finds the index (the `i_` stands for index) of the opening and closing angle brackets on the first tag. You may think this state is unnecessary, since XML requires that there be no text before an opening tag. However, there may be whitespace that needs to be consumed; this is why we search for the opening angle bracket instead of assuming it is the first character in the document. Note that this code is assuming a valid input file. A proper implementation would be religiously testing for invalid input, and would attempt to recover or display a very descriptive error message.

The method extracts the name of the tag and assigns it to the root node of the parser. It also assigns it as the `current_node`, since that's the one we'll be adding children to next.

Then comes the important part; the method changes the current state on the parser object to a `ChildNode` state. It then returns the remainder of the string (after the opening tag) to allow it to be processed.

The `ChildNode` state, which seems quite complicated, turns out to require nothing but a simple conditional:

```python
class ChildNode:
    def process(self, remaining_string, parser):
        stripped = remaining_string.strip()
        if stripped.startswith("</"):
            parser.state = CloseTag()
        elif stripped.startswith("<"):
            parser.state = OpenTag()
        else:
            parser.state = TextNode()
        return stripped
```

The `strip()` call removes whitespace from the string. Then the parser determines if the next item is an opening or closing tag, or a string of text. Depending on which possibility occurs, it sets the parser to a particular state, and then tells it to parse the remainder of the string.

The `OpenTag` state is similar to the `FirstTag` state, except that it adds the newly created node to the previous `current_node` object's `children` and sets it as the new `current_node`. It places the processor back in the `ChildNode` state before continuing:

```
class OpenTag:
    def process(self, remaining_string, parser):
        i_start_tag = remaining_string.find('<')
        i_end_tag = remaining_string.find('>')
        tag_name = remaining_string[i_start_tag+1:i_end_tag]
        node = Node(tag_name, parser.current_node)
        parser.current_node.children.append(node)
        parser.current_node = node
        parser.state = ChildNode()
        return remaining_string[i_end_tag+1:]
```

`CloseTag` basically does the opposite; it sets the parser's `current_node` back to the parent node so any further children in the outside tag can be added to it:

```
class CloseTag:
    def process(self, remaining_string, parser):
        i_start_tag = remaining_string.find('<')
        i_end_tag = remaining_string.find('>')
        assert remaining_string[i_start_tag+1] == "/"
        tag_name = remaining_string[i_start_tag+2:i_end_tag]
        assert tag_name == parser.current_node.tag_name
        parser.current_node = parser.current_node.parent
        parser.state = ChildNode()
        return remaining_string[i_end_tag+1:].strip()
```

The two `assert` statements help ensure that the parse strings are consistent. The `if` statement at the end of the method simply ensures that the processor terminates when it is finished. If the parent of a node is `None`, it means that we are working on the root node.

Finally, the `TextNode` state very simply extracts the text before the next close tag and sets it as a value on the current node:

```
class TextNode:
    def process(self, remaining_string, parser):
        i_start_tag = remaining_string.find('<')
        text = remaining_string[:i_start_tag]
```

```
parser.current_node.text = text
parser.state = ChildNode()
return remaining_string[i_start_tag:]
```

Now we just have to set up the initial state on the parser object we created. The initial state is a `FirstTag` object, so just add the following to the __init__ method:

```
self.state = FirstTag()
```

To test the class, let's add a main script that opens an file from the command line, parses it, and prints the nodes:

```
if __name__ == "__main__":
    import sys
    with open(sys.argv[1]) as file:
        contents = file.read()
        p = Parser(contents)
        p.start()

        nodes = [p.root]
        while nodes:
            node = nodes.pop(0)
            print(node)
            nodes = node.children + nodes
```

All it does is open the file, load the contents, and parse them. Then it prints each node and its children in order. The __str__ method we originally added on the node class takes care of formatting the nodes for printing. If we run the script on the earlier example, it outputs the tree as follows:

```
book
author: Dusty Phillips
publisher: Packt Publishing
title: Python 3 Object Oriented Programming
content
chapter
number: 1
title: Object Oriented Design
chapter
number: 2
title: Objects In Python
```

Comparing this to the original simplified XML document tells us the parser is working.

State versus strategy

State pattern looks very similar to strategy pattern, indeed the UML diagrams for the two are identical. The implementation, too, is identical; we could even have written our states as first-class functions instead of wrapping them in objects, as was suggested for strategy.

While the two patterns have identical structures, their purposes are very different. The strategy pattern is used to choose an algorithm at runtime; generally, only one of those algorithms is going to be chosen for a particular use case. The state pattern, on the other hand is designed to allow switching between different states dynamically, as some process evolves. In code, the primary difference is that the strategy pattern is not typically aware of other strategy objects. In the state pattern, either the state or the context needs to know which other states that it can switch to.

Singleton pattern

The singleton pattern is one of the most controversial patterns; many have accused it of being an "anti-pattern"; a pattern that should be avoided, not promoted. In Python, if someone is using the singleton pattern, they're almost certainly doing something wrong, probably because they're coming from a more restrictive programming language.

So why discuss it at all? Singleton is one of the most famous of all design patterns. It is very useful in overly object-oriented languages, and is a vital part of object-oriented programming. Finally, the idea behind singleton is useful, even if we implement that idea in a totally different way in Python.

The basic idea behind the singleton pattern is to allow exactly one instance of a certain object to exist. Typically, this object is a sort of manager class like those we discussed in *Chapter 5*. Such objects often need to be referenced by a wide variety of other objects, and passing references to the manager object around to the methods and constructors that need them can make code hard to read.

Instead, when a singleton is used, the separate objects request the single instance of the manager object from the class, so a reference to it does not need to be passed around. The UML diagram doesn't fully describe it, but here it is for completeness:

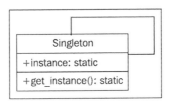

In most programming environments, singletons are enforced by making the constructor private (so no-one can create additional instances of it) and then providing a static method to retrieve the single instance. This method will create a new instance the first time it is called, and then return that same instance whenever it is called again.

Singleton implementation

Python doesn't have private constructors, but for this purpose, it has something even better. We can use the __new__ class method to ensure that only one instance is ever created:

```python
class OneOnly:
    _singleton = None
    def __new__(cls, *args, **kwargs):
        if not cls._singleton:
            cls._singleton = super(OneOnly, cls
                ).__new__(cls, *args, **kwargs)
        return cls._singleton
```

When __new__ is called, it normally constructs a new instance of that class. When we override it, we first check if our singleton instance has been created; if not, we create it using a super call. Thus, whenever we call the constructor on OneOnly, we always get the exact same instance:

```python
>>> o1 = OneOnly()
>>> o2 = OneOnly()
>>> o1 == o2
True
>>> o1
<__main__.OneOnly object at 0xb71c008c>
>>> o2
<__main__.OneOnly object at 0xb71c008c>
```

The two objects are equal and located at the same address; they are the same object. This particular implementation isn't very transparent, since it's not obvious that a singleton object has been created. Whenever we call a constructor, we expect a new instance of that object; in this case we do not get that. Perhaps, good docstrings on the class could alleviate this problem if we really think we need a singleton.

But we don't need it. Python coders frown on forcing the users of their code into a specific mindset. We may think only one instance of a class will ever be required, but other programmers may have different ideas. Singletons can interfere with distributed computing, parallel programming, and automated testing, for example. In all those cases it can be very useful to have multiple or alternative instances of a specific object, even though "normal' operation may never require one.

Module variables can mimic singletons

Normally, in Python, the singleton pattern can be sufficiently mimicked by using module-level variables. It's not as "safe" as a singleton in that people could reassign those variables at any time, but like our discussion of private variables in *Chapter 2*, this is acceptable in Python. If someone has a valid reason to change those variables, why should we stop them? It also doesn't stop people from instantiating multiple instances of the object, but again, if they have a valid reason to do so, why interfere?

Ideally, we should give them a mechanism to get access to the "default singleton" value, while also allowing them to create other instances if they need them. While, technically, it is not a singleton at all, it provides the most Pythonic mechanism for behaving **like** a singleton.

To use module-level variables instead of a singleton, we simply instantiate an instance of the class after we've defined it. We can improve our state pattern to use singletons. Instead of creating a new object every time we change states, we can create a module-level variable that is always accessible:

```python
class FirstTag:
    def process(self, remaining_string, parser):
        i_start_tag = remaining_string.find('<')
        i_end_tag = remaining_string.find('>')
        tag_name = remaining_string[i_start_tag+1:i_end_tag]
        root = Node(tag_name)
        parser.root = parser.current_node = root
        parser.state = child_node
        return remaining_string[i_end_tag+1:]


class ChildNode:
    def process(self, remaining_string, parser):
        stripped = remaining_string.strip()
        if stripped.startswith("</"):
            parser.state = close_tag
        elif stripped.startswith("<"):
            parser.state = open_tag
        else:
```

```
                    parser.state = text_node
            return stripped

    class OpenTag:
        def process(self, remaining_string, parser):
            i_start_tag = remaining_string.find('<')
            i_end_tag = remaining_string.find('>')
            tag_name = remaining_string[i_start_tag+1:i_end_tag]
            node = Node(tag_name, parser.current_node)
            parser.current_node.children.append(node)
            parser.current_node = node
            parser.state = child_node
            return remaining_string[i_end_tag+1:]

    class TextNode:
        def process(self, remaining_string, parser):
            i_start_tag = remaining_string.find('<')
            text = remaining_string[:i_start_tag]
            parser.current_node.text = text
            parser.state = child_node
            return remaining_string[i_start_tag:]

    class CloseTag:
        def process(self, remaining_string, parser):
            i_start_tag = remaining_string.find('<')
            i_end_tag = remaining_string.find('>')
            assert remaining_string[i_start_tag+1] == "/"
            tag_name = remaining_string[i_start_tag+2:i_end_tag]
            assert tag_name == parser.current_node.tag_name
            parser.current_node = parser.current_node.parent
            parser.state = child_node
            return remaining_string[i_end_tag+1:].strip()

first_tag = FirstTag()
child_node = ChildNode()
text_node = TextNode()
open_tag = OpenTag()
close_tag = CloseTag()
```

All we've done is create instances of the various state classes that can be reused. Notice how we can access these module variables inside the classes, even before the variables have been defined? This is because the code inside the classes is not executed until the method is called, and by that point, the entire module will have been defined.

The difference in this example is that instead of wasting memory creating a bunch of new instances that must be garbage collected, we are reusing a single state object for each state. Even if multiple parsers are running at once, only these state classes need to be used. Of course, if someone wants to create their own instances, they can. So it's not a true singleton, but convention can strongly suggest that a singleton paradigm be used. If someone wants to mess with that paradigm... well, they'll have to deal with the consequences, beneficial or detrimental.

When we originally created the state-based parser, you may have wondered why we didn't pass the parser object to `__init__` on each individual state, instead of passing it into the process method as we did. The state could then have been referenced as `self.parser`. This is a perfectly valid implementation of the state pattern, but it would not have allowed leveraging the singleton pattern. If the state objects maintain a reference to the parser, then they cannot be used simultaneously to reference other parsers.

The thing to remember is that these are two very different patterns with different purposes; the fact that singleton's purpose may be useful for implementing the state pattern does not, in any way, mean the two patterns are related.

Template pattern

The template pattern is useful for removing duplicate code; it's an implementation to support the "Don't Repeat Yourself" principle we discussed in *Chapter 5*. It is designed for situations where we have several different tasks to accomplish that have some, but not all, steps in common. The common steps are implemented in a base class, and the different steps are overridden in subclasses to provide custom behavior. In some ways, it's like a generalized strategy pattern, except similar sections of the algorithms are shared using a base class. Here it is in UML format:

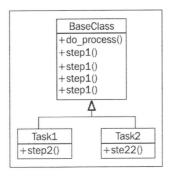

Template example

Let's create a car sales reporter as an example. We can store records of sales in an SQLite database table. SQLite is a simple file-based database engine that allows us to store records using SQL syntax. Python 3 includes SQLite in its standard library, so there is no setup involved.

We have two common tasks we need to perform:

- Select all sales of new vehicles and output them to the screen in a comma-delimited format
- Output a comma-delimited list of all salespeople with their gross sales and save it to a file that can be imported to a spreadsheet

These seem like quite different tasks, but they have some common features. In both cases, we need to perform the following steps:

1. Connect to the database.
2. Construct a query for new vehicles or gross sales.
3. Issue the query.
4. Format the results into a comma-delimited string.
5. Output the data to a file or e-mail.

The query construction and output steps are different for the two tasks, but the other steps are identical for both. We can use the template pattern to put the common steps in a base class, and the varying steps in two subclasses.

Before we start, let's create a database and put some sample data in it, using a few lines of SQL:

```python
import sqlite3

conn = sqlite3.connect("sales.db")

conn.execute("CREATE TABLE Sales (salesperson text, "
        "amt currency, year integer, model text, new boolean)")
conn.execute("INSERT INTO Sales values"
        " ('Tim', 16000, 2010, 'Honda Fit', 'true')")
conn.execute("INSERT INTO Sales values"
        " ('Tim', 9000, 2006, 'Ford Focus', 'false')")
conn.execute("INSERT INTO Sales values"
        " ('Gayle', 8000, 2004, 'Dodge Neon', 'false')")
conn.execute("INSERT INTO Sales values"
        " ('Gayle', 28000, 2009, 'Ford Mustang', 'true')")
```

```
conn.execute("INSERT INTO Sales values"
        " ('Gayle', 50000, 2010, 'Lincoln Navigator', 'true')")
conn.execute("INSERT INTO Sales values"
        " ('Don', 20000, 2008, 'Toyota Prius', 'false')")
conn.commit()
conn.close()
```

Hopefully you can see what's going on here even if you don't know SQL; we've created a table to hold the data, and used six insert statements to add sales records. The data is stored in a file named `sales.db`. Now we have a sample we can work with in developing our template pattern.

Since we've already outlined the steps that the template has to perform, we can start by defining the base class that contains the steps. Each step gets its own method (to make it easy to selectively override any one step), and we have one more all-encompassing method that calls the steps in turn. Without any method contents, here's how it might look:

```
class QueryTemplate:
    def connect(self):
        pass
    def construct_query(self):
        pass
    def do_query(self):
        pass
    def format_results(self):
        pass
    def output_results(self):
        pass

    def process_format(self):
        self.connect()
        self.construct_query()
        self.do_query()
        self.format_results()
        self.output_results()
```

The `process_format` method is the primary method to be called by an outside client. It ensures each step is executed in order, but it does not care if that step is implemented in this class or in a subclass. For our examples, we know that three methods are going to be identical between our two classes:

```python
import sqlite3

class QueryTemplate:
    def connect(self):
        self.conn = sqlite3.connect("sales.db")

    def construct_query(self):
        raise NotImplementedError()

    def do_query(self):
        results = self.conn.execute(self.query)
        self.results = results.fetchall()

    def format_results(self):
        output = []
        for row in self.results:
            row =[str(i) for i in row]
            output.append(", ".join(row))
        self.formatted_results = "\n".join(output)

    def output_results(self):
        raise NotImplementedError()
```

To help with implementing subclasses, the two methods that are not specified raise `NotImplementedError`. This is a common way to specify abstract interfaces in Python. The methods could have empty implementations (with `pass`), or could even be fully unspecified. Raising `NotImplementedError`, however, helps the programmer understand that the class is meant to be subclassed and these methods overridden; empty methods or methods that simply do not exist are harder to identify as needing to be implemented and to debug if we forget to implement them.

Now we have a template class that takes care of the boring details, but is flexible enough to allow the execution and formatting of a wide variety of queries. The best part is, if we ever want to change our database engine from SQLite to another database engine (such as py-postgresql), we only have to do it here, in this template class, and don't have to touch the two (or two hundred) subclasses we've written.

Let's have a look at the concrete classes now:

```
import datetime
class NewVehiclesQuery(QueryTemplate):
    def construct_query(self):
        self.query = "select * from Sales where new='true'"

    def output_results(self):
        print(self.formatted_results)

class UserGrossQuery(QueryTemplate):
    def construct_query(self):
        self.query = ("select salesperson, sum(amt) " +
        " from Sales group by salesperson")

    def output_results(self):
        filename = "gross_sales_{0}".format(
                datetime.date.today().strftime("%Y%m%d")
                )
        with open(filename, 'w') as outfile:
            outfile.write(self.formatted_results)
```

These two classes are actually pretty short, considering what they're doing: connecting to a database, executing a query, formatting the results, and outputting them. The superclass takes care of the repetitive work, but lets us easily specify those steps that vary between tasks. Further, we can also easily change steps that are provided in the base class. For example, if we wanted to output something other than a comma-delimited string (for example: an HTML report to be uploaded to a website), we can still override `format_results`.

Exercises

While writing this chapter, I discovered that it can be very difficult, and extremely educational to come up with good examples where specific design patterns should be used. Instead of going over current or old projects to see where you can apply these patterns, as I've suggested in previous chapters, think about the patterns and different situations where they might come up. Try to think outside your own experiences. If your current projects are in the banking business, consider how you'd apply these design patterns in a retail or point-of-sale application. If you normally write web applications, think about using design patterns while writing a compiler.

Start with the iterator pattern. We've been looking at iterators all through this book, including the special comprehension and generator syntaxes. Consider places where you'd want to implement the iterator pattern from scratch; what objects would you want to implement __iter__ or __next__ on?

Look at the decorator pattern and come up with some good examples of when to apply it. Focus on the pattern itself, not the Python syntax we discussed; it's a bit more general than the actual pattern. The special syntax for decorators is, however, something you might want to look for places to apply in existing projects too.

What are some good areas to use the observer pattern? Why? Think about not only how you'd apply the pattern, but how you would implement the same task without using observer? What do you gain, or lose, by choosing to use it?

Consider the difference between the strategy and state patterns. Implementation-wise, they look very similar, yet they have different purposes. Can you think of cases where the patterns could be interchanged? Would it be reasonable to redesign a state-based system to use strategy instead, or vice-versa? How much different would the design actually be?

The template pattern is such an obvious application of inheritance to reduce duplicate code that you may have used it before, without knowing its name. Try to think of at least half a dozen different scenarios where it would be useful. If you can do that, you'll be finding places for it in your daily coding all the time.

Summary

In this chapter, we learned that design patterns are useful abstractions that provide "best practice" solutions for common programming problems. We understood that design patterns in Python, due to its dynamic nature and built-in syntax, can look very different from their usual renditions in other languages. We discussed several patterns in detail, with examples, UML diagrams and a discussion of the differences between Python and statically typed object-oriented languages. We covered:

- What design patterns are
- The iterator pattern
- The decorator pattern
- The observer pattern
- The strategy and state patterns
- The template pattern

In the next chapter, we'll discuss several more useful design patterns and their application in Python.

9
Python Design Patterns II

This chapter carries on from the previous chapter by introducing several more design patterns. Once again, we'll cover the canonical examples as well as any common alternative implementations in Python. We'll be discussing:

- The adapter pattern
- The facade pattern
- Lazy initialization and the flyweight pattern
- The command pattern
- The abstract factory pattern
- The composition pattern

Adapter pattern

Unlike most of the patterns we reviewed in *Chapter 8*, the adapter pattern is designed to interact with existing code. We would not design a brand new set of objects that implement the adapter pattern. Adapters are used to allow two pre-existing objects to work together, even if their interfaces are not compatible. Like the keyboard adapters that allow USB keyboards to be plugged into PS/2 ports, an adapter object sits between two different interfaces, translating between them on the fly. The adapter object's sole purpose is to perform this translating job; translating may entail a variety of tasks, such as converting arguments to a different format, rearranging the order of arguments, calling a differently named method, or supplying default arguments.

In structure, the adapter pattern is similar to a simplified decorator pattern. Decorators typically provide the same interface that they replace, whereas adapters map between two different interfaces. Here it is in UML form:

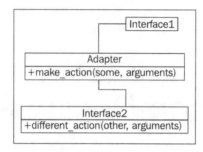

Here, **Interface1** is expecting to call a method called **make_action(some, arguments)**. We already have this perfect **Interface2** class that does everything we want (and to avoid duplication, we don't want to rewrite it!), but it provides a method called **different_action(other, arguments)** instead. The **Adapter** class implements the **make_action** interface and maps the arguments to the existing interface.

The advantage here is that the code that maps from one interface to another is all in one place. The alternative would be to translate it directly in multiple places whenever we need to access this code.

For example, imagine we have the following pre-existing class, which takes a string date in the format "YYYY-MM-DD" and calculates a person's age on that day:

```python
class AgeCalculator:
    def __init__(self, birthday):
        self.year, self.month, self.day = (
                int(x) for x in birthday.split('-'))

    def calculate_age(self, date):
        year, month, day = (
                int(x) for x in date.split('-'))
        age = year - self.year
        if (month,day) < (self.month,self.day):
            age -= 1
        return age
```

This is a pretty simple class that does what it's supposed to do. But we have to wonder what the programmer was thinking, using a specifically formatted string instead of using Python's incredibly useful built-in `datetime` library. Most programs we write are going to be interacting with `datetime` objects, not strings.

We have several options to address this scenario; we could rewrite the class to accept `datetime` objects, which would probably be more accurate anyway. But if this class has been provided by a third party and we don't know what its internals are, or we simply aren't allowed to change them, we need to try something else. We could use the class as it is, and whenever we want to calculate the age on a `datetime.date` object, we could call `datetime.date.strftime('%Y-%m-%d')` to convert it to the proper format. But that conversion would be happening in a lot of places, and worse, if we mistyped the `%m` as `%M` it would give us the current instead of the entered month! Imagine if you wrote that in a dozen different places only to have to go back and change it when you realized your mistake. It's not maintainable code, and it breaks the DRY principle.

Or, we can write an adapter that allows a normal date to be plugged into a normal `AgeCalculator`:

```
import datetime
class DateAgeAdapter:
    def _str_date(self, date):
        return date.strftime("%Y-%m-%d")

    def __init__(self, birthday):
        birthday = self._str_date(birthday)
        self.calculator = AgeCalculator(birthday)

    def get_age(self, date):
        date = self._str_date(date)
        return self.calculator.calculate_age(date)
```

This adapter converts `datetime.date` and `datetime.time` (they have the same interface to `strftime`) into a string that our original `AgeCalculator` can use. Now we can use the original code with our new interface. I changed the method signature to `get_age` to demonstrate that the calling interface may also be looking for a different method name, not just a different type of argument.

Creating a class as an adapter is the usual way to implement this as a pattern, but, as usual, there are other ways to do it. Inheritance and multiple inheritance can be used to add functionality to a class. For example, we could add an adapter on the `date` class so that it works with the original `AgeCalculator`:

```
import datetime
class AgeableDate(datetime.date):
    def split(self, char):
        return self.year, self.month, self.day
```

It's code like this that makes one wonder if Python should even be legal. All we've done here is add a `split` method that takes a single argument (which we ignore) and returns a tuple of year, month, day. This works flawlessly with our `AgeCalculator`, because that code calls `strip` on a specially formatted string, and `strip`, in that case returns a tuple of year, month, day. The `AgeCalculator` code only cares if `strip` exists and returns acceptable values; it doesn't care if we really passed in a string. It really works:

```
>>> bd = AgeableDate(1975, 6, 14)
>>> today = AgeableDate.today()
>>> today
AgeableDate(2010, 2, 23)
>>> a = AgeCalculator(bd)
>>> a.calculate_age(today)
34
```

In this particular instance, such an adapter would be hard to maintain, as we'll soon forget why we needed to add a `strip` method to a `date` class. The method name is quite ambiguous. That can be the nature of adapters, but if we had created an adapter explicitly instead of using inheritance, it's more obvious what its purpose is.

Instead of inheritance, you can sometimes also use monkey-patching to add a method to an existing class. It won't work with the `datetime` object, as it won't allow attributes to be added at runtime, but in normal classes, we can just add a new method that provides the adapted interface that is required by calling code.

It can also be possible to use a function as an adapter; this doesn't really fit the adapter pattern properly, but often, you can simply pass data into a function and return it in the proper format for entry into another interface.

Facade pattern

The facade pattern is designed to provide a simple interface to a complex system of components. The objects in this system may need to be interacted with directly for complex tasks and interactions. Often, however, there is 'typical' usage for the system, and these complicated interactions aren't necessary in that common scenario. The facade pattern allows us to define a new object that wraps this typical usage of the system. Any code that wants to use the typical functionality can use the single object's simplified interface. If another project or part of the project finds this interface is too simple and needs to access more complicated functionality, it is still able to interact with the system directly. The UML diagram for the facade pattern is really dependent on the subsystem, but in a cloudy way, it looks like this:

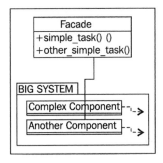

Facade is, in many ways, like adapter. The primary difference is that the facade is trying to abstract a simpler interface out of a complex system; the adapter is only trying to map one existing interface to another.

Let's write a simple facade for an e-mail application. The low-level library for sending e-mail in Python, as we saw in *Chapter 7*, is quite complicated. The two libraries for receiving messages are even worse.

It would be nice to have a simple class that allows us to send a single e-mail, and list the e-mails currently in the inbox on an IMAP or POP3 connection. To keep our example short, we'll stick with IMAP and SMTP: two totally different subsystems that happen to deal with e-mail. Our facade will perform only two tasks; sending an e-mail to a specific address, and checking the inbox on an IMAP connection. It will make some common assumptions about the connection, such as the host for both SMTP and IMAP is the same machine, that the username and password for both is the same, and that they use standard ports. This will cover the case for many e-mail servers, but if a programmer needs more flexibility, they can always bypass the facade and access the two subsystems directly.

The class is initialized with the hostname of the e-mail server and a username and password to log in:

```python
import smtplib
import imaplib

class EmailFacade:
    def __init__(self, host, username, password):
        self.host = host
        self.username = username
        self.password = password
```

The `send_email` method simply formats the e-mail address and message and sends it using `smtplib`. This isn't a complicated task, but it requires quite a bit of fiddling to massage the "natural" input parameters that are passed into the facade to put them in the correct format for `smtplib` to send the message:

```python
def send_email(self, to_email, subject, message):
    if not "@" in username:
        from_email = "{0}@{1}".format(
                self.username, self.host)
    else:
        from_email = self.username
    message = ("From: {0}\r\n"
            "To: {1}\r\n"
            "Subject: {2}\r\n\r\n{3}").format(
                from_email,
                to_email,
                subject,
                message)

    smtp = smtplib.SMTP(self.host)
    smtp.login(self.username, self.password)
    smtp.sendmail(from_email, [to_email], message)
```

The `if` statement at the beginning of the method is catching whether or not the `username` is the entire from e-mail address or just the part on the left side of the @ symbol; different hosts treat the login details differently. Finally, the code to get the messages currently in the inbox is a ruddy mess; the IMAP protocol is painfully over-engineered, and the `imaplib` standard library is only a thin layer over the protocol:

```python
def get_inbox(self):
    mailbox = imaplib.IMAP4(self.host)
    mailbox.login(bytes(self.username, 'utf8'),
        bytes(self.password, 'utf8'))
    mailbox.select()
    x, data = mailbox.search(None, 'ALL')
    messages = []
    for num in data[0].split():
        x, message = mailbox.fetch(num, '(RFC822)')
        messages.append(message[0][1])
    return messages
```

Now, if we add all this together, we have a simple facade class that can send and receive messages in a fairly straightforward manner, much simpler than if we had to interact with the complex libraries directly.

Flyweight pattern

The flyweight pattern is a memory optimization pattern. Novice Python programmers tend to ignore memory optimization, assuming the built-in garbage collector will take care of them. This is often perfectly acceptable, but when developing larger applications with many related objects, paying attention to memory concerns can have a huge payoff.

In real life, the flyweight pattern is often implemented only after a program has demonstrated memory problems. It may make sense to design an optimal configuration from the beginning in some situations, but bear in mind that premature optimization is the most effective way of ensuring that your program is too complicated to maintain.

The basic idea behind the flyweight pattern is to ensure that objects that share a state can use the same memory for that shared state. Think of an inventory system for car sales. Each individual car has a specific serial number and is a specific color. But most of the details about that car are the same for all cars of a particular model. For example, the Honda Fit DX model is a bare-bones car with few features. The LX model has A/C, tilt, cruise, and power windows and locks. The Sport model has fancy wheels, a USB charger, and a spoiler. (I recently bought a Fit LX, which I love; that's why we're looking at a second car sales example in as many chapters!) Without the flyweight pattern, each individual car object would have to store a long list of which features it did and did not have. Considering the number of cars Honda sells in a year, this would add up to a huge amount of wasted memory. Using the flyweight pattern, we can instead have shared objects for the list of features associated with a model, and then simply reference that model, along with a serial number and color, for individual vehicles.

Let's have a look at the UML diagram for the flyweight pattern:

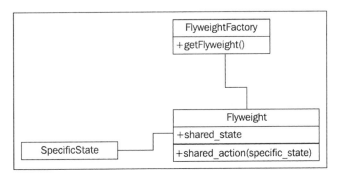

Each **Flyweight** has no specific state; any time it needs to perform an operation on **SpecificState**, that state needs to be passed into the **Flyweight** by the calling code. Traditionally, the factory that returns a flyweight is a separate object; its purpose is to return a flyweight for a given key identifying that flyweight. It works like the singleton pattern we discussed in *Chapter 8*; if the flyweight exists, we return it; otherwise we create a new one. In many languages, the factory is implemented, not as a separate object, but as a static method on the `Flyweight` class itself.

Both of these options work, but in Python, the flyweight factory is often implemented using that funky __new__ constructor, similar to what we did with the singleton pattern. Unlike singleton, which only needs to return one instance of the class, we need to be able to return different instances depending on the keys. We could store the items in a dictionary and look them up based on the key. This solution is problematic, however, because the item will remain in memory so long as it is in the dictionary. If we sold out of LX model Fits, the Fit flyweight is no longer necessary, yet it will still be in the dictionary. We could, of course, clean this up whenever we sell a car, but isn't that what a garbage collector is for?

The Python `weakref` module comes to our rescue. This module provides a `WeakValueDictionary` object, which basically allows us to store items in a dictionary without the garbage collector caring about them. If a value is in a weak referenced dictionary and there are no other references to that object stored anywhere (that is, we sold out of LX models), the garbage collector will eventually clean up for us.

Let's build the factory for our car flyweights first:

```python
import weakref

class CarModel:
    _models = weakref.WeakValueDictionary()

    def __new__(cls, model_name, *args, **kwargs):
        model = cls._models.get(model_name)
        if not model:
            model = super().__new__(cls)
            cls._models[model_name] = model

        return model
```

Basically, whenever we construct a new flyweight with a given name, we first look up that name in the weak referenced dictionary; if it exists, we return that model, if not, we create a new one. Either way, we know the __init__ method on the flyweight will be called every time, regardless of whether it is a new or existing object. Our __init__ can therefore look like this:

```
def __init__(self, model_name, air=False, tilt=False,
        cruise_control=False, power_locks=False,
        alloy_wheels=False, usb_charger=False):
    if not hasattr(self, "initted"):
        self.model_name = model_name
        self.air = air
        self.tilt = tilt
        self.cruise_control = cruise_control
        self.power_locks = power_locks
        self.alloy_wheels = alloy_wheels
        self.usb_charger = usb_charger
        self.initted=True
```

The `if` statement ensures that we only initialize the object the first time `__init__` is called. This means we can call the factory later with just the model name and get the same flyweight object back. However, because the flyweight will be garbage-collected if no external references to it exist, we have to be careful not to accidentally create a new flyweight with null values.

Let's add a method to our flyweight that hypothetically looks up a serial number on a specific model of vehicle, and determines if it has been involved in any accidents. This method needs access to the car's serial number, which varies from car to car; it cannot be stored with the flyweight. Therefore, this data must be passed into the method by the calling code:

```
def check_serial(self, serial_number):
    print("Sorry, we are unable to check "
            "the serial number {0} on the {1} "
            "at this time".format(
                serial_number, self.model_name))
```

We can define a class that stores the additional information, as well as a reference to the flyweight:

```
class Car:
    def __init__(self, model, color, serial):
        self.model = model
        self.color = color
        self.serial = serial

    def check_serial(self):
        return self.model.check_serial(self.serial)
```

We can also keep track of the available models as well as the individual cars on the lot:

```
>>> dx = CarModel("FIT DX")
>>> lx = CarModel("FIT LX", air=True, cruise_control=True,
... power_locks=True, tilt=True)
>>> car1 = Car(dx, "blue", "12345")
>>> car2 = Car(dx, "black", "12346")
>>> car3 = Car(lx, "red", "12347")
```

Now, let's demonstrate the weak referencing at work:

```
>>> id(lx)
3071620300
>>> del lx
>>> del car3
>>> import gc
>>> gc.collect()
0
>>> lx = CarModel("FIT LX", air=True, cruise_control=True,
... power_locks=True, tilt=True)
>>> id(lx)
3071576140
>>> lx = CarModel("FIT LX")
>>> id(lx)
3071576140
>>> lx.air
True
```

The id function tells us the unique identifier for an object. When we call it a second time, after deleting all references to the LX model and forcing garbage collection, we see that the ID has changed. The value in the CarModel __new__ factory dictionary was deleted and a fresh one created. If we then try to construct a second CarModel instance, however, it returns the same object (the IDs are the same), and, even though we did not supply any arguments in the second call, the air variable is still set to True. This means the object was not initialized the second time, just as we designed.

Obviously, using the flyweight pattern can be more complicated than just storing features on a single car class. When should we choose to use it? The flyweight pattern is designed for conserving memory; if we have tens or hundreds of thousands of similar objects, combining similar properties into a flyweight can have an enormous impact on memory consumption.

Command pattern

The command pattern adds a level of abstraction between actions that must be done, and the object that invokes those actions, normally at a later time. In the command pattern, client code creates a Command object that can be executed at a later date. This object knows about a receiver object that manages its own internal state when the command is executed on it. The Command object implements a specific interface (typically it has an execute or do_action method, and also keeps track of any arguments required to perform the action. Finally, one or more Invoker objects execute the command at the correct time. Here's the UML diagram:

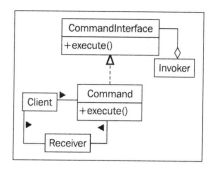

A common example of command pattern in action is actions on a graphical window. Often, an action can be invoked by a menu item on the menu bar, a keyboard shortcut, a toolbar icon, or a context menu. These are all examples of Invoker objects. The actions that actually occur, such as Exit, Save, or Copy are all command implementations of CommandInterface. A GUI Window to receive exit, document to receive save, and ClipboardManager to receive copy commands are all examples of possible Receivers.

Let's implement a simple command pattern that provides commands for Save and Exit actions. We'll start with some modest receiver classes:

```python
import sys

class Window:
    def exit(self):
        sys.exit(0)

class Document:
    def __init__(self, filename):
        self.filename = filename
```

```
            self.contents = "This file cannot be modified"

    def save(self):
        with open(self.filename, 'w') as file:
            file.write(self.contents)
```

These mock classes model objects that would likely be doing a lot more in a working environment. The window would need to handle mouse movement and keyboard events, and the document would need to handle character insertion, deletion, and selection. But for our purposes these two classes will do what we need.

Now let's define some invoker classes. These will model toolbar, menu, and keyboard events that can happen; again, they aren't actually hooked up to anything, but we can see how they are decoupled from the command, receiver, and client code:

```
    class ToolbarButton:
        def __init__(self, name, iconname):
            self.name = name
            self.iconname = iconname

        def click(self):
            self.command.execute()

    class MenuItem:
        def __init__(self, menu_name, menuitem_name):
            self.menu = menu_name
            self.item = menuitem_name

        def click(self):
            self.command.execute()

    class KeyboardShortcut:
        def __init__(self, key, modifier):
            self.key = key
            self.modifier = modifier

        def keypress(self):
            self.command.execute()
```

Notice how the various action methods each call the execute method on their respective commands? The commands haven't actually been set on the objects; they could be passed into the __init__ function, but because they may be changed (for example, with a customizable keybinding editor), we can set the attributes on the objects afterwards. Different situations call for different designs, but Python gives us the flexibility to do what makes the most sense to us, the programmers.

Now, let's hook up the commands:

```
class SaveCommand:
    def __init__(self, document):
        self.document = document

    def execute(self):
        self.document.save()

class ExitCommand:
    def __init__(self, window):
        self.window = window

    def execute(self):
        self.window.exit()
```

These commands are extremely straightforward; they demonstrate the basic pattern, but it is important to note that we can store state and other information with the command if necessary. For example, if we had a command to insert a character, we could maintain state for the character currently being inserted.

Now all we have to do is hook up some client and test code to make the commands work. For basic testing, we can just include this at the end of the script as follows:

```
window = Window()
document = Document("a_document.txt")
save = SaveCommand(document)
exit = ExitCommand(window)

save_button = ToolbarButton('save', 'save.png')
save_button.command = save
save_keystroke = KeyboardShortcut("s", "ctrl")
save_keystroke.command = save
exit_menu = MenuItem("File", "Exit")
exit_menu.command = exit
```

First we create two receivers and the two commands. Then we create several of the available invokers and set the correct command on each of them. To test, we can use `python3 -i filename.py` and run code like `exit_menu.click()`, which will end the program, or `save_keystroke.keystroke()`, which will save the fake file.

The above examples, however, do not feel terribly Pythonic, do they? They have a lot of "boilerplate code" (code that does not accomplish anything, but only provides structure to the pattern), and the Command classes are all very similar to each other. Perhaps we could create a generic command object that takes a function as a callback?

Wait, why bother with that, even; maybe we can just use a function or method object for each command? Instead of an object with an `execute()` method, we can write a function and use that as the command, directly. This is a common paradigm for the command pattern in Python:

```python
import sys

class Window:
    def exit(self):
        sys.exit(0)

class MenuItem:
    def click(self):
        self.command()

window = Window()
menu_item = MenuItem()
menu_item.command = window.exit
```

Now that looks a lot more like Python. At first glance, it looks like we've removed the command pattern altogether, and we've tightly connected the `menu_item` and `Window` classes. But look closer, there is no tight coupling at all. Any callable can be set up as the command on the `MenuItem`, just as before. And the `Window.exit` method can be attached to any invoker. Most of the flexibility of the command pattern has been maintained. We have sacrificed complete decoupling for readability, but this code is, in my opinion, and that of many Python programmers, more maintainable than the fully abstracted version.

Of course, since we can add a __call__ method to any object, we aren't restricted to only functions. The above example is a useful shortcut when the method being called doesn't have to maintain a state, but in more advanced usage, we can use this code as well:

```python
class Document:
    def __init__(self, filename):
        self.filename = filename
        self.contents = "This file cannot be modified"

    def save(self):
        with open(self.filename, 'w') as file:
            file.write(self.contents)

class KeyboardShortcut:
    def keypress(self):
        self.command()
```

```
class SaveCommand:
    def __init__(self, document):
        self.document = document

    def __call__(self):
        self.document.save()

document = Document("a_file.txt")
shortcut = KeyboardShortcut()
save_command = SaveCommand(document)
shortcut.command = save_command
```

Here we have something that looks like the first command pattern, but a bit more Pythonic. As you can see, changing the invoker to call a callable instead of a command object with an execute method has not restricted us in any way; in fact, it's given us more flexibility. We can link to functions directly when that works, yet we can build a complete callable command object when the situation calls for it.

The command pattern is often extended to support undoable commands. For example, a text program may wrap each insertion in a separate command with not only an `execute` method, but also an `undo` method that will delete that insertion. A graphics program may wrap each drawing action (rectangle, line, freehand pixels, and so on) in a command that has an `undo` method that resets the pixels to their original state. In such cases, the decoupling of the command pattern is much more obviously useful, because each action has to maintain enough of its state to undo that action at a later date.

Abstract factory pattern

The abstract factory pattern is normally used when we have multiple possible implementations of a system that depend on some configuration or platform issue. The calling code requests an object from the abstract factory, not knowing exactly what class of object will be returned. The underlying implementation returned may depend on a variety of factors, such as current locale, operating system, or local configuration.

Common examples of the abstract factory pattern at work include code for operating system independent toolkits, database backends, and country-specific formatters or calculators. An operating system independent GUI toolkit might use an abstract factory pattern that returns a set of Winform widgets under Windows, Cocoa widgets under Mac, GTK widgets under Gnome, and QT widgets under KDE. Django provides an abstract factory that returns a set of object relational classes for interacting with a specific database backend (MySQL, PostgreSQL, SQLite, and others) depending on a configuration setting for the current site. If the application needs to be deployed in multiple places, each one can use a different database backend by changing only one configuration variable. Different countries have different systems for calculating taxes, subtotals, and totals on retail merchandise; an abstract factory can return a particular tax calculation object.

The UML class diagram for an abstract factory pattern is hard to understand without a specific example, so let's turn things around and create a concrete example first. We'll create a set of formatters that depend on a specific locale, and help us format dates and currencies. There will be an abstract factory class that picks the specific factory, as well as a couple example concrete factories, one for France and one for the USA. Each of these will create formatter objects for dates and times, which can be queried to format a specific value. Here's the diagram:

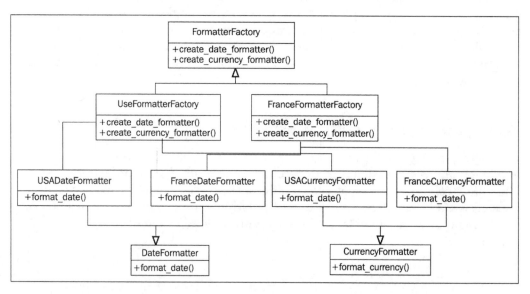

Comparing that image to the simpler text above it shows that a picture is not always worth a thousand words, after all, especially considering we haven't even allowed for factory selection code here.

Of course, in Python, we don't have to implement any interface classes, so we can discard `DateFormatter`, `CurrencyFormatter`, and `FormatterFactory`. The formatting classes themselves are pretty simple:

```python
class FranceDateFormatter:
    def format_date(self, y, m, d):
        y, m, d = (str(x) for x in (y,m,d))
        y = '20' + y if len(y) == 2 else y
        m = '0' + m if len(m) == 1 else m
        d = '0' + d if len(d) == 1 else d
        return("{0}/{1}/{2}".format(d,m,y))


class USADateFormatter:
    def format_date(self, y, m, d):
        y, m, d = (str(x) for x in (y,m,d))
        y = '20' + y if len(y) == 2 else y
        m = '0' + m if len(m) == 1 else m
        d = '0' + d if len(d) == 1 else d
        return("{0}-{1}-{2}".format(m,d,y))


class FranceCurrencyFormatter:
    def format_currency(self, base, cents):
        base, cents = (str(x) for x in (base, cents))
        if len(cents) == 0:
            cents = '00'
        elif len(cents) == 1:
            cents = '0' + cents

        digits = []
        for i,c in enumerate(reversed(base)):
            if i and not i % 3:
                digits.append(' ')
            digits.append(c)
        base = ''.join(reversed(digits))
        return "{0}€{1}".format(base, cents)


class USACurrencyFormatter:
    def format_currency(self, base, cents):
        base, cents = (str(x) for x in (base, cents))
        if len(cents) == 0:
            cents = '00'
        elif len(cents) == 1:
            cents = '0' + cents
```

```
        digits = []
        for i,c in enumerate(reversed(base)):
            if i and not i % 3:
                digits.append(',')
            digits.append(c)
        base = ''.join(reversed(digits))
        return "${0}.{1}".format(base, cents)
```

These classes use some basic string manipulation to try to turn a variety of possible inputs (integers, strings of different lengths, and others) into the following formats:

	USA	France
Date	Mm-dd-yyyy	dd/mm/yyyy
Currency	$14,500.50	14 500€50

There could be more validation on the input in this code, but let's keep it simple and dumb for this example!

Now that we have the formatters set up, we just need to create the formatter factories:

```
class USAFormatterFactory:
    def create_date_formatter(self):
        return USADateFormatter()
    def create_currency_formatter(self):
        return USACurrencyFormatter()

class FranceFormatterFactory:
    def create_date_formatter(self):
        return FranceDateFormatter()
    def create_currency_formatter(self):
        return FranceCurrencyFormatter()
```

Now we simply need to set up the code that picks the appropriate formatter. Since this is the kind of thing that only needs to be set up once, we could make it a singleton—except singletons aren't very useful in Python. Let's just make the current formatter a module-level variable instead:

```
country_code = "US"
factory_map = {
        "US": USAFormatterFactory,
        "FR": FranceFormatterFactory}
formatter_factory = factory_map.get(country_code)()
```

In this example, we hardcode the current country code; in practice, it would likely introspect the locale, operating system, or a configuration file to choose the code. It uses a dictionary to associate the country codes with factory classes. Then we simply get the correct class from the dictionary and instantiate it.

It is easy to see what needs to be done when we want to add support for more countries; just create new formatter classes and the abstract factory itself.

Abstract factories often return a singleton object, but this is not required; in our code, it's returning a new instance of each formatter every time it's called. There's no reason the formatters couldn't be stored as instance variables and the same instance returned for each factory.

Looking back at these examples, we see that, once again, there appears to be a lot of boilerplate code for factories that just doesn't feel necessary in Python. Often, the requirements that might call for an abstract factory can be more easily fulfilled by using a separate module for each factory type (example: USA, France), and then ensuring that the correct module is being accessed in a factory module. The package structure for such modules often looks like this:

```
localize/
    __init__.py
    backends/
            __init__.py
        USA.py
        France.py
        ...
```

The trick is that __init__.py in the localize package can contain code that redirects all requests to the correct backend. There is a variety of ways this could be done. Obviously, we could duplicate each of the methods in the backend modules and route them through __init__.py as a proxy module. But we can do it a bit more cleanly as well. If we know that the backend is never going to change dynamically (that is without a restart), we can simply put some if statements in __init__.py that check the current country code, and use the usually unacceptable from .backends.USA import * syntax to import all variables from the appropriate backend. Or, we could import each of the backends and set a current_backend variable to point at a specific module:

```
from .backends import USA, France


if country_code == "US":
    current_backend = USA
```

Depending on which solution we choose, our client code would simply have to call either `localize.format_date` or `localize.current_backend.format_date` to get a date formatted in the current country's locale. The end result is much more Pythonic than the original abstract factory pattern, and, in typical usage, just as flexible.

Composite pattern

The composite pattern allows complex tree-like structures to be built from simple components. Composite objects are simply container objects, where the content may actually be another composite object.

Traditionally, each component in a composite object must be either a leaf node (that cannot contain other objects) or a composite node. The key is that both composite and leaf nodes can be treated identically. The UML diagram is very simple:

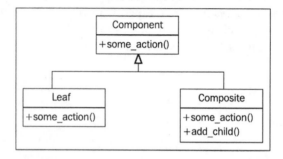

This simple pattern, however, allows us to create very complex arrangements of elements, all of which satisfy the interface of the component object. As an example, here is one such complicated arrangement:

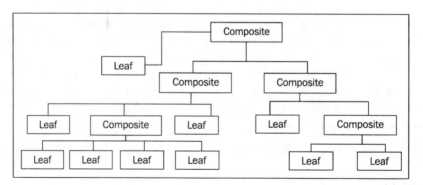

The composite pattern is commonly useful in file/folder-like trees. Regardless of whether a node in the tree is a normal file or a folder, it is still subject to operations such as moving, copying, or deleting the node. We can create a component interface that supports these operations, and then use a composite object to represent folders, and leaf nodes to represent normal files.

Of course, in Python, once again, we can take advantage of duck typing to implicitly provide the interface, so we only need to write two classes. Let's define these interfaces first:

```python
class Folder:
    def __init__(self, name):
        self.name = name
        self.children = {}

    def add_child(self, child):
        pass

    def move(self, new_path):
        pass

    def copy(self, new_path):
        pass

    def delete(self):
        pass

class File:
    def __init__(self, name, contents):
        self.name = name
        self.contents = contents

    def move(self, new_path):
        pass

    def copy(self, new_path):
        pass

    def delete(self):
        pass
```

For each folder (composite) object, we maintain a dictionary of children. Often, a list is sufficient, but in this case, a dictionary will be useful for looking up children by name. Our paths will be specified as node names separated by the / character, similar to paths in a UNIX shell.

Thinking about the methods involved, we can see that moving or deleting a node will behave in a similar way, regardless of whether or not it is a file or folder node. Copying, however, will have to do a recursive copy for folder nodes, where copying a file node is a trivial operation.

To take advantage of the similar operations, let's extract some of the common methods into a parent class. Let's take that discarded Component interface and change it to a base class:

```python
class Component:
    def __init__(self, name):
        self.name = name

    def move(self, new_path):
        new_folder =get_path(new_path)
        del self.parent.children[self.name]
        new_folder.children[self.name] = self
        self.parent = new_folder

    def delete(self):
        del self.parent.children[self.name]

class Folder(Component):
    def __init__(self, name):
        super().__init__(name)
        self.children = {}

    def add_child(self, child):
        pass

    def copy(self, new_path):
        pass

class File(Component):
    def __init__(self, name, contents):
        super().__init__(name)
        self.contents = contents

    def copy(self, new_path):
        pass

root = Folder('')
def get_path(path):
    names = path.split('/')[1:]
    node = root
    for name in names:
        node = node.children[name]
    return node
```

Here we've created the `move` and `delete` methods on the `Component` class. Both of them access a mysterious `parent` variable that we haven't set yet. The `move` method uses a module-level `get_path` function that finds a node from a predefined root node, given a path. All files will be added to to this root node or a child of that node. For the move method, the target should be a currently existing folder, or we'll get an error. As with many of the examples in this book, error handling is woefully absent, to help focus on the principles under consideration.

Let's set up that mysterious `parent` variable first; this happens, of course, in the folder's `add_child` method:

```
def add_child(self, child):
    child.parent = self
    self.children[child.name] = child
```

Well, that was simple enough. Let's see if our composite file hierarchy is working properly:

```
$ python3 -i 1261_09_18_add_child.py

>>> folder1 = Folder('folder1')
>>> folder2 = Folder('folder2')
>>> root.add_child(folder1)
>>> root.add_child(folder2)
>>> folder11 = Folder('folder11')
>>> folder1.add_child(folder11)
>>> file111 = File('file111', 'contents')
>>> folder11.add_child(file111)
>>> file21 = File('file21', 'other contents')
>>> folder2.add_child(file21)
>>> folder2.children
{'file21': <__main__.File object at 0xb7220a4c>}
>>> folder2.move('/folder1/folder11')
>>> folder11.children
{'folder2': <__main__.Folder object at 0xb722080c>, 'file111': <__main__
.File object at 0xb72209ec>}
>>> file21.move('/folder1')
>>> folder1.children
{'file21': <__main__.File object at 0xb7220a4c>, 'folder11': <__main__
.Folder object at 0xb722084c>}
>>>
```

Yes, we can create folders, add folders to other folders, add files to folders, and move them around! What more could we ask for in a file hierarchy?

Well, we could ask for copying to be implemented, but to conserve space, let's leave that as an exercise!

The composite pattern is extremely useful for such tree-like structures, including GUI widget hierarchies, file hierarchies, tree sets, graphs, and HTML DOM. It can be a useful pattern in Python when implemented according to the traditional implementation, as the example earlier demonstrates. Sometimes, if only a shallow tree is being created, we can get away with a list of lists or dictionary of dictionaries and do not need to implement custom component, leaf, and composite classes as we did earlier. Other times, we can get away with implementing only one composite class, and treating leaf and composite objects as one class. Alternatively, Python's duck typing can make it easy to add other objects to a composite hierarchy, as long as they have the correct interface.

Exercises

Before diving into exercises for each design pattern, take a moment to implement the `copy` method for the `File` and `Folder` objects in the previous section. The `File` method should be quite trivial; just create a new node with the same name and contents, and add it to the new parent folder. The `copy` method on `Folder` is quite a bit more complicated, as you first have to duplicate the folder, and then recursively copy each of it's children to the new location. You can call the `copy()` method on the children indiscriminately, regardless of whether each is a file or a folder object. This will drive home just how powerful the composite pattern can be.

Now, as with the previous chapter, look at the patterns we've discussed, and consider ideal places where you might implement them. You may want to apply the adapter pattern to existing code, as it is most often applicable when interfacing with existing libraries, rather than new code. How can you use an adapter to force two interfaces to interact with each other correctly?

Can you think of a system complex enough to justify using the facade pattern? Consider how facades are used in real-life situations, such as the driver-facing interface of a car, or the control panel in a factory. It is similar in software, except the users of the facade interface are other programmers, rather than people trained to use them. Are there complex systems in your latest project that could benefit from the facade pattern?

It's possible you don't have any huge, memory-consuming code that would benefit from the flyweight pattern, but can you think of situations where it might be useful? Anywhere that large amounts of overlapping data need to be processed, a flyweight is waiting to be used. Would it be useful in the banking industry? In web applications? At what point does the flyweight pattern make sense? When is it overkill?

What about the command pattern? Can you think of any common (or better yet, uncommon) examples of places where the decoupling of action from invocation would be useful? Look at the programs you use on a daily basis, and imagine how they are implemented internally. It's likely that many of them use the command pattern for some purpose or another.

The abstract factory pattern, or the somewhat more Pythonic derivatives we discussed, can be very useful for creating one-touch-configurable systems. Can you think of places where such systems are useful?

Finally, consider the composite pattern. There are tree-like structures all around us in programming; some of them, like our file hierarchy example, are blatant; others are fairly subtle. What situations might arise where the composite pattern would be useful? Can you think of places where you can use it in your own code? What if you adapted the pattern slightly, for example to contain different types of leaf or composite nodes for different types of objects?

Summary

In this chapter, we went into detail on several more design patterns, covering their canonical descriptions as well as alternatives for implementing them in Python, which is often more flexible and versatile than traditional object-oriented languages. In particular, we covered:

- The adapter pattern for matching interfaces
- The facade pattern for simplifying complex systems
- The flyweight pattern for reducing memory consumption
- The command pattern for isolating invokers
- The abstract factory pattern for separating implementation
- The composition pattern for tree-like structures

In the next chapter, we'll cover some of the common tools for manipulating files, configuration, and processes.

10
Files and Strings

Let's take a step back from the higher-level patterns now, and cover several Python constructs we've used in all our examples, but without any details. We'll be looking at files, IO, and serializing and loading data. Along the way, we'll find out how complicated Python's excessively simple strings really are. In particular, we'll see:

- The complexities of strings, bytes, and byte array
- The ins and outs of string formatting
- How to open files
- Context managers
- A few ways to serialize data

Strings

Strings are a basic primitive in Python; we've used them in nearly every example we've discussed so far. All they do is represent an immutable sequence of characters. Of course, "character" is a bit of an ambiguous word; can Python strings represent sequences of accented characters? Chinese characters? What about Greek, Cyrillic, or Farsi?

In Python 3, the answer is yes. Python strings are all represented in Unicode, a special character definition that can represent virtually any character in any language on the planet. This is done seamlessly, for the most part. For now, let's think of Python 3 strings as an immutable sequence of Unicode characters.

So what can we do with this immutable sequence? We've touched on many of the ways they can be manipulated in previous examples, but let's quickly cover it all in one place: a crash course in string theory!

String manipulation

As you know, strings can be created in Python by wrapping a sequence of characters in single or double quotes. Multi-line strings can easily be created using three quote characters, and multiple hard-coded strings can be concatenated together by placing them side by side (this is useful for placing long strings in function calls without exceeding a text width limit on your editor). Here are some examples:

```
a = "hello"
b = 'world'
c = '''a multiple
line string'''
d = """More
multiple"""
e = ("Three " "Strings "
        "Together")
```

That's about all that can be said about creating strings. That last string is automatically composed into a single string by the interpreter. It is also possible to concatenate strings using the + operator (as in `"hello " + "world"`).

Strings don't have to be hard-coded, of course. They can also come from various outside sources such as text files, user input, or the network.

Like other sequences, strings can be iterated over (character by character), sliced, or concatenated. The syntax is the same as for lists.

The `str` class has numerous methods on it to make manipulating strings easier. The `dir` and `help` commands in the Python interpreter can tell us how to use all of them; we'll consider some of the more common ones directly.

Several Boolean convenience methods help us identify whether or not the characters in a string match a certain pattern. Here is a summary of these methods:

Method	Purpose
`isalpha`	Return `True` if all characters in the string are alphabet characters in some language. If any spaces, punctuation, or numbers appear in the string, return `False`.
`isdigit` `isdecimal` `isnumeric`	These methods tell us if all characters in the string are numeric digits, Unicode decimal characters, or have the Unicode numeric value set, respectively. Be careful with these ones; the period character is not a decimal, so `'45.2'.isdecimal()` returns `False`! The real decimal character is represented by Unicode value 0660, as in 45.2.
`isalnum`	Return `True` if the string contains only alphabet or number characters, `False` if there is any punctuation or whitespace.

Method	Purpose
isspace	Return True if the string contains only whitespace characters (space, tab, newline, and so on). Otherwise, return False.
isupper islower	Return True if all alphabetic characters in the string are either upper or lower case, depending on which method is called.
istitle	Return True if the string is in title case. Title case means only the first character of every word is capitalized, all others are lower case. Be careful with this one, as it does not strictly fit the grammatical definition of title formatting. For example the poem "The Glove and the Lions" is a valid title, even though not all words are capitalized. "The Cremation Of Sam McGee" is also a valid title, even though there is an uppercase letter in the middle of the last word.
isidentifier	Return True if the string contains a value that can be used as a variable name in Python. If it has spaces, hyphens, or starts with a number, it will return False.
isprintable	Return True if all characters in the string can be printed on the screen or a printer. Excludes terminal control characters such as the escape key. Notably, whitespace characters are printable, even though they are not visible when printed.

Other methods can be used to determine if a string matches a specific pattern. The startswith and endswith methods return True if the string starts or ends with the string of characters passed into the function. The count method tells us how many times a given substring shows up in the string, while find, index, rfind, and rindex tell us the position of a given substring within the original string. The two 'r' (for 'right') methods start searching from the end of the string. The find methods return -1 if the substring can't be found, while index raises a ValueError in this situation. Have a look at some of these methods in action:

```
>>> s = "hello world"
>>> s.startswith('hi')
False
>>> s.endswith('ld')
True
>>> s.find('l')
2
>>> s.index('m')
Traceback (most recent call last):
  File "<stdin>", line 1, in <module>
ValueError: substring not found
>>>
```

Several of the remaining string methods return transformations of the string. The upper, lower, capitalize, and title methods create new strings with all alphabetic characters in the given format. The translate method can use a dictionary to map arbitrary input characters to specified output characters.

For each of these methods, note that the input string remains unmodified; a brand new str instance is returned instead. If we need to manipulate the resultant string, we should assign it to a new variable, as in new_value = value.capitalize(). Often, once we've performed the transformation, we don't need the old value anymore, so a frequent idiom is to assign it to the same variable, as in value = value.title().

Finally, certain string methods return or operate on lists. The split method accepts a substring and splits the string into a list of strings wherever that substring occurs. The partition method splits the string at only the first occurrence of the substring, and returns a tuple of three values: characters before the substring, the substring itself, and the characters after the substring.

As the inverse of split, the join method accepts a list of strings, and returns all of those strings combined together by placing the original string between them. The replace method accepts two arguments, and returns a string where each instance of the first argument has been replaced with the second. Here are some of these methods in action:

```
>>> s = "hello world, how are you"
>>> s2 = s.split(' ')
>>> s2
['hello', 'world,', 'how', 'are', 'you']
>>> '#'.join(s2)
'hello#world,#how#are#you'
>>> s.replace(' ', '**')
'hello**world,**how**are**you'
>>> s.partition(' ')
('hello', ' ', 'world, how are you')
```

That's it: a whirlwind tour of the most common methods on the str class! Now let's look at Python 3's method for composing strings and variables together into new strings.

String formatting

Python 3 has a versatile string formatting mechanism that allows us to easily construct strings comprised of hard-coded text and interspersed variables. We've used it in many previous examples, but it is much more versatile than the simple formatting specifiers we've used.

Any string can be turned into a format string by calling the `format()` method on it. This method returns a new string where specific characters in the input string have been replaced with values provided in the arguments and keyword arguments passed into the function. There is no fixed set of arguments required by the `format` method; internally, it uses the `*args` and `**kwargs` syntax that we discussed in *Chapter 7*.

The special characters that are replaced in formated strings are the opening and closing brace characters: { and }. We can insert pairs of these in a string and they will be replaced, in order, by any positional arguments passed to the `str.format` method:

```
template = "Hello {}, you are currently {}."
print(template.format('Dusty', 'writing'))
```

If we run these statements, it replaces the braces with variables, in order:

```
Hello Dusty, you are currently writing.
```

This basic syntax is not terribly useful if we want to reuse variables within one string or decide to use them in a different position. We can place zero-indexed integers inside the curly braces to tell the formatter which positional variable gets inserted at a given position in the string. Let's repeat the name:

```
template = "Hello {0}, you are {1}. Your name is {0}."
print(template.format('Dusty', 'writing'))
```

If we do use these integer indexes, we have to use them in all the variables. We can't mix empty braces with positional indexes. For example, this code fails:

```
template = "Hello {}, you are {}. Your name is {0}."
print(template.format('Dusty', 'writing'))
```

Running this raises an appropriate exception:

```
Traceback (most recent call last):
  File "1261_10_04_format_some_positions_broken.py", line 2, in
<module>
    print(template.format('Dusty', 'writing'))
ValueError: cannot switch from automatic field numbering to manual
field specification
```

Escaping braces

Brace characters are often useful in strings, aside from formatting. We need a way to escape them in situations where we want them to be displayed as themselves, rather than being replaced. This can be done by doubling the braces. For example, we can use Python to format a basic Java program:

```
template = """
public class {0} {{
    public static void main(String[] args) {{
        System.out.println({1});
    }}
}}"""

print(template.format("MyClass", "print('hello world')"));
```

Wherever we see the {{ or }} sequence in the template, that is, the braces enclosing the Java class and method definition, we know the `format` method will replace them with single braces, rather than some argument passed into the format method. Here's the output:

```
public class MyClass {
    public static void main(String[] args) {
        System.out.println("print('hello world')");
    }
}
```

The class name and contents of the output have been replaced with two parameters, while the double braces have been replaced with single braces, giving us a valid Java file. Turns out, this is about the simplest possible Python program to print the simplest possible Java program that can print the simplest possible Python program!

Keyword arguments

If we're formatting complex strings, it can become tedious to remember the order of the arguments or to update the template if we choose to insert another argument at the beginning of the list. The `format` method therefore allows us to specify names inside the braces instead of numbers. The named variables are then provided to the `format` method as keyword arguments instead of positional arguments:

```
template = """
From: <{from_email}>
To: <{to_email}>
Subject: {subject}

{message}"""
print(template.format(
    from_email = "a@example.com",
    to_email = "b@example.com",
```

```
message = "Here's some mail for you. "
" Hope you enjoy the message!",
subject = "You have mail!"
))
```

 Notice how Python automatically concatenates the two strings we're passing as a message argument? Very useful for line wrapping, but be careful not to do this at the top level of a file. You need to be inside a set of parenthesis (whether grouping a tuple, a function call, or just explicitly grouping several strings together) for the concatenation to be enabled.

We can also mix index and keyword arguments (as with all Python function calls, the keyword arguments must follow the positional ones). We can even mix unlabeled positional braces with keyword arguments:

```
print("{} {label} {}".format("x", "y", label="z"))
```

As expected, this code outputs:

```
x z y
```

Container lookups

We aren't restricted to passing simple string variables into the `format` method. Any primitive, such as integers or floats can be printed. More interestingly, complex objects including lists, tuples, dictionaries, and arbitrary objects can be used, and we can access indexes and variables (but not methods) on those objects from within the `format` string.

For example, if our e-mail message had grouped the from and to e-mail addresses into a tuple, and placed the subject and message in a dictionary, for some reason (perhaps because that's the input required for an existing `send_mail` function we want to use), we can format it like so:

```
emails = ("a@example.com", "b@example.com")
message = {
        'subject': "You Have Mail!",
        'message': "Here's some mail for you!"
        }
template = """
From: <{0[0]}>
To: <{0[1]}>
Subject: {message[subject]}
{message[message]}"""
print(template.format(emails, message=message))
```

The variables inside the braces in the template string look a little weird, so let's look at what they're doing. We have passed one argument as a position-based parameter and one as a keyword argument. The two e-mail addresses are looked up by `0[x]` where x is either `0` or `1`. The initial zero represents, as with other position-based arguments, the first positional argument passed to `format` (the `emails` tuple, in this case). The square brackets with a number inside are the same kind of index lookup we see in regular Python code, so `0[0]` maps to `emails[0]`, in the `emails` tuple. The indexing syntax works with any indexable object, so we see similar behavior when we access `message[subject]`, except this time we are looking up a string key in a dictionary. Notice that unlike in Python code, we do not need to put quotes around the string in the dictionary lookup.

We can even do multiple levels of lookup if we have nested data structures. I would recommend against doing this too often, as template strings rapidly become difficult to understand. If we have a dictionary that contains a tuple, we can do this:

```python
emails = ("a@example.com", "b@example.com")
message = {
        'emails': emails,
        'subject': "You Have Mail!",
        'message': "Here's some mail for you!"
        }
template = """
From: <{0[emails][0]}>
To: <{0[emails][1]}>
Subject: {0[subject]}
{0[message]}"""
print(template.format(message))
```

In this example, we access only one variable, at position zero; we look up values in the dictionary, and for e-mail addresses, we do a second index lookup based on position. The formatting index system is very flexible, but we have to bear in mind that the primary goal is to make our code, including templates, as readable as possible. We need to look at the variables we are passing into a template, and how we access them inside it. Would we be better off breaking them into separate positional or keyword arguments to the format method, instead of passing a single massive object? It depends on what structure the object has to begin with, as well as the structure and amount of variable content in the format string.

Object lookups

Indexing makes `format` lookup powerful, but we're not done yet! We can also pass arbitrary objects as parameters, and use the dot notation to look up attributes on those objects. Let's change our e-mail message data once again, this time to a class:

```
class EMail:
    def __init__(self, from_addr, to_addr, subject, message):
        self.from_addr = from_addr
        self.to_addr = to_addr
        self.subject = subject
        self.message = message

email = EMail("a@example.com", "b@example.com",
        "You Have Mail!",
          "Here's some mail for you!")

template = """
From: <{0.from_addr}>
To: <{0.to_addr}>
Subject: {0.subject}

{0.message}"""
print(template.format(email))
```

The template in this example is more readable than the previous examples, but the overhead of creating an e-mail class adds complexity to the Python code. We wouldn't normally create a class for the express purpose of including the object in a template. Typically, we'd use this sort of lookup if the object we are trying to format already exists. This is true of all the examples; if we have a tuple, list, or dictionary, perhaps we'll pass it into the template directly. Otherwise we'd just create a simple set of positional and keyword arguments.

Making it look right

It's nice to be able to include variables in template strings, but sometimes the variables need a bit of coercion to make them look right in the output. For example, if we are doing calculations with currency, we may end up with a long decimal that we don't want to show up in our template:

```
subtotal = 12.32
tax = subtotal * 0.07
total = subtotal + tax

print("Sub: ${0} Tax: ${1} Total: ${total}".format(
    subtotal, tax, total=total))
```

If we run this formatting code, the output doesn't quite look like proper currency:

```
Sub: $12.32 Tax: $0.8624 Total: $13.1824
```

 Technically, we should never use floating-point numbers in currency calculations like this; we should construct `decimal.Decimal()` objects instead. Floats are dangerous because their calculations are inherently inaccurate beyond a specific level of precision. But we're looking at strings, not floats, and currency is a great example for formatting!

To fix the `format` string above, we can include some additional information inside the curly braces to adjust the formatting of the parameters. There are tons of things we can customize, but the basic syntax inside the braces is the same; first we use whichever of the earlier layouts (positional, keyword, index, attribute access) is suitable to specify the variable that we want to place in the template string. We follow this with a colon, and then the specific syntax for the formatting. Here's an improved version:

```
subtotal = 12.32
tax = subtotal * 0.07
total = subtotal + tax

print("Sub: ${0:0.2f} Tax: ${1:0.2f} "
      "Total: ${total:0.2f}".format(
          subtotal, tax, total=total))
```

The `0.2f` format specifier after the colons basically says, from left to right: for values lower than one, make sure a zero is displayed on the left side of the decimal point; show two places after the decimal; format the input value as a float.

We can also specify that each number should take up a particular number of characters on the screen by placing a value before the period in the precision. This can be useful for outputting tabular data, for example:

```
orders = [('burger', 2, 5),
          ('fries', 3.5, 1),
          ('cola', 1.75, 3)]

print("PRODUCT    QUANTITY    PRICE    SUBTOTAL")
for product, price, quantity in orders:
    subtotal = price * quantity
    print("{0:10s}{1: ^9d}    ${2: <8.2f}${3: >7.2f}".format(
        product, quantity, price, subtotal))
```

OK, that's a pretty scary looking format string, so let's see how it works before we break it down into understandable parts:

```
PRODUCT      QUANTITY     PRICE      SUBTOTAL
burger          5         $2.00      $   10.00
fries           1         $3.50      $    3.50
cola            3         $1.75      $    5.25
```

Nifty! So how is this actually happening? We have four variables we are formatting, in each line in the `for` loop. The first variable is a string and is formatted with `{0:10s}`. The `s` means it is a string variable, the `10` means it should take up ten characters. By default, with strings, if the string is shorter than the specified number of characters, it appends spaces to the right side of the string to make it long enough (beware, however: if the original string is too long, it won't be truncated!). We can change this behavior (to fill with other characters or change the alignment in the format string), as we do for the next value, `quantity`.

The formatter for the `quantity` value is `{1: ^9d}`. The `d` represents an integer value. The `9` tells us the value should take up nine characters. But with integers, instead of spaces, the extra characters are zeros, by default. That looks kind of weird. So we explicitly specify a space (immediately after the colon) as a padding character. The carat character `^` tells us that the number should be aligned in the center of this available padding; this makes the column look a bit more professional. The specifiers have to be in the right order, although all are optional: Fill first, then align, then the size, and finally, the type.

We do similar things with the specifiers for price and subtotal. For `price` we use `{2: <8.2f}` and for `subtotal`, `{3: >7.2f}`. In both cases, we're specifying a space as the fill character, but we use the `<` and `>` symbols, respectively, to represent that the numbers should be aligned to the left or right within the minimum space of eight or seven characters. Further, each float should be formatted to two decimal places.

The 'type' character for different types can affect formatting output as well. We've seen the `s`, `d`, and `f` types, for strings, integers, and floats. Most of the other format specifiers are alternative versions of these; for example, `o` represents octal format and `x` represents hexadecimal for integers. The `n` type specifier can be useful for formatting integer separators in the current locale's format. For floating-point numbers, the `%` type will multiply by 100 and format a float as a percentage.

We've barely scratched the surface of string formatting. These standard formatters apply to most built-in objects, but it is actually possible for other objects to define non-standard specifiers. For example, if we pass a `datetime` object into `format`, we can format it using the specifiers used in the `datetime.strftime` function as follows:

```
import datetime
print("{0:%Y-%m-%d %I:%M%p }".format(
    datetime.datetime.now()))
```

It is even possible to write custom formatters for objects we create ourselves, but that is beyond the scope of this book. Look into overriding the __format__ special method if you need to do this in your code. The most comprehensive instructions can be found in PEP 3101 at `http://www.python.org/dev/peps/pep-3101/` although the details are a bit dry. You can find more digestible tutorials using a web search.

Strings are Unicode

At the beginning of this section, we defined strings as collections of immutable Unicode characters. This actually makes things very complicated at times, because Unicode isn't really a storage format. If you get a string of bytes from a file or a socket, for example, they won't be in Unicode. They will, in fact, be the built-in type `bytes`. Bytes are immutable sequences of... well, bytes. Bytes are the lowest-level storage format in computing. They represent 8 bits, and are generally described as an integer between 0 and 255, or a hexadecimal equivalent between 0 and FF. Bytes don't specifically represent anything; a sequence of bytes may store characters in an encoded string, or pixels in an image.

If we print a byte object, any bytes that map to ASCII representations will be printed as their original character, while non-ASCII bytes (whether they are binary data or other characters) are printed as hex codes escaped by the \x escape sequence. You may find it odd that a byte, represented as an integer, can map to an ASCII character. But ASCII is really just a code where each letter is represented by a different byte pattern, and therefore, a different integer. The character "a" is represented by the same byte as the number 97, which is the hexadecimal number 0x61. Specifically, all of these are an interpretation of the binary pattern 01100001.

Many IO operations only know how to deal with `bytes`, even if the bytes object refers to textual data. It is therefore very important to know how to convert between `bytes` and Unicode.

The problem is that there are many ways to map bytes to Unicode text. Bytes are machine-readable values, while text is a human-readable format. Sitting in between is an encoding that maps a given sequence of bytes to a given sequence of text characters.

However, there are multiple such encodings (ASCII is only one of them). The same sequence of bytes can represent completely different text characters when mapped using different encodings! It is important to decode bytes using the same character set in which it was encoded, or we will get garbage data. It's not possible to get text from bytes without knowing how the bytes should be encoded. If we receive unknown bytes without a specified encoding, the best we can do is guess what format they are encoded in, and we may be wrong.

Converting bytes to text

If we have an array of bytes from somewhere, we can convert it to Unicode using the .decode method on the bytes class. This method accepts a string for the name of the character encoding. There are many such names; common ones for European languages include ASCII, UTF-8, and latin-1.

The sequence of bytes (in hex) 63 6c 69 63 68 e9 actually represent the characters of the word cliché in the latin-1 encoding. The following example will encode this sequence of bytes and convert it to a Unicode string using the latin-1 encoding:

```
characters = b'\x63\x6c\x69\x63\x68\xe9'
print(characters)
print(characters.decode("latin-1"))
```

The first line creates a bytes object; the b immediately before the string tells us that we are defining a bytes object instead of a normal Unicode string. Within the string, each byte is specified using—in this case—a hexadecimal number. The \x escapes within the byte string each say, "the next two characters represent a byte using hexadecimal digits".

Provided we are using a shell that understands the latin-1 encoding, the two print statements will output the following strings:

```
b'clich\xe9'
cliché
```

The first print statement shows that the bytes for ASCII characters are displayed as those characters. The unknown (unknown to ASCII, that is) character stays in its escaped hex format. The output includes a b at the beginning of the line to remind us that it is a bytes representation, not a string.

The next statement decodes the string using latin-1. The decode method returns a normal (Unicode) string with the correct characters. However, if we had decoded this same string using the Cyrillic "iso8859-5" encoding, we'd have ended up with the sequence of characters 'clichщ'! This is because the \xe9 byte maps to different characters in the two encodings.

Converting text to bytes

If we need to convert incoming bytes into Unicode, clearly we're also going to have situations where we convert outgoing Unicode into byte sequences. This is done with the encode method on the str class, which, in parallel to the decode method, also requires a character set. The following code creates a Unicode string and encodes it in a few different character sets:

```
characters = "cliché"
print(characters.encode("UTF-8"))
print(characters.encode("latin-1"))
print(characters.encode("CP437"))
print(characters.encode("ascii"))
```

The first three encodings create a different set of bytes for the accented character. The fourth one can't even handle it:

```
b'clich\xc3\xa9'
b'clich\xe9'
b'clich\x82'
Traceback (most recent call last):
  File "1261_10_16_decode_unicode.py", line 5, in <module>
    print(characters.encode("ascii"))
UnicodeEncodeError: 'ascii' codec can't encode character '\xe9' in
position 5: ordinal not in range(128)
```

Do you understand the importance of encoding now? The accented character is represented in a different way for each encoding; if we use the wrong one when we are decoding bytes to text, we get the wrong character.

The exception in the last case is not always the desired behavior; there may be cases where we want the unknown characters to be handled in a different way. The encode method takes an optional string argument named errors that can define how such characters should be handled. This string can be one of:

- strict
- replace
- ignore
- xmlcharrefreplace

The `strict` replacement strategy is the default we just saw. When a byte sequence is encountered that does not have a valid representation in the requested encoding, an exception is raised. When the `replace` strategy is used, the character is replaced with a different character; in ASCII it is a question mark; other encodings may use different symbols, such as an empty box. The `ignore` strategy simply discards any bytes it doesn't understand, while the `xmlcharrefreplace` strategy creates an `xml` entity representing the Unicode character. This can be useful when converting unknown strings for use in an XML document. Here's how each of the strategies affects our sample word:

Strategy	"cliché".encode("ascii", strategy)
replace	b'clich?'
ignore	b'clich'
xmlcharrefreplace	b'cliché'

It is possible to call the `str.encode` and `bytes.decode` methods without passing an encoding string. The encoding will be set to the default encoding for the current platform. This will depend on the current operating system and locale or regional settings; you can look it up using the `sys.getdefaultencoding()` function. It is usually a good idea to specify the encoding explicitly, though, since the default encoding for a platform may change, or the program may one day be extended to work on text from a wider variety of sources.

If you are encoding text and don't know which encoding to use, it is probably best to use the UTF-8 encoding. UTF-8 is able to represent any Unicode character. In modern software, it is a de facto standard encoding to ensure documents in any language—or even multiple languages—can be exchanged. The various other possible encodings are useful for legacy documents or in regions that still use different character sets by default.

The UTF-8 encoding uses one byte to represent ASCII and other common characters, and up to four bytes for more complex characters. UTF-8 is special because it is backwards-compatible with ASCII; any ASCII document encoded using UTF-8 will be identical to the original ASCII document.

Mutable byte strings

The `bytes` type, like `str`, is immutable. We can use index and slice notation on a `bytes` object and search for a particular sequence of bytes, but we can't extend or modify them. This can be very inconvenient when dealing with IO, as it is often necessary to buffer incoming or outgoing bytes until they are ready to be sent. For example, if we are receiving data from a socket, it may take several `recv` calls before we have received an entire message.

This is where the `bytearray` built-in comes in. This type behaves, more or less, like a list, except it only holds bytes. The constructor for the class can accept a `bytes` object to initialize it. The `extend` method can be used to append another `bytes` object to the existing array (for example, when more data comes from a socket or other IO channel).

Slice notation can be used on `bytearray` to modify the item inline. For example, this code constructs a `bytearray` from a `bytes` object and then replaces two bytes using:

```
b = bytearray(b"abcdefgh")
b[4:6] = b"\x15\xa3"
print(b)
```

Be careful though, if we want to manipulate a single element in the `bytearray`, it will expect us to pass an integer between 0 and 255 inclusive. This integer represents a specific `bytes` pattern. If we try to pass a character or `bytes` object, it will raise an exception.

A single byte character can be converted to an integer using the `ord` (short for ordinal) function. This function returns the integer representation of a single character:

```
b = bytearray(b'abcdef')
b[3] = ord(b'g')
b[4] = 68
print(b)
```

After constructing the array, we replace the character at index 3 (the fourth character, as indexing starts at 0, as with lists) with byte 103. This integer was returned by the `ord` function and is the ASCII character for the lowercase g. For illustration, we also replaced the next character up with the byte number 68, which maps to the ASCII character for the uppercase D.

The `bytearray` type has methods that allow it to behave like a list (we can append integer bytes to it, for example), but also like a `bytes` object; we can use methods like `count` and `find` the same way they would behave on a `bytes` or `str` object. The difference is that `bytearray` is a mutable type, which can be useful for building up complex sequences of bytes from a specific input source.

File IO

So far through this book, when our examples touch files, we've operated entirely on text files. Operating systems, however, actually represent files as a sequence of bytes, not text.

Because reading bytes and converting the data to text is one of the more common operations on files, Python wraps the incoming (or outgoing) stream of bytes with appropriate decode (or encode) calls so we can deal directly with str objects. This saves us a lot of boilerplate code to be constantly encoding and decoding text.

The open() function is used to open a file. For reading text from a file, we only need to pass the filename into the function. The file will be opened for reading, and the bytes will be converted to text using the platform default encoding. As with decode and encode on bytes and str objects, the open function can accept encoding and errors arguments to open a text file in a specific character encoding or to choose a specific replacement strategy for invalid bytes in that encoding. These are normally supplied to open as keyword arguments. For example, we can use the following code to read the contents of a text file in ASCII format, converting any unknown bytes using the replace strategy:

```
file = open('filename', encoding='ascii', errors='replace')
print(file.read())
file.close()
```

Of course, we don't always want to **read** files; often we want to **write** data to them! The encoding and errors arguments can also be passed when writing text files. In addition, to open a file for writing, we need to pass a mode argument as the second positional argument, with a value of "w":

```
contents = "an oft-repeated cliché"
file = open("filename", "w", encoding="ascii", errors="replace")
file.write(contents)
file.close()
```

We could also supply the value "a" as a mode argument, to append to the file, rather than completely overwriting existing file contents.

These files with their wrappers for converting bytes to text are great, but it'd be awfully inconvenient if the file we wanted to open was an image, executable, or other binary file, wouldn't it?

To open a binary file, we simply need to append a `'b'` to the mode string. So `'wb'` would open a file for writing bytes, while `'rb'` allows us to read them. They will behave like text files, but without the automatic encoding of text to bytes. When we read such a file, it will return `bytes` instead of `str`, and when we write to it, it will fail if we try to pass a Unicode object.

Once a file is opened for reading, we can call the `read`, `readline`, or `readlines` methods to get the contents of the file. The `read` method returns the entire contents of the file as an `str` or `bytes` object, depending on whether there is a `'b'` in the mode. Be careful not to use this method without arguments on huge files. You don't want to find out what happens if you try to load that much data into memory!

It is also possible to read a fixed number of bytes from a file; we simply pass an integer argument to the `read` method describing how many bytes we want to read. The next call to `read` will load the next sequence of bytes, and so on. We can do this inside a `while` loop to read the entire file in manageable chunks.

The `readline` method returns a single line from the file; we can call it repeatedly to get more lines. The plural `readlines` method returns a list of all the lines in the file. Like the `read` method, it's not safe to use on very large files. These two methods even work when the file is open in `bytes` mode, but it only makes sense if we are parsing text-like data. An image or audio file, for example, will not have newlines in it (unless the newline byte happened to represent a certain pixel or sound), so applying `readline` wouldn't make sense.

For readability and to avoid reading a large file into memory at once, we can also use a `for` loop directly on a file object to read each line, one at a time, and process it.

Writing to a file is just as easy; the `write` method on file objects simply writes a string (or bytes, for binary data) object to the file; it can be called repeatedly to write multiple strings, one after the other. The `writelines` method accepts an iterator and writes each of the iterated values to the file. It specifically does **not** turn the arguments into multiple lines by appending a newline after each one. If each item in the iterator is expected to be a separate line, they should all have newline characters at the end. The `writelines` method is basically a convenience to write the contents of an iterator without having to explicitly iterate over it using a `for` loop.

A final important method on file objects is the `close` method. This method should be called when we are finished reading or writing the file to ensure any buffered writes are written to the file, that the file has been properly cleaned up, and that all resources associated with the file are released back to the operating system. Technically, this will happen automatically when the script exits, but it's better to be explicit and clean up after ourselves.

Placing it in context

This need to always close a file can make for some ugly code. Because an exception may occur during file IO, we ought to wrap all calls to a file in a `try...finally` clause, and close the file in `finally`, regardless of whether IO was successful. This isn't very Pythonic; there must be a more elegant way to do it.

If we run `dir` on a file-like object, we see that it has two special methods named `__enter__` and `__exit__`. These methods turn the file object into what is known as a **context manager**. Basically, if we use a special syntax called the `with` statement, these methods will be called before and after nested code is executed. On file objects, the `__exit__` method ensures the file is closed, even if an exception is raised. We no longer have to explicitly manage the closing of the file. Here is what the `with` statement looks like in practice:

```
with open('filename') as file:
    for line in file:
        print(line, end='')
```

The `open` call returns a file object, which has `__enter__` and `__exit__` methods. The returned object is assigned to the variable named `file` by the `as` clause. We know the file will be closed when the code returns to the outer indentation level, and that this will happen even if an exception is raised.

The `with` statement is used in several places in the standard library where startup or cleanup code needs to be executed. For example, the `urlopen` call returns an object that can be used in a `with` statement to clean up the socket when we're done. Locks in the threading module can automatically release the lock when the statement has been executed.

Most interestingly, because the `with` statement can apply to any object that has the appropriate special methods, we can use it in our own frameworks. Keeping with our string examples, let's create a simple context manager that allows us to construct a sequence of characters and automatically convert it to a string upon exit:

```
class StringJoiner(list):
    def __enter__(self):
        return self

    def __exit__(self, type, value, tb):
        self.result = "".join(self)
```

This code simply adds the two special methods required of a context manager to the list class it inherits from. The __enter__ method performs any required setup code (in this case, there isn't any) and then returns the object that will be assigned to the variable after as in the with statement. Often, as we've done here, this is just the context manager object itself.

The __exit__ method accepts three arguments. In a normal situation, these are all given a value of None. However, if an exception occurs inside the with block, they will be set to values related to the type, value, and traceback for the exception. This allows the __exit__ method to do any cleanup code that may be required even if an exception occurred. In our example, we simply create a result string by joining the characters in the string, regardless of whether an exception was thrown.

While this is one of the simplest context managers we could write, and its usefulness is dubious, it does work with a with statement. Have a look at it in action:

```
import random, string
with StringJoiner() as joiner:
    for i in range(15):
        joiner.append(random.choice(string.ascii_letters))

print(joiner.result)
```

This code simply constructs a string of fifteen random characters. It appends these to a StringJoiner using the append method it inherited from list. When the with statement goes out of scope (back to the outer indentation level), the __exit__ method is called, and the result attribute becomes available on the joiner object. We print this value to see a random string.

Faking files

Sometimes we need code that provides a file-like interface but doesn't actually read from or write to any real files. For example, we might want to retrieve a string from a third-party library that only knows how to write to a file. This is an example of the adapter pattern in action; we need an adapter that converts the file-like interface into a string-like one.

Two such adapters already exist in the standard library, StringIO and BytesIO. They behave in much the same way, except that one deals with text characters and the second deals with bytes data. Both classes are available in the io package. To emulate a file open for reading, we can supply a string or bytes object to the constructor. Calls to read or readline will then parse that string as if it was a file. To emulate a file opened for writing, we simply construct a StringIO or BytesIO object and call the write or writelines methods. When writing is complete, we can discover the final contents of the written "file" using the getvalue method. It's really very simple:

```
# coding=utf-8
from io import StringIO, BytesIO
source_file = StringIO("an oft-repeated cliché")
dest_file = BytesIO()

char = source_file.read(1)
while char:
    dest_file.write(char.encode("ascii", "replace"))
    char = source_file.read(1)

print(dest_file.getvalue())
```

This piece of code is, technically, doing nothing more than encoding a str to a bytes. But it is performing this task using a file-like interface. We first create a source "file" that contains a string, and a destination "file" to write it to. Then we read one character at a time from the source, encode it to ASCII using the "replace" error replacement strategy, and write the resulting byte to the destination file. This code doesn't know that the object it is calling write on is not a file, nor does it care.

The file interface is common for reading and writing data, even if it's not to a file or a string. Network IO often uses the same protocol (set of methods) for reading and writing data to the network, and compression libraries use it to store compressed data, for example. This is duck typing at work; we can write code that operates on a file-like object, and it will never need to know if the data actually came from a compressed file, a string, or the internet.

Storing objects

Nowadays, we take the ability to write data to a file and retrieve it at an arbitrary later date for granted. As convenient as this is (imagine the state of computing if we couldn't store anything!), we may often find ourselves converting data we have stored in a nice object or design pattern in memory into some kind of clunky text or binary format for storage.

The Python pickle module, allows us to store objects directly in a special object storage format. It essentially converts an object (and all the objects it holds as attributes) into a format that can be stored in a file or file-like object or a string of bytes that we can do whatever we want with.

For basic work, the pickle module has an extremely simple interface. It is comprised of four basic functions for storing and loading data; two for manipulating file-like objects, and two for manipulating bytes objects (the latter are just shortcuts to the file-like interface so we don't have to create a BytesIO file-like object ourselves).

The dump method accepts an object to be written and a file-like object to write the serialized bytes to. This object must have a write method (or it wouldn't be file-like), and that method must know how to handle a bytes argument (so a file opened for text output wouldn't work).

The load method does exactly the opposite; it reads a serialized object from a file-like object. This object must have the proper file-like read and readline arguments, each of which must, of course, return bytes. The pickle module will load the object from these bytes and the load method will return the fully reconstructed object. Here's an example that stores and then loads some data in a list object:

```
import pickle

some_data = ["a list", "containing", 5,
        "values including another list",
        ["inner", "list"]]

with open("pickled_list", 'wb') as file:
    pickle.dump(some_data, file)

with open("pickled_list", 'rb') as file:
    loaded_data = pickle.load(file)

print(loaded_data)
assert loaded_data == some_data
```

This code works as advertised: the objects are stored in the file and then loaded from the same file. In each case, we open the file using a with statement so that it is automatically closed. The file is first opened for writing and then a second time for reading, depending on whether we are storing or loading data.

The assert statement at the end would raise an error if the newly loaded object is not equal to the original object. Equality does not imply that they are the same object. Indeed, if we print the id() of both objects, we would discover they are different. However, because they are both lists whose contents are equal, the two lists are also considered equal.

The dumps and loads functions behave much like their file-like counterparts, except they return or accept bytes instead of file-like objects. The dumps function requires only one argument; the object to be stored, and it returns a serialized bytes object. The loads function requires a bytes object and returns the restored object. The 's' in the method names is short for string; it's a legacy name from older versions of Python where str objects were used instead of bytes.

Both `dump` methods accept an optional `protocol` argument. If we are saving and loading pickled objects that are only going to be used in Python 3 programs, we don't need to supply this argument. Unfortunately, if we are storing objects that may be loaded by older versions of Python, we have to use an older and less efficient protocol. This should not normally be an issue. Usually, the only program that would load a pickled object would be the same one that stored it. Pickle is an unsafe format, so we don't want to be sending them unsecured over the internet to unknown interpreters.

The argument supplied is an integer version number. The default version is number 3, representing the current highly efficient storage system used by Python 3 pickling. The number 2 is the older version, which will store an object that can be loaded on all interpreters back to Python 2.3. As 2.3 is the oldest version of Python that is still widely used in the wild, version 2 pickling is normally sufficient. Versions 0 and 1 are supported on older interpreters; 0 is an ASCII format, while 1 is a binary format.

As a rule of thumb, then, if you know that the objects you are pickling will only be loaded by a Python 3 program (for example, only your program will be loading them), use the default pickling protocol. If they may be loaded by unknown interpreters, pass a protocol value of 2, unless you really believe they may need to be loaded by an archaic version of Python.

If we do pass a protocol to `dump` or `dumps`, we should use a keyword argument to specify it: `pickle.dumps(my_object, protocol=2)`. This is not strictly necessary, as the method only accepts two arguments, but typing out the full keyword argument reminds readers of our code what the purpose of the number is. Having a random integer in the method call would be hard to read. Two what? Store two copies of the object, maybe? Remember, code should always be readable. In Python, less code is often more readable than longer code, but not always. Be explicit.

It is possible to call `dump` or `load` on a single open file more than once. Each call to `dump` will store a single object (plus any objects it is composed of or contains), while a call to `load` will load and return just one object. So for a single file, each separate call to `dump` when storing the object should have an associated call to `load` when restoring at a later date.

Customizing pickles

With many common Python objects, pickling "just works". Basic primitives such as integers, floats, and strings can be pickled, as can any container object, such as lists or dictionaries, provided the contents of those containers are also picklable. Further, and importantly, any object can be pickled, so long as all of its attributes are also picklable.

So what makes an attribute unpicklable? Usually, it has something to do with time-sensitive attributes that it would not make sense to load in the future. For example, if we have an open network socket, open file, running thread, or database connection stored as an attribute on an object, it would not make sense to pickle these objects; a lot of operating system state would simply be gone when we came to reload them later. We can't simply pretend a thread or socket connection exists and make it appear! No, we need to somehow customize how such data is stored and restored.

Here's a class that loads the contents of a web page every hour to ensure that they stay up-to-date. It uses the `threading.Timer` class to schedule the next update:

```python
from threading import Timer
import datetime
from urllib.request import urlopen

class UpdatedURL:
    def __init__(self, url):
        self.url = url
        self.contents = ''
        self.last_updated = None
        self.update()

    def update(self):
        self.contents = urlopen(self.url).read()
        self.last_updated = datetime.datetime.now()
        self.schedule()

    def schedule(self):
        self.timer = Timer(3600, self.update)
        self.timer.setDaemon(True)
        self.timer.start()
```

The `url`, `contents`, and `last_updated` are all pickleable, but if we try to pickle an instance of this class, things go a little nutty on the `self.timer` instance:

```python
>>> u = UpdatedURL("http://news.yahoo.com/")
>>> import pickle
>>> serialized = pickle.dumps(u)
Traceback (most recent call last):
  File "<stdin>", line 1, in <module>
  File "/usr/lib/python3.1/pickle.py", line 1358, in dumps
    Pickler(f, protocol, fix_imports=fix_imports).dump(obj)
_pickle.PicklingError: Can't pickle <class 'method'>:
attribute lookup builtins.method failed
```

That's not a very useful error, but it looks like we're trying to pickle something we shouldn't be. That would be the `Timer`; we're storing a reference to `self.timer` in the schedule method, and that attribute cannot be serialized.

When `pickle` tries to serialize an object, it simply tries to store the object's `__dict__` attribute; `__dict__` is a dictionary mapping all the attribute names on the object to their values. Luckily, before checking `__dict__`, `pickle` checks to see if a `__getstate__` method exists. If it does, it will store the return value of that method instead of the `__dict__`.

Let's add a `__getstate__` method to our `UpdatedURL` class that simply returns a copy of the `__dict__` without a timer:

```
def __getstate__(self):
    new_state = self.__dict__.copy()
    if 'timer' in new_state:
        del new_state['timer']
    return new_state
```

If we pickle the object now, it will no longer fail. And we can even successfully restore that object using `loads`. However, the restored object doesn't have a timer attribute, so it will not be refreshing the content like it is designed to do. We need to somehow create a new timer (to replace the missing one) when the object is unpickled.

As we might expect, there is a complementary `__setstate__` method that can be implemented to customize unpickling. This method accepts a single argument, which is simply the object returned by `__getstate__`. If we implement both methods, `__getstate__` is not required to return a dictionary, since `__setstate__` will know what to do with whatever object `__getstate__` chooses to return. In our case, we simply want to restore the `__dict__`, and then create a new timer:

```
def __setstate__(self, data):
    self.__dict__ = data
    self.schedule()
```

The `pickle` module is very flexible and provides other tools to further customize the pickling process if you need them. However, these are beyond the scope of this book. The tools we've covered are sufficient for basic pickling tasks. Objects to be pickled are normally relatively simple data objects; we would not typically pickle an entire running program or complicated design pattern, for example.

Serializing web objects

It is not a good idea to load a pickled object from an unknown or untrusted source. It is possible to inject arbitrary code into a pickled file. This can be used to maliciously attack a computer via the pickle. Another disadvantage of pickles is that they can only be loaded by other Python programs, and cannot be easily shared with other systems.

JavaScript Object Notation (JSON) is a special format for exchanging primitive data. JSON is a standard format that can be interpreted by a wide array of heterogeneous client systems. Hence, JSON can be very useful for transmitting data between completely decoupled systems. Further, JSON does not have any support for executable code, only data can be serialized; thus it is much more difficult to inject malicious statements into it.

Because JSON can be easily interpreted by JavaScript engines, it is most often used for transmitting data from a web server to a JavaScript-capable web browser. If the web application serving the data is written in Python, it needs a way to convert internal data into the JSON format.

There is a module to do this, named, as we might expect, `json`. This module provides a similar interface to the `pickle` module, with `dump`, `load`, `dumps`, and `loads` functions. The default calls to these functions are nearly identical to those in `pickle`, so we won't repeat the details. There are a couple differences; obviously the output of these calls is valid JSON notation, rather than a pickled object. In addition, the `json` functions operate on `str` objects, rather than `bytes`. Therefore, when dumping to or loading from a file, we need to create text files rather than binary ones.

The JSON serializer is not as robust as the `pickle` module; it can only serialize basic types such as integers, floats, and strings, and simple containers such as dictionaries and lists. Each of these has a direct mapping to a JSON representation, but JSON is unable to represent classes, methods, or functions. It is not possible to transmit complete objects in this format. Because the receiver of an object we have dumped to JSON format is normally not a Python object, it would not be able to understand classes or methods in the same way that Python does, anyway. JSON is a **data** notation; objects, as you will recall, are composed of both data and behavior.

If we do have objects for which we want to serialize only the data, we can always serialize the object's `__dict__` attribute. Or we can semi-automate this task by supplying custom code to create or parse a JSON serializable dictionary from certain types of objects.

In the `json` module, both the object storing and loading functions accept optional arguments to customize the behavior. The `dump` and `dumps` methods accept a `cls` keyword argument. If passed, this should be a subclass of the `JSONEncoder` class, with the `default` method overridden. This method accepts an object and converts it to a dictionary that `json` can digest. If it doesn't know how to process the object, it's generally good to call the `super()` method, so that it can take care of serializing basic types.

The `load` and `loads` methods also accept such a `cls` argument that can be a subclass of the inverse class, `JSONDecoder`. However, it is normally sufficient to pass a function into these methods using the `object_hook` keyword argument. This function accepts a dictionary and returns an object; if it doesn't know what to do with the input dictionary, it can simply return it unmodified.

But that's enough theory, let's look at an example! Imagine we have the following simple contact class that we want to serialize:

```
class Contact:
    def __init__(self, first, last):
        self.first = first
        self.last = last

    @property
    def full_name(self):
        return("{} {}".format(self.first, self.last))
```

We could just serialize the `__dict__`:

```
>>> c = Contact("John", "Smith")
>>> json.dumps(c.__dict__)
'{"last": "Smith", "first": "John"}'
```

But accessing special (double-underscore) attributes in this fashion is kind of crude. Also, what if the receiving code (perhaps some JavaScript on a web page) wanted that `full_name` property to be supplied? Of course, we could construct the dictionary by hand, but if we need to do a lot of that, it can be useful to create a custom encoder instead:

```
import json
class ContactEncoder(json.JSONEncoder):
    def default(self, obj):
        if isinstance(obj, Contact):
            return {'is_contact': True,
                    'first': obj.first,
                    'last': obj.last,
                    'full': obj.full_name}
        return super().default(obj)
```

The `default` method basically checks to see what kind of object we're trying to serialize; if it's a contact, we convert it to a dictionary manually, otherwise we let the parent class handle serialization (by assuming that it is a basic type that `json` knows how to handle). Notice that we pass an extra attribute to identify this object as a contact, since there would be no way to tell upon loading it. This is just a convention; for a more generic serialization mechanism it might make more sense to store a string type in the dictionary, or possibly even the full class name, including package and module. Remember that the format of the dictionary depends on the code at the receiving end; there has to be an agreement as to how the data is going to be specified.

We can use this class to encode a contact by passing the class (not an instantiated object) to the `dump` or `dumps` function:

```
>>> c = Contact("John", "Smith")
>>> json.dumps(c, cls=ContactEncoder)
'{"is_contact": true, "last": "Smith", "full": "John Smith",
"first": "John"}'
```

For decoding, we can write a function that accepts a dictionary and checks the existence of the `is_contact` variable to decide whether to convert it to a contact:

```
def decode_contact(dic):
        if dic.get('is_contact'):
            return Contact(dic['first'], dic['last'])
        else:
            return dic
```

We can pass this function to the `load` or `loads` function using the `object_hook` keyword argument:

```
>>> data = '{"is_contact": true, "last": "smith",
        "full": "john smith", "first": "john"}'
>>> c = json.loads(data, object_hook=decode_contact)
>>> c
<__main__.Contact object at 0xa02918c>
>>> c.full_name
'john smith'
```

Exercises

We've covered a wide variety of topics in this chapter, from strings to files, to object serialization, and back again. Now it's time to consider how these ideas can be applied to your own code.

Python strings are very flexible, and Python is an extremely powerful tool for string-based manipulations. If you don't do a lot of string processing in your daily work, try designing a tool that is exclusively intended for manipulating strings. Try to come up with something innovative, but if you're stuck, consider writing a web log analyzer (how many requests per hour? How many people visit more than five pages?) or a template tool that replaces certain variable names with the contents of other files.

Spend a lot of time toying with the string formatting operators. Simply write a bunch of template strings and objects to pass into the format function, and see what kind of output you get. Try the exotic formatting operators, like percentage or hexadecimal notation. Try out the fill and alignment operators, and see how they behave differently for integers, strings, and floats. Consider writing a class of your own that has a __format__ method; we didn't discuss this in detail, but explore just how much you can customize formatting.

Make sure you understand the difference between bytes and str objects. The distinction is very complicated in older versions of Python (there was no bytes, and str acted like both bytes and str unless we needed non-ASCII characters in which case there was a separate unicode object, which was similar to Python 3's str class. It's even more confusing than it sounds!). It's clearer nowadays; bytes is for binary data, and str is for character data. The only tricky part is knowing how and when to convert between the two. For practice, try writing text data to a file opened for writing bytes (you'll have to encode the text yourself), and then reading from the same file.

Do some experimenting with bytearray; see how it can act both like a bytes object and a list or container object at the same time. Try writing a buffer that holds data in the bytes array until it is a certain length before returning it. You can simulate the code that puts data into the buffer by using time.sleep calls to ensure data doesn't arrive too quickly.

If you don't use the with statement in your daily coding, go through all your code and find all the places you have opened files and forgotten to close them. Pay special attention to places where you did close the files, but only under the assumption that no exception was raised. For every one you find, replace the code with a with statement.

Have you ever written code where a custom context manager might be useful? Think about cases where you have to do arbitrary setup or cleanup around an unknown or partially known task. That task will be implemented inside the with statement, while the setup or cleanup code is taken care of in __enter__ and __exit__ methods on the object. This is a very useful construct, although it's not an overly common pattern; if you can't think of any places it would suit an old project, try writing one for a new situation of your devising, just as an exercise.

If you've ever written an adapter to load small amounts of data from a file or database and convert it to an object, consider using a pickle instead. Pickles are not efficient for storing massive amounts of data, but they can be useful for loading configuration or other simple objects. Try coding it multiple ways; using a pickle, a text file, or a small database. Which is easiest to work with?

Try experimenting with pickling data, then modifying the class that holds the data, and loading the pickle into the new class. What works? What doesn't? Is there a way to make drastic changes to a class, such as renaming an attribute or splitting it into two new attributes and still get the data out of an older pickle? (Hint: try placing a private pickle version number on each object and update it each time you change the class; you can then put a migration path in `__setstate__`.)

If you do any web development at all, especially Web 2.0 applications, do some experimenting with the JSON serializer. Personally, I prefer to serialize only standard JSON serializable objects, rather than writing custom encoders or `object_hooks`, but the desired effect really depends on the interaction between the frontend (JavaScript, typically) and backend code. The JSON format isn't very common outside of JavaScript and web notation, so if you don't do web development you may want to skip this exercise. Note, however, that JSON is a subset of YAML, so if you have occasion to generate valid YAML, the JSON serializer can still be useful!

Summary

We've covered string manipulation, file IO, and object serialization. We discussed how to combine hard-coded strings and program variables into outputtable strings using the powerful string formatting system, and learned the difference between binary and textual data. All told, we've seen:

- How to use the various `str` methods
- String formatting
- `bytes` versus `str`
- Mutable `bytearrays`
- Files in binary and textual formatters
- Context managers and the `with` statement
- Serializing data with `pickle` and `json`

In the next chapter, we'll cover one of the most important topics in Python programming: how to test our code to ensure it's doing what we think it is doing.

11

Testing Object-oriented Programs

Most skilled Python programmers agree that testing is one of the most important aspects of software development in Python. Even though this chapter is placed near the end of the book, it is not an afterthought; everything we have studied so far will help us when writing tests. We'll be studying:

- The importance of unit testing and test-driven development
- The standard `unittest` module
- The `py.test` automated testing suite
- Code coverage

Why test?

More and more programmers are learning how important testing their code is. If you're among them, feel free to skim this section. You'll find the next section, where we actually learn how to do the tests in Python, more scintillating. If you're not convinced of the importance of testing, I promise that your code is broken, you just don't know it. Read on!

Some people argue that testing is more important in Python code because of its dynamic nature; compiled languages such as Java and C++ are occasionally thought to be somehow 'safer' because they enforce type checking at compile time. The thing is, Python tests rarely, if ever, check types. They're checking values. They're making sure that the right attributes have been set at the right time or that the sequence has the right length, order, and values. They aren't checking to make absolutely sure that a list was returned if a tuple or custom container would suffice. These higher-level things need to be tested in any language. The real reason Python programmers test more than programmers of other languages is that it is so easy to test in Python!

But why test? Do we really need to test? What if we didn't test? To answer those questions, write a program from scratch without any testing at all. Don't run it until it is completely written, start to finish. Don't pick a large program, just a few classes interacting. If you can't come up with anything, try a two player tic-tac-toe game; it's fairly simple if you make both players human players (no artificial intelligence). You don't even have to try to calculate who the winner is.

Now run your program. And fix all the errors. How many were there? I recorded eight on my tic-tac-toe implementation, and I'm not sure I caught them all. Did you?

We need to test our code to make sure it works. Running the program, as we just did, and fixing the errors is one crude form of testing. Most programmers tend to write a few lines of code and run the program to make sure those lines are doing what they expect. But changing a few lines of code can affect parts of the program that the developer hadn't considered as being influenced by the changes. Because they weren't thinking of this influence, they won't test the other functionality. As we can see from the the program we just wrote, if they haven't tested it, it's almost certainly broken.

To handle this, we write automated tests. Written tests are simply programs that automatically run certain inputs through other programs (or, more often, parts of other programs, such as one function or class). We can run these test programs in seconds and cover more possible user inputs than one programmer would think to test every time they change something.

There are four main reasons to write tests:

- To ensure that code is working the way the developer thinks it should
- To ensure that code continues working when we make changes
- To ensure the developer understood the requirements
- To ensure that the code we are writing has a maintainable interface

The first point really doesn't justify the time it takes to write a test; we can simply test the code directly (perhaps through the interactive interpreter). But as soon as we have to perform the same sequence of test actions multiple times, it takes less time to automate those steps once and then run them whenever necessary. It is a good idea to run tests whenever we have to change code, whether it is during initial development or maintenance releases. When we have a comprehensive set of automated tests, we can run them after code changes and know that we didn't inadvertently break anything that was tested.

However, the most interesting points in the list are the last two. When we write tests for code, it can actually help us design the API, interface, or pattern that code takes. Thus, if we, as the programmers, misunderstood the requirements from management or the client, writing a test can help highlight that misunderstanding. On the other side, if we're not certain how we want to design a class, we can write a test that interacts with that class so we have an idea what the most natural way to test it would be. In fact, it is often beneficial to write the tests before we write the code we are testing!

Test-driven development

Writing tests first is the mantra of test-driven development. Test-driven development takes the "untested code is broken code" concept one step further and suggests that only unwritten code should be untested. Do not write any code until you have written the tests for this code. So the first step is to write a test that proves the code would work. Obviously, the test is going to fail, since the code hasn't been written. Then write the code that ensures the test passes. Then write another test for the next segment of code.

Test-driven development is fun. It allows us to build little puzzles to solve; these are the tests. Then we implement the code to solve the puzzles. Then we make a more complicated puzzle, and we write code that solves the new puzzle without unsolving the previous one.

There are two goals to the test-driven methodology. The first is to ensure that tests really get written. It's so very easy, after we have written code, to say: "Hmm, it seems to work, I don't have to write any tests for this. It was just a small change, nothing could have broken." If the test is already written before we write the code, we will know exactly when it works (because the test will pass), and we'll know in the future if it is ever broken by a change we, or someone else has made.

Secondly, writing tests first forces us to consider exactly how the code is going to be interacted with. It tells us what methods we need objects to have and how attributes will be accessed. It helps us break up the initial problem into smaller, testable problems, and then to recombine the tested solutions into larger, also tested solutions. Writing tests can thus become a part of the design process. Often, if we're writing a test for a not-fully-specified object, we will discover anomalies in the design that force us to consider new aspects of the software.

As a concrete example, we may be writing code that uses an object-relational mapper to store object properties in a database. It is common to use an automatically assigned database ID in such objects, and our code might be using this ID for various purposes, say as a key in a dictionary. If we are writing a test for such code, before we write it, we may realize that our design is faulty because objects do not have these IDs until they have been saved to the database. If we want to manipulate an object without saving it in our test, it will highlight this problem before we have written any code.

Testing makes software better. Writing tests before we release the software makes it better before the end user sees or purchases the buggy version (I have worked for companies that thrive on the "the users can test it" philosophy. It's not a healthy business model!). Writing tests before we write the software makes it better the first time it is written.

Unit testing

Let's start our exploration with Python's built-in test library. This library provides a common interface for **unit tests**. Unit tests are a special kind of automated test that focuses on testing the least amount of code possible in any one test. Each test tests a single unit of the total amount of available code.

The Python library for this is called, unsurprisingly: unittest. It provides several tools for creating and running unit tests, the most important being the TestCase class. This class provides a set of methods that allow us to compare values, set up tests, and clean up after running them.

When we want to write a set of unit tests for a specific task, we create a subclass of TestCase, and write methods that accept no arguments to do the actual testing. These methods must all start with the string test. If this convention is followed, they'll automatically be run as part of the test process. Normally, the tests set some values on an object and then run a method, and use the built-in comparison methods to ensure that the right results were calculated. Here's a very simple example:

```python
import unittest

class CheckNumbers(unittest.TestCase):
    def test_int_float(self):
        self.assertEquals(1, 1.0)

if __name__ == "__main__":
    unittest.main()
```

This code simply subclasses the `TestCase` class and adds a method that calls the `TestCase.assertEquals` method. This method will either succeed or raise an exception, depending on whether the two parameters are equal. If we run this code, the `main` function from `unittest` will give us the following output:

```
.
----------------------------------------------------------------
Ran 1 test in 0.000s

OK
```

Did you know that floats and integers can compare as equal? Let's add a new test that fails:

```
def test_str_float(self):
    self.assertEquals(1, "1")
```

If we run this code, the output is a bit more sinister, since floats and strings can not be considered equal:

```
.F
================================================================
FAIL: test_str_float (__main__.CheckNumbers)
----------------------------------------------------------------
Traceback (most recent call last):
  File "simplest_unittest.py", line 8, in test_str_float
    self.assertEquals(1, "1")
AssertionError: 1 != '1'

----------------------------------------------------------------
Ran 2 tests in 0.001s

FAILED (failures=1)
```

The dot on the first line indicates that the first test (the one we wrote before) passed successfully; the F after it shows that the second test failed. Then at the end, it gives us some informative output telling us how and where the test failed, along with a summary of the number of failures.

We can have as many test methods on one TestCase class as we like; as long as the method name begins with test the test runner will execute each one as a separate test. Each test should be completely independent of other tests. Results or calculations from a previous test should have no impact on the current test. The key to writing good unit tests is to keep each test method as short as possible, testing a small unit of code with each test case. If your code does not seem to naturally break up into such testable units, it's probably a sign that your design needs rethinking. Writing tests allows us not only to ensure our code works, but also helps test our design as well.

Assertion methods

The general layout of a test case is to set certain variables to known values, run one or more functions, methods, or processes, and then "prove" that the correct results were returned or calculated by using TestCase assertion methods.

There are a few different assertion methods available to confirm that specific results have been achieved. We just saw assertEqual, which will cause a test failure if the two parameters do not pass an equality check. The inverse, assertNotEqual, will fail if the two parameters do compare as equal. The assertTrue and assertFalse methods each accept a single expression, and fail if the expression does not pass an if test. These tests are not checking for the Boolean values True or False; they return the same value that would be returned if an if statement were used: False, None, 0, or an empty list, dictionary, or tuple would pass an assertFalse, while nonzero numbers, containers with values in them, or the value True would pass an assertTrue.

The assertRaises method accepts an exception class, a callable object (function, method, or an object with a __call__ method), and arbitrary arguments and keyword arguments to be passed into the callable. The assertion method will invoke the function with the supplied arguments, and will fail or raise an error if the method does not raise the expected exception class.

In addition, each of these methods accepts an optional argument named msg; if supplied, it will be included in the error message if the assertion fails. This is useful for clarifying what was expected or explaining where a bug may have occurred to cause the assertion to fail.

Additional assertion methods in Python 3.1

The `unittest` library has been extensively updated in Python 3.1. It now contains several new assertion methods, and allows the `assertRaises` method to take advantage of the `with` statement. The following code only works on Python 3.1 and later. It illustrates the two ways that `assertRaises` can be called:

```python
import unittest

def average(seq):
    return sum(seq) / len(seq)

class TestAverage(unittest.TestCase):
    def test_python30_zero(self):
        self.assertRaises(ZeroDivisionError,
            average,
            [])

    def test_python31_zero(self):
        with self.assertRaises(ZeroDivisionError):
            average([])

if __name__ == "__main__":
    unittest.main()
```

The context manager allows us to write the code the way we would normally write it (by calling functions or executing code directly) rather than having to wrap the function call in another function call.

In addition, Python 3.1 provides access to several useful new assertion methods:

- `assertGreater`, `assertGreaterEqual`, `assertLess`, and `assertLessEqual` all accept two comparable objects, and ensure that the named inequality holds.

- `assertIn` ensures that the first of two arguments is an element in the container object (list, tuple, dictionary, and so on) that is passed as a second argument. The `assertNotIn` method does the inverse.

- `assertIsNone` tests that a value is `None`. Unlike `assertFalse`, it will not pass for values of zero, `False`, or empty container objects; the value must be `None`. The `assertIsNotNone` method does, of course, the opposite.

- `assertSameElements` accepts two container objects as arguments, and ensures that they contain the same set of elements, regardless of order.

- `assertSequenceEqual` does enforce order. Further, if there's a failure, it will show a diff comparing the two lists to see exactly how it failed.

- `assertDictEqual`, `assertSetEqual`, `assertListEqual`, and `assertTupleEqual` all do the same thing as `assertSequenceEqual`, except they also ensure that the container objects are the correct type.

- `assertMultilineEqual` accepts two multiline strings and ensures they are identical. If they are not, a diff is displayed in the error message.

- `assertRegexpMatches` accepts text and a regular expression and confirms that the text matches the regular expression.

Reducing boilerplate and cleaning up

After writing a few small tests, we often find that we have to do the same setup code for several related tests. For example, the following simple `list` subclass has three methods for simple statistical calculations:

```python
from collections import defaultdict

class StatsList(list):
    def mean(self):
        return sum(self) / len(self)

    def median(self):
        if len(self) % 2:
            return self[int(len(self) / 2)]
        else:
            idx = int(len(self) / 2)
            return (self[idx] + self[idx-1]) / 2

    def mode(self):
        freqs = defaultdict(int)
        for item in self:
            freqs[item] += 1
        mode_freq = max(freqs.values())
        modes = []
        for item, value in freqs.items():
            if value == mode_freq:
                modes.append(item)
        return modes
```

Clearly, we're going to want to test situations with each of these three methods that have very similar inputs; we'll want to see what happens with empty lists or with lists containing non-numeric values or with lists containing a normal dataset. We can use the `setUp` method on the `TestCase` class to do initialization for each test. This method accepts no arguments, and allows us to do arbitrary setup before each test is run. For example, we can test all three methods on identical lists of integers as follows:

```python
from stats import StatsList
import unittest

class TestValidInputs(unittest.TestCase):
    def setUp(self):
        self.stats = StatsList([1,2,2,3,3,4])

    def test_mean(self):
        self.assertEqual(self.stats.mean(), 2.5)

    def test_median(self):
        self.assertEqual(self.stats.median(), 2.5)
        self.stats.append(4)
        self.assertEqual(self.stats.median(), 3)

    def test_mode(self):
        self.assertEqual(self.stats.mode(), [2,3])
        self.stats.remove(2)
        self.assertEqual(self.stats.mode(), [3])

if __name__ == "__main__":
    unittest.main()
```

If we run this example, it indicates that all tests pass. Notice first that the `setUp` method is never explicitly called inside the three `test_*` methods. The test suite does this on our behalf. More importantly notice how `test_median` alters the list, by adding an additional 4 to it, yet when `test_mode` is called, the list has returned to the values specified in `setUp` (if it had not, there would be two fours in the list, and the mode method would have returned three values). This shows that `setUp` is called individually before each test, to ensure the test class has a clean slate for testing. Tests can be executed in any order, and the results of one test do not depend on results from another.

In addition to the `setUp` method, `TestCase` offers a no-argument `tearDown` method, which can be used for cleaning up after each and every test on the class has run. This is useful if cleanup entails more than just letting an object be garbage collected. For example, if we are testing code that does file IO, our tests may create new files as a side effect of testing; the `tearDown` method can be used to remove these files and ensure the system is in the same state it was before the tests ran. Test cases should never have side effects.

In general, we group test methods into separate `TestCase` subclasses depending on what setup code they have in common. Several tests that require the same or similar setup will be placed in one class, while tests that require unrelated setup go in their own class.

Organizing and running tests

It doesn't take long for a collection of unit tests to grow very large and unwieldy. It quickly becomes complicated to load and run all the tests at once. This is a primary goal of unit testing; it should be trivial to run all tests on our program and get a quick, "yes or no", answer to the question, "Did my recent changes break any existing tests?"

It is possible to collect groups of `TestCase` objects or modules containing tests into collections called `TestSuites`, and to load specific tests at specific times. In older versions of Python, this resulted in a lot of boilerplate code just to load and execute all the tests on a project. If this much control is needed, the functionality is still available, but most programmers can use test discovery, which will automatically find and run tests in the current package or subpackages.

Test discovery is built into Python 3.2 (and the simultaneously developed Python 2.7) and later, but can also be used in Python 3.1 or older versions of Python by installing the `discover` module available from `http://pypi.python.org/pypi/discover/`.

The `discover` module basically looks for any modules in the current folder or subfolders with names that start with the characters `test`. If it finds any `TestCase` or `TestSuite` objects in these modules, the tests are executed. It's a painless way to ensure you don't miss running any tests. To use it, simply ensure your test modules are named `test_<something>.py` and then run one of the following two commands, depending on which version of Python you have installed:

- Python 3.1 or earlier: `python3 -m discover`
- Python 3.2 or later: `python3 -m unittest discover`

Ignoring broken tests

Sometimes a test is known to fail, but we don't want the test suite to report a failure under those conditions. This may be because a broken or unfinished feature has had tests written, but we aren't currently focusing on improving it. More often, it happens because a feature is only available on a certain platform, Python version, or for advanced versions of a specific library. Python provides us with a few decorators to mark tests as expected to fail or to be skipped under known conditions.

These decorators are:

- `expectedFailure()`
- `skip(reason)`
- `skipIf(condition, reason)`
- `skipUnless(condition, reason)`

These are applied using the Python decorator syntax. The first one accepts no arguments, and simply tells the test runner not to record the test as a failure even if it does, in fact, fail. The `skip` method goes one step further and doesn't even bother to run the test. It expects a single string argument describing why the test was skipped. The other two decorators accept two arguments, one a Boolean expression that indicates whether or not the test should be run, and a similar description. In use, these three decorators might be applied like this:

```python
import unittest
import sys

class SkipTests(unittest.TestCase):
    @unittest.expectedFailure
    def test_fails(self):
        self.assertEqual(False, True)

    @unittest.skip("Test is useless")
    def test_skip(self):
        self.assertEqual(False, True)

    @unittest.skipIf(sys.version_info.minor == 1,
            "broken on 3.1")
    def test_skipif(self):
        self.assertEqual(False, True)

    @unittest.skipUnless(sys.platform.startswith('linux'),
            "broken on linux")
    def test_skipunless(self):
        self.assertEqual(False, True)

if __name__ == "__main__":
    unittest.main()
```

The first test fails, but it is reported as an expected failure; the second test is never run. The other two tests may or may not be run depending on the current Python version and operating system. On my Linux system running Python 3.1 the output looks like this:

```
xssF
================================================================
FAIL: test_skipunless (__main__.SkipTests)
----------------------------------------------------------------
Traceback (most recent call last):
  File "skipping_tests.py", line 21, in test_skipunless
    self.assertEqual(False, True)
AssertionError: False != True


----------------------------------------------------------------
Ran 4 tests in 0.001s

FAILED (failures=1, skipped=2, expected failures=1)
```

The x on the first line indicates an expected failure; the two s characters represent skipped tests, and the F indicates a real failure, since the conditional to skipUnless was True on my system.

Testing with py.test

The Python unittest module is very verbose and requires a lot of boilerplate code to set up and initialize tests. It is based on the very popular JUnit testing framework for Java. It even uses the same method names (you may have noticed they don't conform to the PEP-8 naming standard, which suggests underscores be used to separate words in a method name, rather than CamelCase) and test layout. While this is effective for testing in Java, it's not necessarily the best design for Python testing.

Because Python programmers like their code to be elegant and simple, other test frameworks have been developed, outside the standard library. Two of the more popular ones are **py.test** and **nose**. The latter is not yet supported on Python 3, so we'll focus on py.test here.

Since py.test is not part of the standard library, you'll need to download and install it yourself; you can get it from the py.test homepage at http://pytest.org/. The website has comprehensive installation instructions for a variety of interpreters and platforms.

`py.test` has a substantially different layout from the `unittest` module. It doesn't require test cases to be classes. Instead, it takes advantage of the fact that functions are objects, and allows any properly named function to behave like a test. Rather than providing a bunch of custom methods for asserting equality, it simply uses the `assert` statement to verify results. This makes tests more readable and maintainable.

When we run `py.test`, it will start in the current folder and search for any modules in that folder or subpackages whose names start with the characters `test_`. If there are any functions in this module that also start with `test`, they will be executed as individual tests.

Further, if there are any classes in the module whose name starts with `Test`, any methods on that class that start with `test_` will also be executed in the test environment.

So let's take the simplest possible `unittest` example we wrote earlier and port it to `py.test`:

```
def test_int_float():
    assert 1 == 1.0
```

For the exact same test, we've written two lines of more readable code, in comparison to the six lines we used in our first `unittest` example.

However, we are not precluded from writing class-based tests. Classes can be useful for grouping related tests together or for tests that need to access related attributes or methods on the class. This example shows an extended class with a passing and a failing test; we'll see that the error output is more comprehensive than that provided by the `unittest` module:

```
class TestNumbers:
    def test_int_float(self):
        assert 1 == 1.0

    def test_int_str(self):
        assert 1 == "1"
```

Notice that the class doesn't have to extend any special objects to be picked up as a test. If we run `py.test` on this file, the output looks like this:

```
=============== test session starts ===============
python: platform linux2 -- Python 3.1.2 -- pytest-1.2.1
test object 1: class_pytest.py

class_pytest.py .F
```

```
=================== FAILURES====================
               TestNumbers.test_int_str _____

self = <class_pytest.TestNumbers object at 0x85b4fac>

    def test_int_str(self):
>         assert 1 == "1"
E         assert 1 == '1'

class_pytest.py:7: AssertionError
====== 1 failed, 1 passed in 0.10 seconds =======
```

The output starts with some useful information about the platform and interpreter. This can be useful for sharing bugs across disparate systems. The third line tells us the name of the file being tested (if there are multiple test modules picked up, they will all be displayed) followed by the familiar `.F` we saw in the `unittest` module; the `.` indicates a passing test, while the `F` demonstrates a failure.

After all tests have run, the error output for each of them is displayed. It presents a summary of local variables (there is only one in this example: the `self` parameter passed into the function), the source code where the error occurred, and a summary of the error message. In addition, if an exception other than an `AssertionError` is raised, `py.test` will present us with a complete traceback including source code references.

By default, `py.test` suppresses output from `print` statements if the test is successful. This is extremely useful for test debugging; if we have a test that is failing, we can add print statements to the test to check the values of specific variables and attributes as the test progresses. If the test fails, the values will be output to help with diagnostics. However, if the test is successful, the output of the print statements will not be displayed, allowing them to easily be ignored. Most importantly, we don't have to "clean up" the output by removing print statements; we can leave them in the tests and if the tests ever fail again, due to changes in our code, the debugging output will be immediately available.

One way to do setup and cleanup

`py.test` supports setup and teardown methods similar to those used in `unittest`, but it provides even more flexibility. We'll discuss these briefly, since they are familiar, but they are not used as extensively as in the `unittest` module, as `py.test` provides us with a powerful funcargs facility, which we'll discuss in the next section.

If we are writing class-based tests, we can use two methods called `setup_method` and `teardown_method` in basically the same way that `setUp` and `tearDown` are called in `unittest`. They are called before and after each method in the class to do any setup and cleanup duties. There is one difference from the `unittest` methods though. Both methods accept an argument: the function object representing the method being called.

In addition, `py.test` provides other setup and teardown functions to give us more control over when setup and cleanup code is executed. The `setup_class` and `teardown_class` methods are expected to be class methods; they accept a single argument (there is no `self` argument) representing the class in question.

Finally, we have the `setup_module` and `teardown_module` methods, which are run immediately before and after all tests (in functions or classes) in that module. These can be useful for "one time" setup, such as creating a socket or database connection that will be used by all tests in the module. Be careful with this one, as it can accidentally introduce dependencies between tests if the object being set up stores state.

That short description probably doesn't do a great job of explaining exactly when these setup and teardown methods are called, so let's look at an example that tells us exactly when it happens:

```python
def setup_module(module):
    print("setting up MODULE {0}".format(
        module.__name__))


def teardown_module(module):
    print("tearing down MODULE {0}".format(
        module.__name__))


def test_a_function():
    print("RUNNING TEST FUNCTION")


class BaseTest:
    def setup_class(cls):
        print("setting up CLASS {0}".format(
            cls.__name__))

    def teardown_class(cls):
        print("tearing down CLASS {0}\n".format(
            cls.__name__))

    def setup_method(self, method):
```

```
        print("setting up METHOD {0}".format(
            method.__name__))

    def teardown_method(self, method):
        print("tearing down  METHOD {0}".format(
            method.__name__))

class TestClass1(BaseTest):
    def test_method_1(self):
        print("RUNNING METHOD 1-1")

    def test_method_2(self):
        print("RUNNING METHOD 1-2")

class TestClass2(BaseTest):
    def test_method_1(self):
        print("RUNNING METHOD 2-1")

    def test_method_2(self):
        print("RUNNING METHOD 2-2")
```

The sole purpose of the `BaseTest` class is to extract four methods that would be otherwise identical to the test classes and use inheritance to reduce the amount of duplicate code. So, from the point of view of `py.test`, the two subclasses have not only two test methods each, but also two setup and two teardown methods (one at the class level, one at the method level).

If we run these tests using `py.test`, the output shows us when the various functions are called in relation to the tests themselves. We also have to disable the suppression of output for the `print` statements to execute; this is done by passing the `-s` (or `--capture=no`) flag to `py.test`:

py.test setup_teardown.py -s

```
setup_teardown.py
setting up MODULE setup_teardown
RUNNING TEST FUNCTION
.setting up CLASS TestClass1
setting up METHOD test_method_1
RUNNING METHOD 1-1
.tearing down  METHOD test_method_1
setting up METHOD test_method_2
RUNNING METHOD 1-2
.tearing down  METHOD test_method_2
tearing down CLASS TestClass1
```

```
setting up CLASS TestClass2
setting up METHOD test_method_1
RUNNING METHOD 2-1
.tearing down  METHOD test_method_1
setting up METHOD test_method_2
RUNNING METHOD 2-2
.tearing down  METHOD test_method_2
tearing down CLASS TestClass2

tearing down MODULE setup_teardown
```

The setup and teardown methods for the module are executed at the beginning and end of the session. Then the lone module-level test function we added is run. Next, the setup method for the first class is executed, followed by the two tests for that class. The tests, however, are each individually wrapped in separate setup_method and teardown_method calls. After the methods have been executed, the class teardown method is called. The same sequence happens for the second class, before the teardown_module method is finally called, exactly once.

A completely different way to set up variables

One of the most common uses for the various setup and teardown functions is to ensure certain class or module variables are available with a known value before each test method is run.

py.test offers a completely different way to do this using what are known as **funcargs**, short for function arguments. Funcargs are basically named variables that are previously set up in a test configuration file. This allows us to separate configuration from execution of tests, and allows the funcargs to be used across multiple classes and modules.

To use them, we simply add parameters to our test function. The names of the parameters are used to look up specific arguments in specially named functions. For example, if we wanted to test the StatsList class we used earlier, while demonstrating unittest, we would again want to repeatedly test a list of valid integers. But we can write our tests like so instead of using setup methods:

```
from stats import StatsList

def pytest_funcarg__valid_stats(request):
    return StatsList([1,2,2,3,3,4])


def test_mean(valid_stats):
    assert valid_stats.mean() == 2.5
```

```
def test_median(valid_stats):
    assert valid_stats.median() == 2.5
    valid_stats.append(4)
    assert valid_stats.median() == 3

def test_mode(valid_stats):
    assert valid_stats.mode() == [2,3]
    valid_stats.remove(2)
    assert valid_stats.mode() == [3]
```

Each of the three test methods accepts a parameter named `valid_stats`; this parameter is created afresh by calling the `pytest_funcarg__valid_stats` function defined at the top of the file. It can also be defined in a file called `conftest.py` if the funcarg is needed by multiple modules. The `conftest.py` file is parsed by `py.test` to load any "global" test configuration; it is a sort of catchall for customizing the `py.test` experience. It's actually normal to put funcargs in this module instead of your test file, in order to completely separate the configuration from the test code.

As with other `py.test` features, the name of the factory for returning a funcarg is important; funcargs are simply functions that are named `pytest_funcarg__<valid_identifier>`, where `<valid_identifier>` is a valid variable name that can be used as a parameter in a test function. This function accepts a mysterious request parameter, and returns the object that should be passed as an argument into the individual test functions. The funcarg is created afresh for each call to an individual test function; this allows us, for example, to change the list in one test and know that it will be reset to its original values in the next test.

Funcargs can do a lot more than return simple variables. That `request` object passed into the funcarg factory gives us some extremely useful methods and attributes to modify the funcarg's behavior. The `module`, `cls`, and `function` attributes allow us to see exactly which test is requesting the funcarg. The `config` attribute allows us to check command-line arguments and other configuration data. We don't have room to go into detail on this topic, but custom command-line arguments can be used to customize the test experience by running certain tests only if an argument is passed (useful for slow tests that need to be run less often) or supplying connection parameters to a database, file, or hardware device.

More interestingly, the request object provides methods that allow us to do additional cleanup on the funcarg or to reuse it across tests. The former allows us to use funcargs instead of writing custom teardown functions to clean up open files or connections, while the latter can help reduce the time it takes to run a test suite if the setup of a common funcarg is time consuming. This is often used for database connections, which are slow to create and destroy and do not need to be reinitialized after each test (although the database still typically needs to be reset to a known state between tests).

The `request.addfinalizer` method accepts a callback function that does any cleanup after each test function that uses a funcarg has been called. This can provide the equivalent of a teardown method, allowing us to clean up files, close connections, empty lists or reset queues. For example, the following code tests the `os.mkdir` functionality by creating a temporary directory funcarg:

```
import tempfile
import shutil
import os.path

def pytest_funcarg__temp_dir(request):
    dir = tempfile.mkdtemp()
    print(dir)

    def cleanup():
        shutil.rmtree(dir)
    request.addfinalizer(cleanup)
    return dir

def test_osfiles(temp_dir):
    os.mkdir(os.path.join(temp_dir, 'a'))
    os.mkdir(os.path.join(temp_dir, 'b'))
    dir_contents = os.listdir(temp_dir)
    assert len(dir_contents) == 2
    assert 'a' in dir_contents
    assert 'b' in dir_contents
```

The funcarg creates a new empty temporary directory for files to be created in. Then it adds a finalizer call to remove that directory (using `shutil.rmtree`, which recursively removes a directory and anything inside it) after the test has completed. The file system is then left in the same state in which it started.

Then we have the `request.cached_setup` method, which allows us to create function argument variables that last longer than one test. This is useful when setting up an expensive operation that can be reused by multiple tests without the resource reuse breaking the atomic or unit nature of the tests (so that one test does not rely on and is not impacted by a previous one). For example, if we want to test the following echo server, we may want to run only one instance of the server in a separate process and then have multiple tests connect to that instance.

```
import socket

s = socket.socket(socket.AF_INET, socket.SOCK_STREAM)
s.setsockopt(socket.SOL_SOCKET, socket.SO_REUSEADDR, 1)
s.bind(('localhost',1028))
```

```
    s.listen(1)

    while True:
        client, address = s.accept()
        data = client.recv(1024)
        client.send(data)
        client.close()
```

All this code does is listen on a specific port and wait for input from a client socket. When it receives input, it just sends the same value back. To test this, we can start the server in a separate process and cache the result for use in multiple tests. Here's how the test code might look:

```
import subprocess
import socket
import time

def pytest_funcarg__echoserver(request):
    def setup():
        p = subprocess.Popen(
                ['python3', 'echo_server.py'])
        time.sleep(1)
        return p

    def cleanup(p):
        p.terminate()

    return request.cached_setup(
            setup=setup,
            teardown=cleanup,
            scope="session")

def pytest_funcarg__clientsocket(request):
    s = socket.socket(socket.AF_INET, socket.SOCK_STREAM)
    s.connect(('localhost', 1028))
    request.addfinalizer(lambda: s.close())
    return s

def test_echo(echoserver, clientsocket):
    clientsocket.send(b"abc")
    assert clientsocket.recv(3) == b'abc'

def test_echo2(echoserver, clientsocket):
    clientsocket.send(b"def")
    assert clientsocket.recv(3) == b'def'
```

We've created two funcargs here. The first runs the echo server in a separate process, and returns the process object. The second instantiates a new socket object for each test, and closes it when the test has completed, using `addfinalizer`. The first funcarg is the one we're currently interested in. It looks much like a traditional unit test setup and teardown. We create a `setup` function that accepts no parameters and returns the correct argument, in this case, a process object that is actually ignored by the tests, since they only care that the server is running. Then we create a `cleanup` function (the name of the function is arbitrary since it's just an object we pass into another function), which accepts a single argument: the argument returned by `setup`. This cleanup code simply terminates the process.

Instead of returning a funcarg directly, the parent function returns the results of a call to `request.cached_setup`. It accepts two arguments for the `setup` and `teardown` functions (which we just created), and a `scope` argument. This last argument should be one of the three strings "function", "module", or "session"; it determines just how long the argument will be cached. We set it to "session" in this example, so it is cached for the duration of the entire `py.test` run. The process will not be terminated or restarted until all tests have run. The "module" scope, of course, caches it only for tests in that module, and the "function" scope treats the object more like a normal funcarg, in that it is reset after each test function is run.

Test skipping with py.test

As with the `unittest` module, it is frequently necessary to skip tests in `py.test`, for a variety of reasons; the code being tested hasn't been written yet, the test only runs on certain interpreters or operating systems, or the test is time consuming and should only be run under certain circumstances.

We can skip tests at any point in our code using the `py.test.skip` function. It accepts a single argument: a string describing why it has been skipped. This function can be called anywhere; if we call it inside a test function, the test will be skipped. If we call it in a module, all the tests in that module will be skipped. If we call it inside a funcarg function, all tests that call that funcarg will be skipped.

Of course, in all these locations, it is often desirable to skip tests only if certain conditions are or are not met. Since we can execute the skip function at any place in Python code, we can execute it inside an `if` statement. So we may write a test that looks like this:

```
import sys
import py.test

def test_simple_skip():
    if sys.platform != "fakeos":
            py.test.skip("Test works only on fakeOS")

    fakeos.do_something_fake()
    assert fakeos.did_not_happen
```

That's some pretty silly code, really. There is no Python platform named fakeos, so this test will skip on all operating systems. It shows how we can skip conditionally, and since the `if` statement can check any valid conditional, we have a lot of power over when tests are skipped. Often, we check `sys.version_info` to check the Python interpreter version, `sys.platform` to check the operating system, or `some_library.__version__` to check if we have a recent enough version of a given API.

Since skipping an individual test method or function based on a certain conditional is one of the most common uses of test skipping, `py.test` provides a convenience decorator that allows us to do this in one line. The decorator accepts a single string, which can contain any executable Python code that evaluates to a Boolean value. For example, the following test will only run on Python 3 or higher:

```
import py.test

@py.test.mark.skipif("sys.version_info <= (3,0)")
def test_python3():
    assert b"hello".decode() == "hello"
```

The `py.test.mark.xfail` decorator behaves similarly, except that it marks a test as expected to fail, similar to `unittest.expectedFailure()`. If the test is successful, it will be recorded as a failure, if it fails, it will be reported as expected behavior. In the case of `xfail`, the conditional argument is optional; if it is not supplied, the test will be marked as expected to fail under all conditions.

py.test extras

py.test is an incredibly powerful library and it can do much much more than the basics we've discussed here. We haven't even started on its distributed testing framework (which allows tests to be run across a network of different platforms and interpreter versions), its numerous built-in or third-party plugins, how incredibly easy it is to write our own plugins, or the extensive customization and configuration architecture the framework supplies. You'll have to read the documentation at http://pytest.org/ for all the juicy details.

However, before we leave for the day, we should discuss some of the more useful command-line arguments built into py.test. As with most command-line applications, we can get a list of the available command-line arguments by running the command py.test --help. However, unlike many programs, the available command-line options depends on what py.test plugins are installed and whether we've written any arguments of our own into the conftest.py for the project.

First, we'll look at a couple of arguments that help us with debugging tests. If we have a large test suite with many tests failing (because we've done invasive code changes, such as porting the project from Python 2 to Python 3), the py.test output can quickly get away from us. Passing the -x or --exitfirst command-line argument to py.test forces the test runner to exit after the first failure. We can then fix whatever problems are causing that test to fail before running py.test again and checking out the next failure.

The --pdb argument is similar, except that instead of exiting after a test fails, it drops to a python debugger shell. If you know how to use the debugger, this feature can allow you to quickly introspect variables or step through broken code.

py.test also supports an interesting --looponfail or -f argument, although it's only available if the py.test xdist plugin is installed. This plugin is available from http://pypi.python.org/pypi/pytest-xdist. If it's installed and we pass the --looponfail option to py.test, the test suite will automatically rerun itself when a failing test is encountered. This means that we can wait for a test to fail, then edit the test and fix the broken code. When we save the file, the test will automatically run again to tell us if our fix was successful. It's basically like using the --exitfirst argument repeatedly as we fix one test at a time, but automates the boring restarting bits!

The most important of the `py.test` arguments is the `-k` argument, which accepts a keyword to search for tests. It is used to run specific tests that contain the given keyword argument in the full name (including package, module, class, and test name). For example, if we have the following structure:

```
package: something/
    module:        test_something.py
          class: TestSomething
                method: test_first
                method: test_second
```

We can run `py.test -k test_first` or even just `py.test -k first` to run just the one `test_first` method. Or, if there are other methods that have that name, we can run `py.test -k TestSomething.test_first` or even `something.test_something.TestSomething.test_first.py.test`, which will first collect the complete test name into a dot-separated string, and then checks to see if the string contains the requested keyword.

How much testing is enough?

We've already established that untested code is broken code. But how can we tell how well our code is tested? How do we know how much of our code is actually being tested? The first question is the more important one, but it's hard to answer. Even if we know we have tested every line of code in our application, we do not know that we have tested it properly. For example, if we write a stats test that only checks what happens when we provide a list of integers, it may still fail spectacularly if used on a list of floats or strings or self-made objects. The onus of designing complete test suites still lies with the programmer.

The second question, how much of our code is actually being tested, is actually easy to verify. **Code coverage** is essentially an estimate of the number of lines of code that are executed by a program. If we know that number and the number of lines that are in the program, we can get an estimate of what percentage of the code was really tested, or covered. If we additionally have an indicator as to which lines were not tested, we can more easily write new tests to ensure those lines are less broken.

There are two popular tools for coverage testing in Python: `figleaf`, and `coverage.py`. Only `coverage.py` is Python 3 compatible as I write this, so we'll focus on it. It can be downloaded from `http://nedbatchelder.com/code/coverage/`.

We don't have space to cover all the details of the coverage API, so we'll just look at a few typical examples. If we have a python script that runs all our unit tests for us (for example, using `unittest.main` or a custom test runner or `discover`), we can use the command below to perform a coverage analysis:

```
>>> coverage run coverage_unittest.py
```

This command will exit normally, but it creates a file named `.coverage` that holds the data from the run. We can now use the `coverage report` command to get an analysis of code coverage:

```
>>> coverage report
```

The output is as follows:

```
Name                      Stmts    Exec   Cover
--------------------------------------------------
coverage_unittest             7       7    100%
stats                        19       6     31%
--------------------------------------------------
TOTAL                        26      13     50%
```

This simple report lists the files that were executed (our unit test and a module it imported). The number of lines of code in each file, and the number that were executed by the test are also listed. The two numbers are then combined to estimate the amount of code coverage. If we pass the `-m` option to the report command, it will additionally add a column that looks like this:

```
Missing
-----------
8-12, 15-23
```

The ranges of lines listed here identify lines in the `stats` module that were not executed during the test run.

The example we just tested code coverage on uses the same `stats` module we've been using throughout the chapter, but uses a single test that deliberately misses testing a lot of code in the file:

```python
from stats import StatsList
import unittest

class TestMean(unittest.TestCase):
    def test_mean(self):
        self.assertEqual(StatsList([1,2,2,3,3,4]).mean(), 2.5)

if __name__ == "__main__":

    unittest.main()
```

This code doesn't test the median or mode functions. These correspond to the line numbers that the coverage output told us were missing.

The simple report earlier is sufficient, but if we use the command `coverage html`, we can get an even fancier interactive HTML report that we can view in a web browser. The web page even highlights which lines in the source code were and were not tested. Here's how it looks:

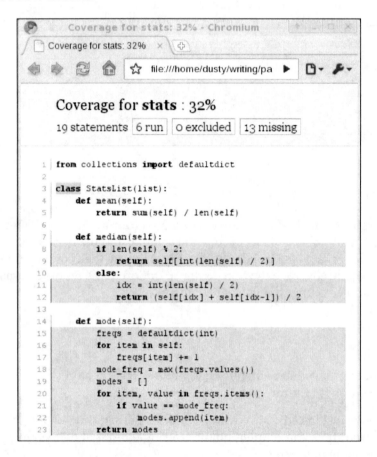

The green lines were executed by the test, the red ones were not. There are some other interactive features of these reports if you want to try them out.

We can use the `coverage.py` module with `py.test` as well. We simply need to install the `py.test` plugin for code coverage, which is available from `http://pypi.python.org/pypi/pytest-coverage/`. This adds several command-line options to `py.test`, the most useful being `--cover-report`, which can be set to either `html`, `report`, or `annotate` (the latter actually modifies the source code to show any lines that were not covered).

If we ran a coverage report on this section of the chapter, we'd find that we have not covered most of what there is to know about code coverage! It is possible to use the coverage API to manage code coverage from our own programs (or test suites), and `coverage.py` accepts numerous configuration options that we haven't touched on. Nor have we discussed the difference between statement coverage and branch coverage (the latter is much more useful, and the default in recent versions of `coverage.py`) or other styles of code coverage.

Bear in mind that while 100% code coverage is a lofty goal that we should all strive for, 100% coverage is not enough! Just because a statement was tested does not mean that it was tested properly for all possible input.

Case Study

Let's take a walk through test-driven development by writing a small, tested, cryptography application. Don't worry, you won't need to understand the mathematics behind complicated modern encryption algorithms such as Threefish or RSA. Instead, we'll be implementing a 16th century algorithm known as the Vigenère cipher. The application simply needs to be able to encode and decode a message, given an encoding keyword, using this cipher.

First we need to understand how the cipher works if we apply it manually (without a computer). We start with a table like this:

```
A B C D E F G H I J K L M N O P Q R S T U V W X Y Z
B C D E F G H I J K L M N O P Q R S T U V W X Y Z A
C D E F G H I J K L M N O P Q R S T U V W X Y Z A B
D E F G H I J K L M N O P Q R S T U V W X Y Z A B C
E F G H I J K L M N O P Q R S T U V W X Y Z A B C D
F G H I J K L M N O P Q R S T U V W X Y Z A B C D E
G H I J K L M N O P Q R S T U V W X Y Z A B C D E F
H I J K L M N O P Q R S T U V W X Y Z A B C D E F G
I J K L M N O P Q R S T U V W X Y Z A B C D E F G H
J K L M N O P Q R S T U V W X Y Z A B C D E F G H I
K L M N O P Q R S T U V W X Y Z A B C D E F G H I J
L M N O P Q R S T U V W X Y Z A B C D E F G H I J K
M N O P Q R S T U V W X Y Z A B C D E F G H I J K L
N O P Q R S T U V W X Y Z A B C D E F G H I J K L M
O P Q R S T U V W X Y Z A B C D E F G H I J K L M N
P Q R S T U V W X Y Z A B C D E F G H I J K L M N O
Q R S T U V W X Y Z A B C D E F G H I J K L M N O P
R S T U V W X Y Z A B C D E F G H I J K L M N O P Q
S T U V W X Y Z A B C D E F G H I J K L M N O P Q R
T U V W X Y Z A B C D E F G H I J K L M N O P Q R S
U V W X Y Z A B C D E F G H I J K L M N O P Q R S T
V W X Y Z A B C D E F G H I J K L M N O P Q R S T U
W X Y Z A B C D E F G H I J K L M N O P Q R S T U V
X Y Z A B C D E F G H I J K L M N O P Q R S T U V W
Y Z A B C D E F G H I J K L M N O P Q R S T U V W X
Z A B C D E F G H I J K L M N O P Q R S T U V W X Y
```

Given a keyword TRAIN, we encode the message ENCODED IN PYTHON as follows:

1. Repeat the keyword and message together such that it is easy to map letters from one to the other:

   ```
   E N C O D E D I N P Y T H O N
   T R A I N T R A I N T R A I N
   ```

2. For each letter in the **plaintext**, find the **row** that begins with that letter in the table.

3. Find the **column** with the letter associated with the **keyword** letter for the chosen plaintext letter.

4. The encoded character is at the intersection of this row and column.

For example, the row starting with E intersects the column starting with T at the character X. So the first letter in the ciphertext is X. The row starting with N intersects the column starting with R at the character E, leading to the ciphertext XE. C intersects A at C, and O intersects I at W. D and N map to Q while E and T map to X. The full encoded message is XECWQXUIVCRKHWA.

Decoding basically follows the opposite procedure. First find the row with the character for the shared keyword (the T row) then find the location in that row where the encoded character (the X) is located. The plaintext character is at the top of the column for that row (the E).

Implementing it

Our program will need an `encode` method that takes a keyword and plaintext and returns the ciphertext, and a `decode` method that accepts a keyword and ciphertext and returns the original message.

But before we write those methods, let's follow a test-driven development strategy. We'll be using `py.test` for our unit testing. We need an encode method, and we know what it has to do; let's write a test for that method first:

```python
def test_encode():
    cipher = VigenereCipher("TRAIN")
    encoded = cipher.encode("ENCODEDINPYTHON")
    assert encoded == "XECWQXUIVCRKHWA"
```

This test, fails, naturally, because we aren't importing a `VigenereCipher` class anywhere. Let's create a new module to hold that class.

Let's start with the following `VigenereCipher` class:

```
class VigenereCipher:
    def __init__(self, keyword):
        self.keyword = keyword

    def encode(self, plaintext):
        return "XECWQXUIVCRKHWA"
```

If we add a `from vigenere_cipher import VigenereCipher` line to the top of our test class and run `py.test`, the above test will pass! We've finished our first test-driven development cycle.

Obviously, returning a hardcoded string is not the most sensible implementation of a cipher class, so let's add a second test:

```
def test_encode_character():
    cipher = VigenereCipher("TRAIN")
    encoded = cipher.encode("E")
    assert encoded == "X"
```

Ah, that test will fail. Looks like we're going to have to work harder. But I just thought of something, what if someone tries to encode a string with spaces or lowercase characters? Before we start implementing the encoding, we better add some tests for these cases, before we forget them. Expected behavior will be to remove spaces, and to convert lowercase letters to capitals:

```
def test_encode_spaces():
    cipher = VigenereCipher("TRAIN")
    encoded = cipher.encoded("ENCODED IN PYTHON")
    assert encoded == "XECWQXUIVCRKHWA"

def test_encode_lowercase():
    cipher = VigenereCipher("TRain")
    encoded = cipher.encoded("encoded in Python")
    assert encoded == "XECWQXUIVCRKHWA"
```

If we run the new test suite, we find that the new tests pass (they expect the same hardcoded string). But they ought to fail later if we forget to account for these cases.

Now we have to think about how to implement our encoding algorithm. Writing code to use a table like we used in the manual algorithm above is possible, but seems complicated, considering that each row is just an alphabet rotated by an offset number of characters.

It turns out that we can use modulo arithmetic to combine the characters instead of doing a table lookup. Given plaintext and keyword characters, if we convert the two letters to their numerical values (with A being 0 and Z being 25), add them together, and take the remainder mod 26, we get the ciphertext character! This is a straightforward calculation, but since it happens on a character-by-character basis, we should probably put it in its own function. And before we do that, we should write a test for the new function:

```python
from vigenere_cipher import combine_character
def test_combine_character():
    assert combine_character("E", "T") == "X"
    assert combine_character("N", "R") == "E"
```

Now, as usual, we can write the code to make this function work. In all honesty, I had to run the test several times before I got this function completely correct; first I returned an integer, and then I forgot to shift the character back up to the normal ASCII scale from the zero-based scale. Having the test available made it easy to test and debug these errors, another bonus of test-driven development.

```python
def combine_character(plain, keyword):
    plain = plain.upper()
    keyword = keyword.upper()
    plain_num = ord(plain) - ord('A')
    keyword_num = ord(keyword) - ord('A')
    return chr(ord('A') + (plain_num + keyword_num) % 26)
```

I thought we'd be ready to implement our encode function. However, the first thing we want inside that function is a repeating version of the keyword string that is as long as the plaintext. Let's implement a function for that first. Or rather, let's implement the test first!

```python
def test_extend_keyword():
    cipher = VigenereCipher("TRAIN")
    extended = cipher.extend_keyword(16)
    assert extended == "TRAINTRAINTRAINT"
```

Before writing this test, I expected to write extend_keyword as a standalone function that accepted a keyword and an integer. But as I started drafting the test, I realized it made more sense to use it as a helper method on the VigenereCipher class. This shows how test-driven development can help us design more sensible APIs. Here's the method implementation:

```python
def extend_keyword(self, number):
    repeats = number // len(self.keyword) + 1
    return (self.keyword * repeats)[:number]
```

Once again, this took a few runs of the test to get right. I actually used two versions of the test, one with fifteen and one with sixteen letters to make sure it works if the integer division has an even number.

Now we're finally ready to write our encode method:

```
def encode(self, plaintext):
    cipher = []
    keyword = self.extend_keyword(len(plaintext))
    for p,k in zip(plaintext, keyword):
        cipher.append(combine_character(p,k))
    return "".join(cipher)
```

That looks correct. Our test suite should pass now, right?

Actually, if we run it, we'll find that two tests are still failing. We totally forgot about the spaces and lowercase characters! It is a good thing we wrote tests to remind us. We'll have to add this line at the beginning of the method:

```
plaintext = plaintext.replace(" ", "").upper()
```

Now all the tests pass successfully. We're running short on space, so we'll condense the examples for decoding. Here are a couple tests:

```
def test_separate_character():
    assert separate_character("X", "T") == "E"
    assert separate_character("E", "R") == "N"

def test_decode():
    cipher = VigenereCipher("TRAIN")
    decoded = cipher.decode("XECWQXUIVCRKHWA")
    assert decoded == "ENCODEDINPYTHON"
```

Here's the `separate_character` function:

```
def separate_character(cypher, keyword):
    cypher = cypher.upper()
    keyword = keyword.upper()
    cypher_num = ord(cypher) - ord('A')
    keyword_num = ord(keyword) - ord('A')
    return chr(ord('A') + (cypher_num - keyword_num) % 26)
```

And the `decode` method:

```
def decode(self, ciphertext):
    plain = []
    keyword = self.extend_keyword(len(ciphertext))
    for p,k in zip(ciphertext, keyword):
        plain.append(separate_character(p,k))
    return "".join(plain)
```

These methods have a lot of similarity to those used for encoding. The great thing about having all these tests written and passing is that we can now go back and modify our code, knowing it is still safely passing the tests. For example, if we replace our existing encode and decode methods with these refactored methods, our tests still pass:

```
def _code(self, text, combine_func):
    text = text.replace(" ", "").upper()
    combined = []
    keyword = self.extend_keyword(len(text))
    for p,k in zip(text, keyword):
        combined.append(combine_func(p,k))
    return "".join(combined)

def encode(self, plaintext):
    return self._code(plaintext, combine_character)

def decode(self, ciphertext):
    return self._code(ciphertext, separate_character)
```

This is the final benefit of test-driven development, and the most important. Once the tests are written, we can improve our code as much as we like and be confident that our changes didn't break anything we have been testing for. Further, we know exactly when our fixes are finished: when the tests all pass.

Of course, our tests may not comprehensively test everything we need them to; maintenance or code refactoring may still cause undiagnosed bugs that don't show up in testing. Automated tests are not foolproof. If bugs do occur, however, it is still possible to follow a test-driven plan; step one is to write a test (or multiple tests) that duplicates or "proves" that the bug in question is occurring. This will, of course, fail. Then write the code to make the tests stop failing. If the tests were comprehensive, the bug will be fixed, and we will know if it ever happens again, as soon as we run the test suite.

Finally, we can try to determine how well our tests operate on this code. With the `py.test`-coverage plugin installed, `py.test -coverage-report=report` tells us that our test suite has 100% code coverage. This is a great statistic, but we shouldn't get too cocky about it. Our code hasn't been tested when encoding messages that have numbers, and its behavior with such inputs is thus undefined. Untested code is broken code. Untested use cases are undefined scenarios.

Exercises

Practice test-driven development. That is your first exercise. It's easier to do this if you're starting a new project, but if you have existing code you need to work on, you can start by writing tests for each new feature you implement. This can become frustrating as you become more enamored with automated tests. The old, untested code will start to feel uncomfortable to maintain; you'll start feeling like changes you make are breaking the code and you have no way of knowing, for lack of tests.

So to get your feet wet with test-driven development, start a fresh project. Once you've started to appreciate the benefits (you will) and realize that the time spent writing tests is quickly regained in terms of more maintainable code, you'll want to start writing tests for existing code. This is when you should start doing it, not before. Writing tests for code that we "know" works is boring. It is hard to get interested in the project until you realize just how broken the code we "thought" was working really is.

Try writing the same set of tests using both the built-in `unittest` module and `py.test`. Which do you prefer? `unittest` is more similar to test frameworks in other languages, while `py.test` is arguably more Pythonic. Both allow us to write object-oriented tests and to test object-oriented programs with ease.

We used `py.test` in our case study, but we didn't touch on any features that wouldn't have been easily testable using `unittest`. Try adapting the tests to use test skipping or funcargs. Try the various setup and teardown methods, and compare their use to funcargs; which feels more natural to you?

In our case study, we have a lot of tests that use a similar `VigenereCipher` object; try reworking this code to use a funcarg. How many lines of code does it save?

Try running a coverage report on the tests you've written. Did you miss testing any lines of code? Even if you have 100% coverage, have you tested all the possible inputs? If you're doing test-driven development, 100% coverage should follow quite naturally, as you will write a test before the code that satisfies that test. However, if writing tests for existing code, it is more likely that there will be edge conditions that go untested.

Think carefully about the values that are somehow different: empty lists when you expect full ones, zero or one or infinity compared to intermediate integers, floats that don't round to an exact decimal place, strings when you expected numerals, or the ubiquitous None value when you expected something meaningful. If your tests cover such edge cases, your code will be in good shape.

Summary

We have finally covered the most important topic in Python programming: automated testing. After proving its importance and considering best design principles, we discussed the basic API for two popular Python 3 test frameworks. In particular we covered:

- Unit testing
- Test-driven development
- The unittest module
- Assertion methods and code setup/cleanup
- The py.test framework
- Code coverage

In the next chapter, we'll wrap up our learning with a compendium of object-oriented frameworks and libraries that work in Python 3.

12

Common Python 3 Libraries

We've covered the principles of object-oriented programming and we've applied them to Python. We've looked at the ins and outs of object-oriented design, and the higher-level design patterns that make up good programs. We've seen Python's tendency to simplify object-oriented solutions. We even know how to test our Python programs. Yet, are we able to do the common tasks of day-to-day programming?

Yes, we know Python's syntax, and we could — in theory — write a web framework or database engine from scratch. Python's true power, however, lies in the work other people have done before us. In the examples throughout this book, we've seen many of the Python standard library's modules at work. Yet, we haven't really covered many of the most common tasks facing Python programmers today. We've completely bypassed graphical applications and their widgets, input boxes and buttons: one of the most common interfaces users see today. And we haven't touched on web backend development: Python's current most prevalent use.

These are complex topics, and we'll see an introduction to each of them here. We'll be focusing on Python libraries that are available for Python 3 as I write this. Many popular libraries, such as Django or wxPython, are currently only compatible with older versions of Python, so they'll be passed over.

In this chapter we'll be covering:

- Database libraries and object-relational managers
- Point-and-click graphical applications
- CherryPy for web applications
- Working with XML

Database access

Talking to databases is a very common task in Python, especially in the web development world. Unfortunately, not many libraries for database access have been ported to Python 3 in a mature state. We'll be looking at a few of the available database solutions.

Python comes with built-in support for SQLite 3. We looked at some examples of it in earlier chapters. SQLite is not suitable for multi-user, multi-threaded access, but it's perfect for storing configuration or local data. It simply stores all the data in a single file and allows us to access that data using SQL syntax. All we need to do to use it is import `sqlite3` and read the help file. Here's a short example to get you started:

```python
import sqlite3
connection = sqlite3.connect("mydb.db")
connection.execute(
        "CREATE TABLE IF NOT EXISTS "
        "pet (type, breed, gender, name)")
connection.execute("INSERT INTO pet VALUES("
        "'dog', 'spaniel', 'female', 'Esme')")
connection.execute("INSERT INTO pet VALUES("
        "'cat', 'persian', 'male', 'Oscar')")
results = connection.execute("SELECT breed, name"
        " from pet where type='dog'")
for result in results:
    print(result[1])
connection.close()
```

This code first connects to a local file named `mydb.db` (it creates the file if it doesn't exist) and runs some SQL query to put a simple table in the database. Then it queries the same relation and prints one of the results.

Results are returned as iterable sequences of tuples. Each tuple represents a matching row in the query results. The order of the values in each result tuple is the same as the order of the values in the query. The `name` is the second column in the query (the first is `type`), so we print `result[1]` to print the name of the queried `pet`.

The Python API SQLite uses conforms to a database API specification known as DBAPI2. This API is a standard, designed to make it easier for code to interact with different types of databases in the same way. There are similar APIs for other databases such as PostgreSQL, MySQL and Oracle, among many others, but at this time, very few of them are mature on Python 3.

Any database API that follows the DBAPI2 specification will have a `connect` function (which may take different arguments for different database connections) that returns a `Connection` object. Queries are executed on the connection using an `execute` method. Often, additional methods to make querying easier or return named tuples as results are provided; however, none of this is required by the DBAPI2 specification.

However, DBAPI2 is fairly low-level and difficult to work with. In object-oriented programming, it is very common to use an **Object-Relational Manager**, or **ORM** to interact with databases. ORMs allow us to use the familiar abstraction called objects that we've been working with throughout this book, while connecting their attributes to the relational database paradigm. One of the most popular ORMs in Python is SQLAlchemy, and it was also the first to be ported to Python 3.

Introducing SQLAlchemy

SQLAlchemy can be downloaded from `http://www.sqlalchemy.org/`. Only the 0.6 version and higher is supported on Python 3, and at the time of writing, the only underlying databases that are supported are SQLite and PostgresSQL.

This isn't a huge deal, as SQLAlchemy provides an abstraction over database APIs, it is (theoretically) possible to write SQLAlchemy code that works on one database system and later use the exact same (or only slightly modified) code on another one. So if you're looking for MySQL support, you could begin to write your code to use SQLAlchemy with SQLite as a backend first, and port it to MySQL when that backend is eventually supported.

SQLAlchemy is a very large and robust library; it allows us to do almost anything imaginable with a database. We'll only be able to touch on the basics in this section.

The idea behind SQLAlchemy, and ORMs in general is to interact with objects that automatically modify and update database tables in the background. SQLAlchemy provides multiple ways to map objects to tables; we'll be using the modern inheritance-based solution. If you need to connect to a legacy database, SQLAlchemy provides an alternative method that allows arbitrary object classes to be explicitly mapped to database tables, but we won't have room to cover that here.

The first thing we need to do is connect to a database. The `sqlalchemy.create_engine` function provides a single point of access for connecting to a database. It takes a huge number of arguments to customize or tune access. The most important one is a string URL defining the kind of backend database to be connected to, the specific database backend to make the connection, the name of the database, the host the database system is running on, and a username and/or password to authenticate with. The basic form of the URL resembles a web URL: `driver://user:password@host/dbname`.

If we want to use a simple SQLite database, which does not require username, password, or host; we can simply specify the filename for the database, as we'll see in the next example.

Then we'll need to create a class that allows objects to store their data in the database, while optionally supplying behavior as methods on the object. Each instance of the object will be stored in a separate row in the database, identified by its primary key (it is usually a good idea to make the primary key a single integer identifier, but SQLAlchemy does not require this).

Each table in the database is normally represented by a separate class, and special attributes on each class map to table columns. When we access these attributes on an object, we get database values, and when we update and save the object, the database is modified. Here's a simple example for our pets database:

```python
import sqlalchemy as sqa
from sqlalchemy.ext.declarative import declarative_base


Base = declarative_base()


class Pet(Base):
    __tablename__ = "pet"
    id = sqa.Column(sqa.Integer, primary_key=True)
    type = sqa.Column(sqa.String(16))
    breed = sqa.Column(sqa.String(32))
    gender = sqa.Column(sqa.Enum("male", "female"))
    name = sqa.Column(sqa.String(64))


engine = sqa.create_engine('sqlite:///mydata.db')
Base.metadata.create_all(engine)
```

SQLAlchemy first asks us to set up a `Base` class by calling a function called `declarative_base`. This function returns a class, which we are able to extend in our declaration. The subclass needs a special attribute named `__tablename__` to specify the name of the table in the database.

This is followed by several column declarations. We add `Column` objects whose first argument is a type object (example `Integer` or `String`), and subsequent arguments depend on the type. All of these type objects are provided in the `sqlalchemy` package. I generally import this package with the alias `sqa` to make it easier to reference the many classes in the package. Some people suggest using `from sqlalchemy import *` syntax, so all the objects are available, but as we discussed in *Chapter 2*, this can make code very confusing to maintain.

After defining one or more mapped classes that extend the `Base` object, we connect to a specific database (in this case, an SQLite file) using the `create_engine` function. The `Base.metadata.create_all` call ensures that all the tables associated with that `Base` class exist. It would typically issue some sort of CREATE TABLE call to the underlying database.

Adding and querying objects

We can create instances of our table objects just like a normal object. The default constructor on the `Base` class accepts no arguments. It can often be useful to add an `__init__` method to our subclass that initializes some or all of the variables on the object. We can also add any other arbitrary methods to the class that we like. Here's how we might instantiate a new `pet` object and set some values:

```
pet = Pet()
pet.id = 1
pet.type = "dog"
pet.breed = "spaniel"
pet.gender = "female"
pet.name = "Esme"
```

This object can be used like any other Python object, but the object is not yet connected to the database in any way. Before we can associate the object with a database table row, we need to create an SQLAlchemy `Session` object. Sessions are like staging areas between objects and the database. We can add multiple objects to the session, as well as use the session to record changes, deletions, and other database operations. When we're ready for this collection of changes to be saved to the database, we can `commit()` them, or, if something goes wrong, we can call `session.rollback()` to make all the changes disappear.

Here's how we can add our new `pet` to the database and save it:

```
Session = sqa.orm.sessionmaker(bind=engine)
session = Session()

session.add(pet)
session.commit()
```

First we have to get a special `Session` class by calling the `sessionmaker` function; this function needs to know which engine to connect to. Then whenever we want a session, we instantiate the resulting class. Each session is partially independent of the others until the changes are committed. Underneath, they basically rely on database transactions, so similar rules apply, and the rules may vary depending on the underlying database.

We can also use session objects to query the database. SQLAlchemy queries are written in a combination of Python functions and raw SQL syntax. We use the `session.query()` method to get a `Query` object. This method accepts arguments representing the tables or columns to be queried. Then methods on that object can be cascaded to get a set of results. These methods include:

- `all()`, which returns all items in the table.
- `first()`, which returns the first item.
- `one()`, which returns the only item. If no items or multiple items are found, it raises an exception.
- `get(primary_key)`, which accepts a primary key value and returns the object matching that key.
- `group_by()`, `order_by()`, and `having()`, which add the related SQL clauses to the query.
- `filter_by()`, which uses keyword arguments to query the session.
- `filter()`, which uses more advanced SQL expressions (which we will discuss shortly) to query.

The `filter_by` method allows us to search for items using keyword arguments. For example, we can say:

```
session.query(Pet).filter_by(name="Esme").one()
```

This `filter_by` argument tries to match a name to a specific string. This returns a new query object, on which we call the `one()` method to get a single value (since there's only one value in our example database, and it matches our criterion, it will return that result). If we'd called `all()` instead, it would have returned a list of items containing, in this case, only one item.

SQL Expression Language

Unlike `filter_by`, which accepts keyword arguments, the `filter` method accepts values in SQLAlchemy's SQL Expression Language. This is a much more powerful form of querying that applies different operators to column objects. It is an interesting application of overloading the operator special methods.

For example, if we use `session.query(Pet).filter(Pet.name=="Esme")` the expression inside the `filter` query does NOT do a typical equality comparison that evaluates to a Boolean value. Instead, it constructs a proper SQL clause that the filter method will use to query the database. This is done by overriding the `__eq__` method on the `Pet.name` column object. So we need to explicitly state the `Pet.name` object for equality comparison. We can't specify `name` as if it was a keyword argument; that would cause an error.

SQL Expression Language allows many related operators to be used to construct queries. Some of the more common ones are:

- `!=` to specify inequality
- `<` for less than comparisons
- `>` for greater than comparisons
- `<=` for less than or equal
- `>=` for greater than or equal
- `&` to combine clauses using an AND query
- `|` to combine clauses using an OR query
- `~` to negate a query using NOT

The SQLAlchemy Expression Language allows almost any SQL statement to be constructed using Python, including creating joins, and aggregate clauses, and using SQL functions. However, we have a lot of topics to cover, so you'll have to look elsewhere to discover how to use them. Entire books have been written on SQL, SQLAlchemy, and databases in Python, so this brief introduction can do nothing more than spark your interest.

Pretty user interfaces

All the examples throughout this book have been run from the command line. This is great for system administrators, Linux tinkerers, and the grandfather programmers of our times, but it doesn't allow us to write the sort of modern desktop programs that everyone is using these days. Indeed, some might argue that even desktop applications are archaic, and that web applications (which we'll discuss soon) and mobile apps are more contemporary!

The reason we haven't looked at graphical applications is that they invariably rely on design patterns that offer such a high level of abstraction over lower-level objects that it's hard to see the objects for the patterns. This isn't terribly useful for learning about object-oriented programming. But now that we know the ins and outs of the object-oriented paradigm, we can briefly discover the world of Graphical User Interfaces, or GUIs, for short.

It would be possible to design graphical interfaces from scratch, interacting with pixels on the screen to cause visual effects to happen. But nobody does that. Instead, we use some kind of widget toolkit that provides us with common graphical elements such as the buttons, textboxes, checkboxes, toolbars, tabbed interfaces, calendars, and more that we see every day when we look at our desktop computer, regardless of operating system.

We'll briefly (very briefly, unfortunately) discuss two of these widget toolkits that run on Python 3. But first, let's discuss a small amount of theory. Graphical programs invariably use an event-driven architecture. This often means they rely heavily on the command pattern we discussed in *Chapter 9*. When interacting with the user, we never know exactly when they are going to press a key, move the mouse, or click an object, nor do we know which of these activities they are going to perform at any time. So we write code to respond to those events only when they occur. This code should be quick and painless so that the program can get back to waiting for the next input from the user. This is the world of event-driven programming in a nutshell. It can be hard to wrap your mind around at first, but it is extremely well suited to the object-oriented principles we've been discussing all along.

TkInter

The Python standard library comes with a built-in graphical library called `tkinter`. It comes preinstalled with Python on most operating systems, although it requires the TCL/TK interpreter and graphical toolkit to be installed.

The most basic configuration of a TkInter application is to create a `Frame` object, add some widget objects to that window, and then let `tkinter` take over in what is called a `mainloop`. This `mainloop` is responsible for waiting for events to happen and dispatching them to the code we write. Here's an extremely basic TkInter application, with nothing displayed on the created window:

```
import tkinter

class EmptyFrame(tkinter.Frame):
    pass

root = tkinter.Tk()
EmptyFrame(master=root).mainloop()
```

First we create a class that extends the `tkinter.Frame` class; this is basically just a container for other widgets. We create a `Tk()` object to provide a window to hold the frame, and then call the `mainloop` to run with this object. If we run this program, it displays a small, empty window. Not too exciting.

Let's look at an example we can really interact with:

```python
import tkinter
import random

class DiceFrame(tkinter.Frame):
    def __init__(self, master):
        super().__init__(master)

        die = tkinter.Button(self,
                text = "Roll!",
                command=self.roll)
        die.pack()
        self.roll_result = tkinter.StringVar()
        label = tkinter.Label(self,
                textvariable=self.roll_result)
        label.pack()
        self.pack()

    def roll(self):
        self.roll_result.set(random.randint(1, 6))

root = tkinter.Tk()
DiceFrame(master=root).mainloop()
```

There are a few things going on here, almost all of them in an overridden __init__ method. After initializing the superclass, we create a new `Button` object, which represents buttons like 'OK' and 'Cancel' that you have seen so often that you've probably never thought of them as objects! All TkInter widgets take a parent widget as their first argument. We pass `self` here, to make the new button a child of the frame. We also supply a `text` argument, representing the string displayed on the button, and the `command` argument, which is a function to be called when the button is clicked. In this case, that function is a method on the same class. Remember that command pattern? Here it is in action!

Then we call the `pack` method on our new button, which, in this basic format, simply sets up a default size and position for the button and window. If we hadn't called this, the button would not be visible.

Later, we use similar code to create and pack a `Label` object. The label is associated with a specially constructed `StringVar` object, provided by TkInter. The neat thing about this class is that whenever its value is updated to a new string, by calling the `set()` method, any widgets that are associated with the object will automatically have their displays updated to the new value. We use this feature to update the label to a new random value every time we click the "**Roll!**" button. When we run this program, we are presented with a very simple electronic die:

So graphical programming is all about constructing widgets, and connecting commands to them to be called when certain events occur. The most complicated part, often, is getting the display to "look right"; that is, to get all the widgets laid out in an aesthetically pleasing manner that is also easy to use and understand. We can customize this using the `pack` method. This method basically allows widgets to be laid out in either rows or columns. If we need to use columns of rows or rows of columns, we can pack multiple objects into separate frames (example: frames containing rows), and then pack those frames into parent frames (example: that are packed using columns). When packing a widget, we can pass the following additional arguments to control how the widget will be placed in its parent:

- `expand`: A boolean value to say whether or not to grow the widget beyond its expected size if the parent window is resized larger. If multiple widgets have `expand` set, the extra space is divided between them.

- `fill`: Set to a string value of `none`, `x`, `y`, or `both` to instruct the widget to fill all available space assigned to it in the specified direction.

- `anchor`: If the widget is not set to fill its space, it can be positioned within that space. The default, `center`, will ensure equal spacing on all sides. Other values can be compass directions such as n, e, s, w, to position the item at the top, right, bottom, or left of available space, and the values ne, se, sw, and nw can be used to position it in one of the four corners.

- `ipadx` and `ipady`: These integer values provide padding inside the widget on either the left and right or top and bottom edges. It has the effect of increasing the size of the widget.

- `padx` and `pady`: These integer values provide padding between the widget and the edge of its available space. It has the effect of placing space between the widget and its neighbors.

- **side:** Use one of `left`, `right`, `top`, or `bottom` to pack the widgets along a specific side. Normally, all widgets in a container frame are packed to the same side; mixing them can have unanticipated effects. If you need more than a single row or column, you can pack frames inside of other frames.

Here's an example of several of these features in action:

```python
import tkinter

class PackFrame(tkinter.Frame):
    def __init__(self, master):
        super().__init__(master)

        button1 = tkinter.Button(self,
                text = "expand fill")
        button1.pack(expand=True, fill="both", side="left")
        button2 = tkinter.Button(self,
                text = "anchor ne pady")
        button2.pack(anchor="ne", pady=5, side="left")
        button3 = tkinter.Button(self,
                text = "anchor se padx")
        button3.pack(anchor="se", padx=5, side="left")

class TwoPackFrames(tkinter.Frame):
    def __init__(self, master):
        super().__init__(master)
        button1 = tkinter.Button(self,
                text="ipadx")
        button1.pack(ipadx=215)
        packFrame1 = PackFrame(self)
        packFrame1.pack(side="bottom", anchor="e")
        packFrame2 = PackFrame(self)
        packFrame2.pack(side="bottom", anchor="w")
        self.pack()

root = tkinter.Tk()
TwoPackFrames(master=root).mainloop()
```

This example creates two instances of a `PackFrame` that contain three buttons each, packed horizontally (by specifying `side="left"`). The buttons are each positioned differently. These frames are then vertically packed into another frame with a very large button, anchored to the left and right sides of the frames. Here's how the previous code would render. It's not remotely pretty, but it illustrates most of the concepts in a single window:

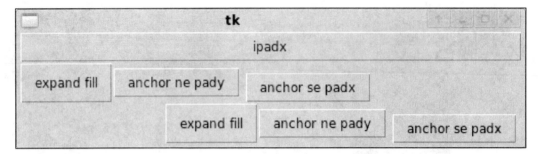

When designing complicated interfaces, packing frames can get monotonous. If you're attempting to do this, you might want to do some research into TkInter's grid style of widget layout instead.

We don't have space to discuss grid layout or the wide array of available TkInter widgets here, but as with SQLAlchemy, hopefully you've had a taste, know what your options are, and are ready to dive in head-first if you need to build a GUI application. Graphical interfaces are not more complicated than command-line ones. They just rely on different design patterns to get their job done.

PyQt

The other major graphical toolkit supported under Python 3 is called PyQt. It is a set of bindings to the popular cross-platform Qt library, which is available under both commercial and open source licenses. PyQt can be downloaded from `http://www.riverbankcomputing.co.uk/software/pyqt/download`. PyQt is an advanced library that supports many features not normally considered part of a GUI toolkit. In some ways, PyQt is a desktop application framework, with extended support for everything from web browser widgets to databases to multimedia.

However, we only have space here to look at the basics of PyQt as a graphical toolkit. Let's start, as before, by displaying an empty window:

```python
from PyQt4 import QtGui

app = QtGui.QApplication([])

class EmptyWidget(QtGui.QWidget):
    pass

window = EmptyWidget()
window.show()
app.exec_()
```

This isn't terribly different from the `tkinter` version. We need to construct the `QApplication` object before we create any windows, since constructing it initializes the Qt internals. We then construct an empty window and call the `mainloop` on the app, which is done with a call to `exec_` in Qt.

Instead of a dice rolling application, we'll build a rudimentary rock/paper/scissors window:

```python
from PyQt4 import QtGui
import random

app = QtGui.QApplication([])

choices = ["Rock", "Paper", "Scissors"]

class RockPaperScissorsWidget(QtGui.QWidget):
    def __init__(self):
        super().__init__()
        rock = RPSButton("Rock", self)
        paper = RPSButton("Paper", self)
        scissors = RPSButton("Scissors", self)
        for button in (rock, paper, scissors):
            button.resize(100, 100)
        rock.move(0,0)
        paper.move(0,100)
        scissors.move(0,200)
        self.response = QtGui.QLabel("", self)
        self.response.setGeometry(110, 0, 200, 300)

class RPSButton(QtGui.QPushButton):
    def mousePressEvent(self, event):
```

```
        computer_choice = random.choice(choices)
        user_choice = self.text()

        comp_idx = choices.index(computer_choice)
        user_idx = choices.index(user_choice)

        message = {
                0: 'Tied',
                1: 'Computer Wins',
                2: 'You Win'}[(comp_idx - user_idx + 3) % 3]


        self.parent().response.setText("You chose {0}<br />"
                "Computer chose {1}<br />"
                "{2}".format(user_choice, computer_choice, message))


    window = RockPaperScissorsWidget()
    window.show()
    app.exec_()
```

This program adds four widgets (three buttons and a results label) to a window. The buttons are each instances of a custom subclass of QPushButton that we have designed. The sole purpose of this inheritance is to override the mousePressEvent method, which is called whenever the user clicks the button. After creating the buttons, we use absolute positioning functions (resize, move, and setGeometry) to place the widgets where we want them. Here's how they look:

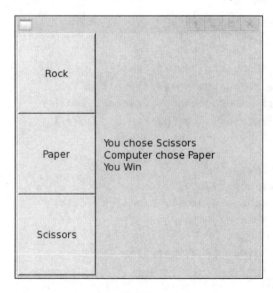

Inside our overridden `mousePressEvent` method, we randomly pick a choice for the computer player, and then calculate the winner. The calculation is done with a simple modulo mathematical function that evaluates to either 0, 1, or 2, depending on who won (I had to do some experimenting to get this value right; my math skills are lacking!). We then use this result to look up a relevant message in a dictionary. Finally, we display the results on the label by calling the `setText` method. Each time a button is pressed, the computer makes a new choice and updates the label.

PyQt supplies numerous widgets, ranging from buttons, checkboxes, and radio buttons to text entry fields, combo boxes, and sliders to advanced widgets like calendars, video players, and syntax highlighted text editors. Generally, if you've seen a widget before, PyQt will supply one. If you need something that's not available, it is possible to create your own widgets. Like TkInter, PyQt also supplies advanced layout schemes so that positioning widgets in resizing windows is painless. (The absolute positioning we used in our example earlier isn't terribly resizable.)

Choosing a GUI toolkit

PyQt and TkInter are the currently available Python 3 capable GUI toolkits. In addition, two Python 2 toolkits are extremely popular: PyGTK and wxPython. The former is in the late stages of being ported and may be available as you read this. The latter is a very advanced cross-platform system that has the advantage of displaying native widgets under whichever operating system it is currently running on. This allows wxPython programs to seamlessly "fit in" with the overall look and feel of the operating system.

But which should you choose for a given task? It really depends on your personal preference. You need to work with each one for a while to decide which provides the programming paradigm you are most comfortable with. It also depends on your specific needs. If you just want to develop a simple interface for a small script or program, TkInter is probably your best bet, simply because it comes bundled with Python and therefore doesn't require any extra work to install or deploy. If you're planning on developing an intense GUI-centric application with complicated widgets, you're probably better off using one of the other libraries. Pick one that supplies the specific widgets you are interested in working with. PyQt is likely the easiest to learn and work with, but if you have experience in wxWidgets or GTK from other programming languages, you may find that wxPython or pyGTK would be a more suitable fit.

XML

Many Python programmers consider working with XML to be a right royal pain. However, XML is extremely popular for a wide range of purposes. Python programs frequently have to interact with it; both as a consumer that needs to interpret XML data from another source, and as a producer that needs to create XML data for other programs or computers to parse.

Python includes three well-documented libraries for interacting with XML documents in its standard library. Two are based on traditional XML parsing techniques, while the third is a nice Pythonic interface.

The **SAX (Simple API for XML)** library is an event-driven system that calls specific functions when specific objects are encountered in the byte stream: opening and closing tags, attributes, and contents. It can be unwieldy to work with, but has the advantage of parsing XML documents "on the fly" without having to load the entire stream into memory. This is useful for huge documents.

The **DOM (Document Object Model)** library takes a different approach. It allows any part of the document to be accessed at any time, and treats the document like a tree of connected nodes. Each node represents an element, attribute, or text in the document. Elements can have child elements and each can be accessed randomly. It allows XML documents to be both read and written as well as modified by dynamically adding new nodes to the tree.

Both of these tools have their uses, but most common XML tasks in Python can be parsed, least painfully, using the third built-in library, `ElementTree`, or a more advanced library that is based on it, called `lxml`. Both libraries allow XML documents to be treated like Python objects, making them easy to read, compose, interact with, and modify.

ElementTree

The `xml.etree.ElementTree` package contains several classes and functions for manipulating XML documents. The most important of these are the `Element` and `ElementTree` classes. An `ElementTree` essentially represents an entire XML document in memory; it uses the composite pattern we discussed in *Chapter 10* to construct a tree of `Element` objects. It has a single pointer to a root node, which contains relevant child nodes, which may contain more children, and so on.

Any one `Element` object contains everything between the opening and associated closing tags in an XML document. It references the tag name, any attributes on the opening tag, the text inside the element, and a list of child elements (nested opening and closing tags) recursively. If the text includes interspersed text and tag elements (as in an HTML document), any text between a closing tag and the following tag (whether it is a new opening tag or the parent's closing tag) is added to a `tail` attribute on the element.

As an example, let's start with a simple HTML document:

```
<!DOCTYPE html>
<html>
    <head>
        <title>This is a web page</title>
        <link rel="stylesheet" href="styles.css" />
    </head>
    <body>
        <h1>Welcome To My Site</h1>
        <article class="simple">
            This is <em>my</em> site. It is rather lame.
            But it's still <strong>mine</strong>. Mine,
            I say.
        </article>
    </body>
</html>
```

If you're interested, this document is valid HTML 5 source code. If you're familiar with XHTML or HTML 4, you'll be relieved to see that they've made the new version much more readable. There must be some Python programmers on the standards development team, reminding the world that readability is important!

Now, the following program will load this HTML document into memory, and illustrate how the various elements are associated:

```python
from xml.etree.ElementTree import fromstring

with open("html_document.html") as file:
    root = fromstring(file.read())

print("ROOT NODE")
print("\ttag:", root.tag)
print("\tnumber of children:", len(root))
```

```
print("\tchildren:", [c.tag for c in root.getchildren()])
head = root[0]
print("HEAD NODE")
print("\tfirst child:", head[0].tag)
print("\tsecond_child:", head[1].tag)
print("\tlink attributes:", head[1].attrib)
article = root[1][1]
print("ARTICLE NODE")
print("\ttag:", article.tag)
print("\ttext:", article.text)
print("\tfirst child:", article[0].tag, article[0].text)
print("\t\tem's tail:", article[0].tail)
print("\tsecond child:", article[1].tag, article[1].text)
print("\tstrong's tail:", article[1].tail)
```

If we run this, we can see how child list access, and tag, text, attrib, and tail attributes work on an element class:

```
ROOT NODE
    tag: html
    number of children: 2
    children: ['head', 'body']
HEAD NODE
    first child: title
    second_child: link
    link attributes: {'href': 'styles.css', 'rel': 'stylesheet'}
ARTICLE NODE
    tag: article
    text:
            This is
    first child: em my
            em's tail:  site. It is rather lame.
            But it's still
    second child: strong mine
    strong's tail: . Mine,
            I say.
```

The important thing to note is that the child of an element is always another element with a similar interface. The list lookup supports iteration over a node (as in for child in element) and slice notation (as in element[1:5]), so it is easy to treat an element like a normal Python sequence.

One thing to be careful of is that ElementTree is a bit ambiguous when it comes to checking for children. Do not use the idiom if element to determine if an element exists or not, because it may return False if the element exists, yet contains no children. If you want to check if an element contains children, use if len(element). Conversely, if you want to check if an element exists, use if element is not None.

This short introduction is almost enough if we need to interpret or work with an element tree we read from a file or was provided across the network. Typically when we read or receive an XML file, we need to do one of two things:

- Parse it node by node and convert it to some other structure
- Find specific elements or attributes and look up their value

The first task can be accomplished by recursively iterating over nodes and looking at their attributes, texts, and tails. The second task usually implies some sort of searching mechanism. The Element class does provide a few methods to help with matching elements. There are three of them. They each return a different value, but all accept a single pattern parameter. This parameter supports a bastardized version of the XPath selection language. Unfortunately, the entire XPath language is not supported. Basic features, such as selecting a tag, selecting a tag recursively, and building a path from the current node work, though:

```
print('search for child tag:', root.find('head'))
print('search children recursively:', root.findall('.//em'))
print('build path:', root.findtext('./body/article/em'))
```

If we run this code it outputs:

```
search for child tag: <Element head at 961f7ac>
search children recursively: [<Element em at 961fb2c>]
build path: my
```

This example also illustrates the three different search methods, each of which accepts the same kind of path. The find method returns the first matching element. The findall method returns a list of matching elements. The findtext method is a bit different; it finds the first matching sub-element (just like find), but then returns the text attribute for that element, instead of the element itself. Thus, e.findtext(path) is identical to e.find(path).text.

Constructing XML documents

ElementTree isn't only good for parsing and searching XML documents. It also provides an intuitive interface for constructing them, using standard list and object access features. We can use the append function on an element to add a child, or the helper function, SubElement, which is a little bit less typing. We can set attributes using dictionary syntax, and text and tails using object attribute access. The following code constructs a simple HTML document using these features:

```
from xml.etree.ElementTree import (Element, SubElement,
        tostring)

root = Element("html")
head = Element("head")
root.append(head)
title = SubElement(head, "title")
title.text = "my page"
link = SubElement(head, "link")
link.attrib['rel'] = "stylesheet"
link.attrib['href'] = "styles.css"
body = Element("body")
body.text = "This is my website."
root.append(body)

print(tostring(root))
```

First we create a root element, then append some children to it in order. The SubElement function does the same thing to append a title to the head. When we create a link element, we also update the attribute dictionary to set attributes on it. Finally, we can use the tostring method to convert the element to an XML string, which looks like this:

```
<html><head><title>my page</title><link href="styles.css"
rel="stylesheet" /></head><body>This is my website.</body></html>
```

There's plenty more to ElementTree than we've considered so far, but unlike the alternative XML libraries, the basics will get you a long ways.

lxml

lxml is an advanced XML parsing library that uses the lightning fast libxml2 library to do the underlying hard work. It can be downloaded from the lxml website at http://codespeak.net/lxml/. It is a third-party library and, in the past, has been difficult to install on some operating systems, although this should not be the case with the latest releases.

If your needs are basic and can be covered by the `ElementTree` API we just discussed, then, by all means, use that. But if you need to parse invalid XML documents, advanced XPath searching, or CSS selectors, lxml is your tool.

lxml has an interface that is very similar to ElementTree, in fact, for basic usage, lxml can be used as a drop-in replacement for ElementTree. This will invariably give your parsing code a speedup, but this compatibility with ElementTree isn't what makes lxml great. lxml is far more advanced and provides numerous features above and beyond ElementTree.

The previous example for parsing and searching our XML file only needs one change to work in lxml; change the import to read `from lxml.etree import fromstring` and the code will run unmodified.

My favorite advanced feature of lxml is its support for advanced XPath and CSS selectors for searching through XML documents. These are far more useful than the basic ElementTree searches. Here are some examples:

```
print('xpath attribute:', root.xpath('//link[@href]'))
print('xpath text filter:', root.xpath('//*[contains(em, "my")]'))
print('xpath first child:', root.xpath('/html/body/article/em[1]'))
from lxml.cssselect import CSSSelector
print('css class selector:', CSSSelector('.simple')(root))
print('css tag selector:', CSSSelector('em')(root))
```

lxml will support any XPath selector that is supported by the underlying `libxml2` library. This basically encompasses the entire XPath language definition, although some of the most exotic selectors may be buggy.

The CSS selectors are very comfortable to anyone used to the jQuery JavaScript library or similar libraries. CSS selectors compile, internally, to equivalent XPath selectors before the selection is run. Both the XPath and the CSS selector functions return a list of all matching elements, similar to the ElementTree `findall` method.

In addition to these advanced search features, lxml provides:

- A parser for badly formed HTML
- A unique library for treating elements like objects, so you can access sub-tags as if they were attributes on objects
- A complete XML validation tool that can utilize DTDs, XMLSchema, and RELAX NG schemas

We don't have space to discuss these, but if you have any advanced or complicated requirements when it comes to XML or HTML parsing, lxml is invariably the tool you want to reach for.

CherryPy

CherryPy version 3.2 is the first major web application server to be made available on the Python 3 platform. It can be downloaded from `http://cherrypy.org/`. It is not a full-stack framework like the very popular Django, TurboGears, or Zope libraries. These frameworks provide extra support for data storage, templating, authentication, and other common web operations. Such features are not impossible in CherryPy, you're just responsible for finding or implementing them yourself.

CherryPy is a very powerful web server that uses a simple design for building web applications. Let's jump in head-first with a simple example that serves the HTML file we developed in the previous section:

```
import cherrypy


class SimplePage:
    @cherrypy.expose
    def index(self):
        with open("html_document.html") as file:
            return file.read()


cherrypy.quickstart(SimplePage())
```

If we run this program, we can visit `http://localhost:8080/` in a web browser to see the web page in action. All we've done here is create a class to pass to the `quickstart` function. That function starts a web server and serves pages from that class. Any methods of the class we created that have been marked as `exposed` will be made available via HTTP at a URL with the same name as the method. Any method not explicitly marked as exposed can be used internally as a helper method, but cannot be accessed at any URL.

The method itself simply opens a file and returns the contents of that file. Ultimately, we've written a web application that serves a single HTML 5 web page.

Of course, having a site that serves only one web page is pretty boring. Let's look at an example that is just a touch more exciting:

```
import cherrypy

template = """<!DOCTYPE html>
<html>
    <body>
        {message}
    </body>
</html>"""
```

```
class AboutPage:
    @cherrypy.expose
    def index(self):
        return template.format(message="""
        I'm not a very interesting person...""")

@cherrypy.expose
def contactPage(self):
    print(self)
    return template.format(
            message="I can't be contacted anywhere.")

class MainPage:
    about = AboutPage()
    contact = contactPage
    @cherrypy.expose
    def index(self):
        return template.format(message="""
        This is the main page.
        <a href="/about/">About Me</a>
        <a href="/contact/">Contact Me</a>
        <a href="/links/">Some Links</a>
        """)

    @cherrypy.expose
    def links(self):
        return template.format(
                message="No Links Yet")

cherrypy.quickstart(MainPage())
```

This example shows three ways that pages can be added to a site. The obvious one is to add an exposed method, such as the `links` method above, to the class. But we can add exposed objects in other ways too:

- By defining a separate function and including the attribute in the class definition as we did with `contactPage`

- By defining a separate class and including an instance of it in the class definition, as we did with `aboutPage`

- By adding the exposed method to the object after the class has been instantiated using code such as `app.some_page = AnExposedClass()`

You've probably figured out already that the `index` method is a special method. It doesn't map to the `/index` URL; instead, it is the method called if no path is added after the ending slash.

We can also accept HTML form arguments. Let's create a real contact page:

```python
import cherrypy

class ContactPage:
    @cherrypy.expose
    def index(self, message=None):
        if message:
            print("The user submitted:\n{0}".format(
                message))
            return "Thank you!"
        return """<form>
            <textarea name="message"></textarea>
            <input type="submit" />
            </form>"""

cherrypy.quickstart(ContactPage())
```

This page displays a different result depending on the presence of a `message` variable in the keyword arguments. If no such argument is supplied, the visitor is presented with a form to enter a message in. If the argument is supplied, the value of the message is printed to the console (normally we'd do something useful with the value, such as e-mailing it somewhere or storing it in a database or file for later retrieval). Then a thank you message is returned to the client.

So how did that `message` parameter get set? Basically, any named inputs in a form (in this case, the message `textarea`) are mapped to keyword arguments when the page is submitted. It's that simple!

A full web stack?

As we discussed, CherryPy is just a web application server; it is not a web framework. It provides a complete web server and the basic features to map HTTP requests to code that must be executed when those requests are made. It also provides, with a bit of configuration, complete SSL support, the ability to set and retrieve cookies, caching support, HTTP authentication, and sessions. However, it is missing two key features that many other frameworks supply: templating and data storage.

Many websites use databases for data storage, but CherryPy does not supply this ability. Do we really need it to? We really just need database connectivity; it doesn't have to be built into the web framework. Indeed, why don't we just use SQLAlchemy, which we discussed earlier in the chapter? In fact, this is what the TurboGears framework uses for its database access.

This then, still leaves us to solve the templating problem, another framework feature that CherryPy lacks. Templating is the process of taking static strings or files, and replacing certain substrings in those files with new strings, based on some kind of context. The `str.format` function we covered in *Chapter 10* is a basic example of templating. It allows us to replace modifiers with variables passed into the function. Indeed, this was the template method we used in the example of a simple CherryPy application earlier.

Most template languages go beyond this ability to allow things like conditionals (including data in the template only if a certain condition is met, such as two variables being equal, or a user being logged in), and looping (including data in a template repeatedly, such as creating a table or unordered list containing multiple items from a Python list). Some even go so far as to allow arbitrary Python code to be executed within the template.

There are a myriad opinions on what a template language should be, which is why, for Python 2, there have been an immeasurable number of different template languages devised. This diversity hasn't spread to Python 3 yet, but one of the most powerful templating languages, Jinja2 is already available on the Python 3 platform. It can be downloaded from `http://jinja.pocoo.org/`.

As a sort of case study, let's take these three tools—CherryPy, SQLAlchemy, and Jinja—and create a quick and dirty blogging engine! We'll start with the SQLAlchemy models; these define the data that will be stored in the database:

```python
import datetime
import sqlalchemy as sqa
from sqlalchemy.ext.declarative import declarative_base

Base = declarative_base()

class Article(Base):
    __tablename__ = "article"
    rowid = sqa.Column(sqa.Integer, primary_key=True)
    title = sqa.Column(sqa.String)
    message = sqa.Column(sqa.String)
    pub_date = sqa.Column(sqa.DateTime)

    def __init__(self, title, message):
```

```
        self.title = title
        self.message = message
        self.pub_date=datetime.datetime.now()

class Comment(Base):
    __tablename__ = "comment"
    rowid = sqa.Column(sqa.Integer, primary_key=True)
    article_id = sqa.Column(sqa.Integer,
            sqa.ForeignKey('article.rowid'))
    article = sqa.orm.relationship(Article, backref="comments")
    name = sqa.Column(sqa.String)
    message = sqa.Column(sqa.String)

    def __init__(self, article_id, name, message):
        self.article_id = article_id
        self.name = name
        self.message = message

engine = sqa.create_engine('sqlite:///blog.db')
Base.metadata.create_all(engine)
Session = sqa.orm.sessionmaker(bind=engine)
```

We create two models with some fields. The two models are associated with a ForeignKey relationship on the Comment class.

The rowid field is a special one; in SQLite, every model is automatically given a unique integer rowid. We don't have to do anything to populate this number, it's simply available from the database. This wouldn't work with PostgreSQL or another engine; we'd have to set up a sequence or autoincrement field instead.

We add an __init__ method to each class to make it easier to construct new instances. Then we associate the engine, create the tables, and create a Session class to interact with the database later.

Jinja Templating

Now, we can set up Jinja to serve some templates from a folder for us:

```
import jinja2
templates = jinja2.Environment(loader=jinja2.FileSystemLoader(
        'blog_templates'))
```

Well that was easy. This gives us a `templates` variable that we can use to load templates based on filename from the given folder. Before we create the CherryPy app server, let's have a look at the templates. Let's scrutinize the simple template for adding a blog article first:

```
{% extends "base.html" %}

{% block title %}New Entry{% endblock %}
{% block content %}
<form method="POST" action="/process_add/">
    Title: <input name="title" type="text" size="40" /><br />
    <textarea name="message" rows="10" cols="40">
    </textarea><br />
    <input type="submit" value="Publish" />
</form>
{% endblock %}
```

This sort of resembles normal HTML, but all those {% things are new. That's Jinja markup (it's also very similar to Django markup, if you have used or are interested in using Django's template system) for a **template tag**. Template tags are instructions to the templating system to do something special here. There are two types of template tags in use: `extends`, and `block`. The `extends` tag essentially tells the template system to start with the `base.html`, but replace any named blocks with the named blocks in this file. And that's what the `block` and `endblock` tags are; named blocks to override whatever is specified in the parent template, `base.html`. This may be a bit clearer if we know what `base.html` looks like:

```
<!DOCTYPE html>
<html>
    <head><title>{% block title %}{% endblock %}</title></head>
    <body>
        <h1>My Blog</h1>
        <ul>
            <li><a href="/">Main</a></li>
            <li><a href="/add/">Add Entry</a></li>
        </ul>
        <hr />
        {% block content %}
        {% endblock %}
    <body>
<html>
```

This looks even more like a normal HTML page; it shows where the two named blocks should go in the context of a larger page.

Extending `base.html` in other templates allows us to ignore the parts of every page that stay the same. Further, if we want to add a link to the menu or otherwise modify the overall site, we only have to do it in this single template file.

The other template, `index.html` is substantially more complex:

```
{% extends "base.html" %}

{% block title %}My Blog{% endblock %}
{% block content %}
    {% for article in articles %}
        <h2>{{article.title}}</h2>
        <em>{{article.pub_date.strftime('%b %d %Y')}}</em>
        <p>{{article.message}}</p>
        <div style="margin-left: 6em">
            <h3>Comments</h3>
            {% for comment in article.comments %}
                <em>{{comment.name}} wrote:</em>
                <p>
                {{comment.message}}
                </p>
            {% endfor %}
            {% include "comment_form.html" %}
        </div>
        <hr />
    {% endfor %}
{% endblock %}
```

It includes the same `extends` and `block` tags as the earlier template. In addition, it introduces us to the `for` template tag, which loops over all the articles (or all the comments in an article) and renders slightly different HTML for each of them. It also renders a bunch of variables using the `{{<variable_name>}}` syntax. The variable names are passed into the template from our CherryPy application or are assigned within the context, as is done inside the `for` loops.

The rendering of the `pub_date` variable on the article is particularly interesting, as the item is a `datetime.datetime` object, and we can see that Jinja allows us to call the `strftime` method on this object directly.

Finally, the `include` tag allows us to render part of the template in a separate file, `comment_form.html`, which looks like this:

```
<form method="POST"
        action="/process_comment/{{article.rowid}}/">
    Name: <input name="name" type="text" size="30" /><br />
    <textarea name="message" rows="5" cols="30">
    </textarea><br />
    <input type="submit" value="Comment" />
</form>
```

That's basic Jinja syntax in a nutshell; there's a lot more that can be done with it, of course, but these basics are enough to get you interested. They're also enough for our simple blog engine!

The CherryPy blog web application

In the interest of understanding how web applications are designed, note that I didn't write those templates before I wrote the CherryPy application we're about to see. Instead, I developed iteratively, creating both the code and templates to add an article, followed by the code and templates to display an article, and finally, setting up the comment system. I grouped all the resulting templates together in the above section so we could focus on Jinja template syntax. Now, let's focus on CherryPy and how those templates are called!

First, here's our blog engine with the index method:

```
import cherrypy
class Blog:
    @cherrypy.expose
    def index(self):
        session = Session()
        articles = session.query(Article).all()
        template = templates.get_template("index.html")
        content = template.render(articles=articles)
        session.close()
        return content
cherrypy.quickstart(Blog())
```

Here's where we start to see our three puzzle pieces merging together. CherryPy, of course, is serving the page. Jinja is creating the page using our templates. And SQLAlchemy is giving Jinja the data it needs to display

First we construct a `session` and use it to search for all the available articles. We then get a template by name; this comes from the `templates` object we set up earlier in the module. Then we render the template, passing one keyword argument into it. Keyword arguments map to variables inside the template context; the template we defined earlier will loop over the articles we passed in this function. Then we return the rendered content to let CherryPy display it.

The code to display the form for adding a new article is even simpler; we just render the template, since it doesn't need any variables:

```
@cherrypy.expose
def add(self):
    template = templates.get_template("add.html")
    return template.render()
```

You may have noticed in our templates that the forms for adding articles and comments have action attributes pointing to `process_add` and `process_comment` URLs. The `process_add` URL simply constructs a new article from the form parameters (title and name), which come to us from CherryPy as keyword arguments. Then it raises an exception to redirect the client to the main view, which will display the new article:

```
@cherrypy.expose
def process_add(self, title=None, message=None):
    session = Session()
    article = Article(title, message)
    session.add(article)
    session.commit()
    session.close()
    raise cherrypy.HTTPRedirect("/")
```

The `process_comment` method is much the same, except it also accepts a positional argument. Positional arguments come between forward slash characters in the URL, so the following method signature would actually map to `/process_comment/3/` if an `article_id` of 3 is passed:

```
@cherrypy.expose
def process_comment(self, article_id, name=None,
        message=None):
    session = Session()
    comment = Comment(article_id, name, message)
    session.add(comment)
    session.commit()
    session.close()
    raise cherrypy.HTTPRedirect("/")
```

And there we have it, a complete, simple blog engine with absolutely no authentication and which will fill up with spam in a matter of minutes. But it works! And we wrote it all using Python 3 objects.

Exercises

We covered a wide variety of material in this chapter, but we didn't cover anything in a lot of detail. These exercises, then, will be all about extra reading. All of the tools we discussed in this chapter have terrific documentation on their websites, including tutorials, API references, and specific examples. If any of the topics we discussed are of special interest to you, review the documentation for those libraries. Try them out, see how far you can push them.

Acquire the knowledge you need to write a complicated GUI program, then write it. Do it in both TkInter and PyQt, and decide which toolkit you prefer. Find out what database backends SQLAlchemy currently supports under Python 3, as this number will grow quickly from the two available at the time of writing. Similarly, do research into available web frameworks, and see how they compare to CherryPy. Is Jinja the best tool for templating available? Try some other products and see what you think of them. Or if you have some free time and would like a challenge, take some of the string manipulation knowledge we gained in *Chapter 10* and write your own templating engine!

Try out ElementTree and lxml and see if you can uncover their similarities and differences. What if you were to merge lxml into the web stack we created above and use it to create the HTML documents instead of rendering them using templates? (Hint: This is a bad idea. But try it anyway!)

There are hundreds of other Python libraries and APIs available out there, and more and more of them are becoming available for Python 3 every day. If you have a specific problem you need to solve, the chances are that there is a support library available that will help you solve it. We touched on some popular ones in the examples throughout this book and most especially in this chapter. But there is so much more out there. For example, we didn't discuss scientific or display packages at all. Do some research into available libraries, find out what's available. You'll never know when it might be useful!

Summary

The variety of topics related in this chapter is quite staggering. We started with databases, graduated to Graphical User Interfaces, diverged into a discussion of XML, and ultimately built a small web application. The goal was to introduce popular, available libraries for major real-world tasks. The number of libraries available for Python 3 is steadily growing as more and more developers choose to support the cleaner syntax used in this version of the Python language. We have seen an overview of:

- SQLAlchemy for databases
- TkInter for graphical interfaces
- PyQt for different graphical interfaces
- ElementTree for XML parsing
- lxml for better XML parsing
- CherryPy for web applications
- Jinja for string templating in web applications

Thus ends our tour through the world of Object-oriented Programming in Python. I sincerely hope you enjoyed the ride, and are excited to test your new skills on innovative new programming problems. Thanks for your attention, and please watch your step as you leave the vehicle.

Index

list.sort method 238
list comprehensions 198-200
lists
  about 168-170
  sorting 171, 172
loads function 304
lower method 286
lxm 366
lxml
  features 366, 367

M

mailing list manager, case study
  about 220
  building 220-223
make_background method 240
menu_item class 270
message variable 370
method overloading 205
Method Resolution Order 72
methods 13
mixin 68
modules
  about 43, 44
  absolute imports 46
  importing 45
  organizing 45
  relative imports 47-50
monkey-patch 69
mousePressEvent method 361
move method 279
multiple inheritance
  about 23, 68
  arguments lists, formatting 75, 77
  diamond problem 71
  example 70
  mixin 68
  options 69
  working 70
multiplicity 11
mutable byte strings 297, 298

N

name attribute 131
namedtuple constructor 161

named tuples
  about 161
  creating 161
network programming example, decorator
    pattern 230
new card catalog program, case study
  about 24-30
  UML diagram 26
  UML sequence diagram 27
next() method 228
no_return function 100
Node objects 242
normalize_url method 184
notebook application, case study 53-61
NotImplementedError 254

O

object
  about 7, 9
  attributes 11, 12
  behaviors 13
  class diagram 9
  classes relationship, describing 9
  data 11
  identifying 125-128
  kinds 9
  managing 137
  storing 303
object-oriented 7
object-oriented Analysis (OOA) 8
object-oriented Design (OOD) 8
Object-Relational Managers(ORMs)
  about 349
  SQLAlchemy 349
object management
  about 137
  composition-based solution 145, 146
  delegation method 139
  duplicate code, removing 140, 141
  example 138
  existing code, reusing 142-144
  extensibility 138
  files, unzipping 139
  files, zipping 139
  partitioning 139
  readability 138

Thank you for buying
Python 3 Object Oriented Programming

About Packt Publishing

Packt, pronounced 'packed', published its first book "*Mastering phpMyAdmin for Effective MySQL Management*" in April 2004 and subsequently continued to specialize in publishing highly focused books on specific technologies and solutions.

Our books and publications share the experiences of your fellow IT professionals in adapting and customizing today's systems, applications, and frameworks. Our solution based books give you the knowledge and power to customize the software and technologies you're using to get the job done. Packt books are more specific and less general than the IT books you have seen in the past. Our unique business model allows us to bring you more focused information, giving you more of what you need to know, and less of what you don't.

Packt is a modern, yet unique publishing company, which focuses on producing quality, cutting-edge books for communities of developers, administrators, and newbies alike. For more information, please visit our website: www.packtpub.com.

About Packt Open Source

In 2010, Packt launched two new brands, Packt Open Source and Packt Enterprise, in order to continue its focus on specialization. This book is part of the Packt Open Source brand, home to books published on software built around Open Source licences, and offering information to anybody from advanced developers to budding web designers. The Open Source brand also runs Packt's Open Source Royalty Scheme, by which Packt gives a royalty to each Open Source project about whose software a book is sold.

Writing for Packt

We welcome all inquiries from people who are interested in authoring. Book proposals should be sent to author@packtpub.com. If your book idea is still at an early stage and you would like to discuss it first before writing a formal book proposal, contact us; one of our commissioning editors will get in touch with you.

We're not just looking for published authors; if you have strong technical skills but no writing experience, our experienced editors can help you develop a writing career, or simply get some additional reward for your expertise.

Expert Python Programming

ISBN: 978-1-847194-94-7   Paperback: 372 pages

Best practices for designing, coding, and distributing
your Python software

1. Learn Python development best practices from
    an expert, with detailed coverage of naming
    and coding conventions

2. Apply object-oriented principles, design
    patterns, and advanced syntax tricks

3. Manage your code with distributed version
    control

4. Profile and optimize your code

Python Testing: Beginner's Guide

ISBN: 978-1-847198-84-6   Paperback: 256 pages

An easy and convenient approach to testing your
powerful Python projects

1. Covers everything you need to test your code
    in Python

2. Easiest and enjoyable approach to learn
    Python testing

3. Write, execute, and understand the result of
    tests in the unit test framework

4. Packed with step-by-step examples and
    clear explanations

Please check **www.PacktPub.com** for information on our titles

open source ✿
community experience distilled
PUBLISHING

Spring Python 1.1

ISBN: 978-1-849510-66-0   Paperback: 264 pages

Create powerful and versatile Spring Python applications using pragmatic libraries and useful abstractions

1. Maximize the use of Spring features in Python and develop impressive Spring Python applications

2. Explore the versatility of Spring Python by integrating it with frameworks, libraries, and tools

3. Discover the non-intrusive Spring way of wiring together Python components

4. Packed with hands-on-examples, case studies, and clear explanations for better understanding

Matplotlib for Python Developers

ISBN: 978-1-847197-90-0   Paperback: 308 pages

Build remarkable publication-quality plots the easy way

1. Create high quality 2D plots by using Matplotlib productively

2. Incremental introduction to Matplotlib, from the ground up to advanced levels

3. Embed Matplotlib in GTK+, Qt, and wxWidgets applications as well as web sites to utilize them in Python applications

4. Deploy Matplotlib in web applications and expose it on the Web using popular web frameworks such as Pylons and Django

Please check **www.PacktPub.com** for information on our titles

CPSIA information can be obtained
at www.ICGtesting.com
Printed in the USA
FFOW01n1732290415
13051FF

9 781849 511126